THE CHURCH FATHERS AS SPIRITUAL MENTORS

| THE CHRISTIAN MENTOR | Volume 1

"Faith is illumined"
THE CHURCH FATHERS
AS SPIRITUAL MENTORS

Michael A.G. Haykin

www.joshuapress.com

Published by
Joshua Press, Kitchener, Ontario, Canada
Distributed by
Sola Scriptura Ministries International
www.sola-scriptura.ca

First published 2017
© 2017 Michael A.G. Haykin. All rights reserved. This book may not be reproduced, in whole or in part, without written permission from the publishers.

Cover and book design by Janice Van Eck

The publication of this book was made possible by the generous support of The Ross-Shire Foundation

Library and Archives Canada Cataloguing in Publication

Haykin, Michael A. G., author
    The church fathers as spiritual mentors : "faith is illumined" / Michael A.G. Haykin.

(The Christian mentor ; volume 1)
Includes bibliographical references and index.
Issued also in electronic formats.
ISBN 978-1-894400-81-7 (softcover).—ISBN 978-1-894400-82-4 (HTML).
—ISBN 978-1-894400-83-1 (PDF)

    1. Fathers of the church—Biography. 2. Fathers of the church. 3. Church history—Primitive and early church, ca. 30–600. I. Title.

BR1706.3.H39 2017   270.2092'2   C2017-903418-9
                                      C2017-903419-7

To David and Carolyn Clark,
dear friends, to whom I am deeply indebted.

I call upon you, Lord, the God of Abraham and the God of Isaac and the God of Jacob and Israel, you who are the Father of our Lord Jesus Christ, who through the abundance of your mercy have been pleased with us so that we may know you, you who made heaven and earth and rule over all things, you who are the only true God, beyond whom there is no other God, you who through our Lord Jesus Christ bestowed upon us the gift of the Holy Spirit, now give to everyone who reads this writing the knowledge that you alone are God and make them strong in you and separate from every heretical, godless and impious doctrine.
—IRENAEUS OF LYONS, *AGAINST HERESIES* 3.6.4

Contents

1. The church fathers as spiritual mentors — 1
   An introductory word
2. "With the Father from all eternity" — 5
   The deity of Christ before Nicæa
3. "The ground and pillar of our faith" — 19
   Irenaeus on the perfection and salvific impact of the Scriptures
4. "On the promises" — 37
   The millennium in the Greek patristic tradition
5. "The *imperium* of the Holy Spirit" — 61
   The Holy Spirit in Cyprian's *To Donatus*
6. "A disciple of the holy God" — 73
   Constantine and his revolution
7. "Restoration…[and] repentance" — 89
   Basil of Caesarea and those who commit abortion
8. "To give glory to Father, Son and Holy Spirit" — 97
   Biblical exegesis in fourth-century Trinitarian debates
9. "Rivers of dragons and mouths of lions and dark forces" — 123
   The Holy Spirit and the holiness of the Christian in Macarius
10. "The most glorious City of God" — 135
    Augustine of Hippo and *The City of God*
11. "The words of the Lord are always sweet" — 163
    Preaching God's Word in the ancient church
12. "O blessed gatekeeper of heaven" — 183
    Petrine texts, bishops and the papacy
13. **A concluding word** — 205

Index — 207

NOTES ON DATES AND ABBREVIATIONS

All translations of the original sources are by the author unless otherwise indicated. It should be assumed that all dates are A.D. unless indicated as B.C.

fl. = *floruit*, that is, "flourished," a nomenclature that is used when the exact dates of birth and death are unknown.

c. = *circa*, that is, "around," a nomenclature that is used when an exact date is unknown.

r. = reigned.

1

The church fathers as spiritual mentors

An introductory word

> Come, O Lord and stir our hearts.
> Call us back to yourself.
> Kindle your fire in us and carry us away.
> Let us scent your fragrance and taste your sweetness.
> Let us love you and hasten to your side.
> —AUGUSTINE[1]

This is a part of a trilogy of books, entitled "The Christian Mentor," dealing with the subject of *ressourcement*, that is, the retrieval of the riches of the church's past to help illuminate the present. The first to be completed, volume 2, *The Reformers and Puritans as Spiritual Mentors: "Hope is Kindled"* appeared in 2012. I fully expected that the other two volumes, the one that you hold in your hands and a volume 3, which deals with the eighteenth and nineteenth centuries, would be published

---

1 Augustine, *Confessions* 8.4.

shortly thereafter. Other literary projects intervened, however, and it has been five years since the appearance of volume 2. Unlike volumes 2 and 3, this volume deals with a period of church history about which evangelicals have tended to be quite ignorant and, regretfully, happy in their ignorance! There are good signs that this is changing and fresh interest is being given to our forebears from that distant time.

The ancient or early church period, which runs from around A.D. 100 to A.D. 600, is indeed a vital era. It was in this period, for example, that the essential shape of the doctrine of the Trinity was hammered out (discussed in chapters 2 and 8). It was also in the latter half of this era that the church found herself leaning upon the arm of the state, a consequence of the Constantinian revolution (see chapters 6 and 10), a marriage that would bear disastrous fruit in the centuries to come, even down to the present time.

The chapters proceed roughly chronologically, although a few of them (notably chapters 4, 8, and 11) deal with a significant range of time. Chapter 2 looks at the church's confession of the deity of Christ in the period before the Council of Nicæa. The following chapter examines the thought of the important second-century theologian Irenaeus of Lyon, especially as it relates to the Scriptures. Chapter 4 looks at early debates about the millennium in the Greek patristic tradition from the second century through to the fourth century. Chapter 5 turns to the Latin tradition, namely, Cyprian of Carthage, and his pneumatology. After examination of the Constantinian revolution in chapter 6, a small chapter looks again at Basil of Caesarea (he was discussed first in chapter 3) and his thinking about how to deal with those who commit abortion. Chapter 8 traces the road to the Niceno-Constantinopolitan Creed of 381 during the Arian crisis of the fourth century. Chapter 9 looks at Macarius, a Syriac-Greek author, and his understanding of spiritual warfare, elements of which have some similarity with the thought of the subject of chapter 10, Augustine. Chapter 10 examines the Augustinian masterpiece, *The City of God*, which I first studied in detail for a master's thesis in 1975–1976. Chapter 11 is an overview of patristic preaching, with special emphasis on Augustine and the Cappadocians, Asterius of Amasea and Basil of Caesarea. The final chapter looks at the development of ecclesial oversight in the Western church and the emergence of the papacy.

A number of the chapters have appeared previously in print, and permission has been sought to have them appear here. The original context of these chapters has been noted in a footnote at the beginning of each chapter. Other chapters originated in talks, some of them going back to the late 1980s and others as recent as January 2017, a period of nearly thirty years. This is the third collection of essays that I have written on the ancient church—the other two are *Defence of the Truth: Contending for the Truth Yesterday and Today* (Evangelical Press, 2004) and *Rediscovering the Church Fathers: Who They Were and How They Shaped the Church* (Crossway, 2011)—and I heartily confess that I still find this era deeply instructive and profoundly attractive.

In writing a book like this, one accumulates a variety of debts. Some I have noted in an introductory footnote in some of the chapters. I would also like to thank Marina Coldwell, Cheri Houghton and Jean Hamelin for typing some of the material in these pages. Ron and Monica White of Port Elgin, Ontario, were kind enough to allow my family and me to "housesit" their home for a week nearly twenty years ago, and in the rest of that locale I found time to do some vital work on one or two of the chapters that appear here. Then, I would like to thank Heinz Dschankilic, the director of Sola Scriptura Ministries International, the parent company of Joshua Press, for pressing me to get this book finished, and also Janice Van Eck, who has supervised every aspect of the production of this book.

I have dedicated this book to David and Carolyn Clark, for their friendship, warm hospitality and deep encouragement over nearly twenty-five years.[2]

Michael A.G. Haykin
Dundas, Ontario
St. Valentine's Day, 2017

---

2 David was instrumental in getting *Defence of the Truth: Contending for the Truth Yesterday and Today* published.

2

"With the Father from all eternity"
The deity of Christ before Nicæa

> He sent him as God, he sent him as [man] to men, he sent him as Saviour.
> —EPISTLE TO DIOGNETUS[1]

A high-speed murder mystery, Dan Brown's monumental bestseller *The Da Vinci Code* was also a perfect example of postmodern historical revisionism in which an art historian, hero Robert Langdon, discovers that contemporary expressions of Christianity, especially that of the Roman Catholic Church, have no sound historical basis.[2] According to Brown's

---

1 *Letter to Diognetus* 7.4.
2 Gene Edward Veith, "The Da Vinci Phenomenon," *World*, 21, no.20 (May 20, 2006): 20–21. The edition of *The Da Vinci Code* used in this chapter is Dan Brown, *The Da Vinci Code* (New York: Anchor Books, 2006). This chapter originated as a

novel, it was not until the reign of the early fourth-century Roman emperor Constantine (r.306–337) that the Bible, in particular the New Testament, was collated. In fact, it was Constantine who had the New Testament as we know it drawn up in order to suppress alternative perspectives on Jesus.[3] It was also not until the early fourth-century Council of Nicæa (325) that Jesus Christ was regarded as anything other than a human prophet. It was at this council, which was astutely manipulated by the power-hungry Constantine for his own ends, that Jesus was "turned...into a deity" and became for the first time an object of worship.[4] Third, both of these events took place in order to conceal the fact that Jesus was actually married to Mary Magdalene,[5] had a child by her[6] and that he intended that Mary be the founder of the church.[7] Key Christian teachings are thus the result of a power move by Constantine and other males in order to squash women. As Brown had one of his characters say, "It was all about power."[8]

Brown clearly intended these claims to be more than key aspects of the conspiratorial ambience of his novel. As Greg Clarke, director of the Centre for Apologetic Scholarship and Education at New College, University of New South Wales, has rightly noted, Dan Brown's book had "evangelistic intentions" and was "meant to change our lives."[9] In the words of R. Albert Mohler, president of The Southern Baptist Theological Seminary, the book was thus a not-so-subtle denial of the central truths of biblical Christianity.[10]

---

lecture at a conference on *The Da Vinci Code* held at Toronto Baptist Seminary in Toronto, Ontario, on Saturday, May 20, 2006.

3   Brown, *Da Vinci Code*, 231–232.
4   Brown, *Da Vinci Code*, 233–235.
5   Brown, *Da Vinci Code*, 244–247.
6   Brown, *Da Vinci Code*, 255–256.
7   Brown, *Da Vinci Code*, 248–249, 254.
8   Brown, *Da Vinci Code*, 233.
9   *Is It Worth Believing? The Spiritual Challenge of* The Da Vinci Code (Kingsford, New South Wales: Matthias Media, 2005), 25.
10 "Historical Propaganda," *Tabletalk* 30, no.5 (May 2006): 12. This issue of *Tabletalk* is subtitled "The Da Vinci Hoax" and contains five articles devoted to examining Brown's book.

A goodly number of book-length responses were made to these claims.[11] What this chapter seeks to do is to respond to one of Brown's assertions, namely that about the person and deity of Christ, and in doing so elucidate a central motif of early Christian theology, namely that Christ is indeed God and worthy of worship. In the words of Sir Leigh Teabing, a key figure in the novel, Christ is a "historical figure of staggering influence, perhaps the most enigmatic and inspirational leader the world has ever seen," but simply "a great and powerful man."[12] It was only at the Council of Nicæa that Jesus' divine status was ratified by a "relatively close vote." Behind this vote was the scheming hand of Constantine and thus in a real sense Constantine "shaped the face of Christianity as we know it today."[13]

If this claim is true, it would eviscerate the heart of Christianity. Without the pre-existent deity of Christ, as American scholar Douglas McCready has shown, "every distinctive Christian belief would have to be discarded" and the Christian faith itself would become, at best, trivial and, at worst, utterly irrelevant.[14] Presbyterian theologian Benjamin B. Warfield was right to maintain, though, that the warp and woof of the New Testament is "saturated" with the presupposition of the deity of Christ.[15] And McCready's 2005 study *He Came Down from Heaven: The Preexistence of Christ and the Christian Faith* amply corroborates Warfield's claim.

---

11 Here are some of the best, in terms of their critique of *The Da Vinci Code*: Darrell L. Bock, *Breaking the Da Vinci Code: Answering the Questions Everybody's Asking* (Nashville: Nelson, 2004); Stephen Clark, *The Da Vinci Code on Trial: Filtering Fact from Fiction* (Bryntirion, Bridgend: Bryntirion Press, 2005); Bart D. Ehrman, *Truth And Fiction in The Da Vinci Code. A Historian Reveals What We Really Know about Jesus, Mary Magdalene, and Constantine* (Oxford: Oxford University Press, 2004); Erwin W. Lutzer, *The Da Vinci Deception* (Carol Stream, Illinois: Tyndale House, 2006); Garry Williams, *The Da Vinci Code: From Dan Brown's Fiction to Mary Magdalene's Faith* (Fearn, Ross-shire: Christian Focus, 2006).

12 Brown, *Da Vinci Code*, 231, 233. See also Brown, *Da Vinci Code*, 234.

13 Brown, *Da Vinci Code*, 233–234.

14 Douglas McCready, *He Came Down from Heaven: The Preexistence of Christ and the Christian Faith* (Downers Grove, Illinois: InterVarsity Press/Leicester, England: Apollos, 2005), 317.

15 "The Deity of Christ" in *The Fundamentals. A Testimony to the Truth* (Chicago: Testimony Publishing Co., 1909), I, 23–26, *passim*.

SOME NEW TESTAMENT EVIDENCE

Apart from James' letter, the earliest New Testament documents are the letters of the apostle Paul. McCready shows that a number of these letters plainly speak of Christ's divine pre-existence.[16] For instance, there is Colossians 1:15–16, which maintains that Christ is "the image of the invisible God."[17] In other words, Christ perfectly represents God. This text goes on to say that Christ created the entire universe: "by him all things were created, in heaven and on earth, visible and invisible," they were "created through him and for him." Being thus the Creator of all things, Christ cannot be included in the created order.[18] Following these claims, there is also the assertion in Colossians 1:19 that in Christ dwelt "all the fullness of God," an assertion that is repeated in Colossians 2:9.[19] As McCready notes of these two latter verses, they declare "about as clearly as can be said that Jesus is God without confusing God the Father and the Son."[20]

Paul also affirms Christ's creatorship in 1 Corinthians 8:5–6—"there is…one Lord, Jesus Christ, through whom are all things"[21]—and his deity in Romans 9:5 where Christ is described as "God over all, blessed forever."[22] With regard to this second Pauline text, McCready cites a comment on it by the third-century Christian exegete Origen (c.185–254): "It is clear from this passage that Christ is the God who is over all."[23]

There is also the much-discussed hymn to Christ in Philippians 2:5–11, which clearly presupposes Christ's pre-existence.[24] While the hymn is focused on the example of Christ's humility and self-sacrifice, it does make two significant ontological statements about the Lord Jesus: first, he "was in the form of God" (2:6). While there are sharp

---

16 McCready, *He Came Down from Heaven*, 70–104.
17 Text from the Scriptures is taken from the ESV.
18 McCready, *He Came Down from Heaven*, 81–82.
19 "In him the whole fullness of deity dwells bodily."
20 McCready, *He Came Down from Heaven*, 82.
21 See McCready's discussion in *He Came Down from Heaven*, 86–87.
22 See also McCready, *He Came Down from Heaven*, 91–92.
23 McCready, *He Came Down from Heaven*, 92. See also Ehrman, *Truth And Fiction in The Da Vinci Code*, 16.
24 For extensive discussion, see McCready, *He Came Down from Heaven*, 73–80.

disagreements among New Testament scholars about the exact meaning of this phrase, the most consistent interpretation of this statement in the context of the hymn is that it is a declaration of Christ's enjoyment of the status or nature of God himself.[25] Then, the hymn goes on to assert that, prior to his descent to the earth during the incarnation, Christ possessed "equality with God" (2:6). It was naturally his and he willingly gave it up when he took on human existence.

McCready notes other New Testament texts that strongly assert the divinity of Christ, including Matthew 11:27[26] and Hebrews 1:1–8.[27] Understandably, though, he devotes a significant amount of text to discussing the Johannine witness.[28] At the very opening of the Gospel of John, John 1:1 and 1:14 speak unequivocally of Christ as a divine being: as the Word he "was with God" and "was God (*theos*)" but he "became flesh and dwelt" in this world. In verse 1 it needs to be noted that the term for God, *theos*, does not have the definite article. As McCready points out, this syntactical construction serves to make the point that while the Word is equal with God—what God the Father is in terms of divine attributes the Word is—he is not identical with God. John thus emphasizes Jesus' deity without committing the error of what would later be called modalism, which removes the distinctions between the persons of the Godhead.[29]

In light of these statements about Christ's deity in the opening chapter of John's Gospel, the statement by Jesus in John 10:30 that he and "the Father are one" is probably to be read as being more than simply an assertion of his union with the Father in thought and intent. In light of the gospel context it seems to affirm a union of being between the Father and the Son.[30] Some of Jesus' hearers, who radically disagreed with him, certainly understood it this way, for we are told in John 10:31–33 that they accused him of the blasphemy of making himself God.

---

25 McCready, *He Came Down from Heaven*, 76–78.
26 McCready, *He Came Down from Heaven*, 108–112.
27 McCready, *He Came Down from Heaven*, 123–130.
28 McCready, *He Came Down from Heaven*, 135–162. See also Ehrman, *Truth and Fiction in The Da Vinci Code*, 16–17.
29 McCready, *He Came Down from Heaven*, 141–142.
30 McCready, *He Came Down from Heaven*, 150–151.

Yet another Johannine text that is affirmative of the deity of Christ is 1 John 5:20, where Jesus is described as "the true God and eternal life." To be sure, there are difficulties with the grammatical construction of the sentence in relation to what precedes it. And while the import of the text is soteriological in intent—we can know God, "him who is true," because of the revelatory work of his Son, who "has given us understanding" of God—yet, as McCready quotes I. Howard Marshall, "it is precisely because Jesus is the true God that the person who is in him is also in the Father."[31]

McCready's examination of the New Testament witness about the person of Christ is an exhaustive one. At the end of it, he states that the evidence of the New Testament points in only one direction: it "consistently presents Jesus Christ as preexistent deity every time the subject arises."[32] Of course, by arguing that Constantine commissioned a Bible "that embellished those gospels that made Him [i.e. Christ] godlike,"[33] Dan Brown hoped to undercut any such argument from the New Testament for the deity of Christ. The testimony of post-apostolic Christianity in the second and third centuries therefore also needs to be considered in a response to Brown's claim that, prior to the Council of Nicæa, Christ was regarded only as a human being. In what follows, due to space, our focus is limited to various second and third-century witnesses to the deity of Christ, both pagan and Christian. The two Christian testimonies, it should be noted, cover a couple of genres: the epistolary writings of Ignatius of Antioch, similar in form to those of Paul; and a work of apologetics, the *Letter to Diognetus*.

THREE PAGAN WITNESSES

Around the year 110, a new governor was appointed for the Roman province of Pontus and Bithynia in what is now northern Turkey. His name was Caius Plinius Caecilius Secundus, better known to history as Pliny the Younger (61/62–c.113). Prior to this appointment he was in charge of the public works for the city of Rome and performed so admirably that the emperor, Trajan (r.98–117), appointed him to clean

---

31 McCready, *He Came Down from Heaven*, 158–159.
32 McCready, *He Came Down from Heaven*, 310.
33 Brown, *Da Vinci Code*, 234.

up an economic mess in the province of Pontus and Bithynia. Like any good leader, Pliny sought first to find out what was happening at ground level before instituting significant changes in the infrastructure of the province. In the course of his tour of the cities and towns of the province, certain Christians were brought to him in one of the towns.[34] From the point of view of the Roman *imperium*, these men and women were members of an illegal religion, part of what Pliny called "a degenerate sort of cult carried to extravagant lengths."[35] Their crime was their steadfast refusal (*contumacia*) to heed the urging of an official of the Roman state, Pliny, to worship the Roman gods and do reverence to a statue of the emperor.

To find out more about the doings of these Christians, Pliny tortured two women whom he terms *ministrae*, that is, "deaconesses."[36] In the process of his torturing these women he learned a number of things about early Christian worship, including the fact, as he later wrote to Trajan, that these Christians would sing "an antiphonal hymn to Christ as to a god."[37] Pliny the pagan might have viewed this worship as "degenerate," but there is no gainsaying the fact that the Roman governor understood Christians to be people who offered adoration to Christ as a divine being.

Another pagan author in the second century who had a similar impression is the satirist Lucian of Samosata (c.125–c.180). In his book *The Passing of Peregrinus*, which satirizes the career of the Cynic philosopher Peregrinus and was written after Peregrinus' self-immolation at the Olympic Games in 165, Lucian noted that at one point Peregrinus joined the Christians. Rising rapidly in their ranks, Peregrinus was soon incarcerated for his faith. Lucian poked fun at the way fellow Christians treated Peregrinus while he was in prison and noted that

---

34 For our knowledge of these events, see Pliny, *Letters* 10.96–97. For a translation of these texts, see Henry Bettenson in his selected and ed., *Documents of the Christian Church*, 2nd ed. (London: Oxford University Press, 1963), 3–4.
35 Pliny, *Letters* 10.96.8.
36 Pliny, *Letters* 10.96.8.
37 Pliny, *Letters* 10.96.8. See also the remarks of Clark, *Da Vinci Code on Trial*, 64–65; Nicky Gumbel, *The Da Vinci Code: A Response* (New York: Alpha North America, 2005), 17.

the efficiency the Christians show whenever something of community interest like this happens is unbelievable; they literally spare nothing. And so, because Peregrinus was in jail, money poured in from them; he picked up a very nice income this way. The poor wretches have convinced themselves, first and foremost, that they're all going to be immortal and live forever, which makes them take death lightly and willingly give themselves up to it. Furthermore, their first lawgiver [i.e. Christ] persuaded them that they are all brothers of one another when they deny the Greek gods (thereby breaking our law) and begin to worship him, the crucified sophist himself, and to live their lives according to his rules. They scorn all possessions without distinction and treat them as common property; doctrines like this they accept strictly on faith. Consequently, if a charlatan and trickster who knows how to capitalize on a situation comes among them, he quickly becomes exceedingly rich while laughing at the simpletons.[38]

This is a fascinating text in many ways, touching on, as it does, a number of aspects of early Christianity. What is important for the subject at hand is that Lucian, who has nothing but scorn for Christians, knew that they refused to participate in the worship of the Græco-Roman pantheon of gods. Instead, he said, they offered "worship" to a "crucified sophist," by which he obviously means Christ. It seems clear that Lucian viewed the worship of Christ as the Christian alternative to the worship of the gods of his pagan world. As such Lucian is another pagan witness to the fact that the second-century church worshipped Christ.

A final pagan witness from the third century is an item of graffiti.[39] In the quarters of the imperial page boys on the Palatine Hill in Rome, there has been found the drawing of a figure of a man on a cross with the head of a donkey. Beneath it is another figure, the figure of a boy, with his arm upraised, a typical gesture of worship found in early Christian art. Underneath these crude drawings are words in Latin, which translated state: "Alexamenos worships his god." There is little

---

38 Lucian, *The Passing of Peregrinus* 13.
39 For this piece of graffiti, see Michael Green, *Evangelism in the Early Church* (Grand Rapids: Eerdmans, 1970), 174–175.

doubt that this is an attack on one of the page boys, one Alexamenos, who was a Christian. And it is clear that the one who made this attack understood Alexamenos' religious beliefs to involve worship of the one who was crucified, namely Jesus Christ. It is interesting that another hand—possibly that of Alexamenos himself or one of his fellow page boys who was impressed with Alexamenos' witness—has scrawled below the above-mentioned statement, "Alexamenos is faithful."

IGNATIUS OF ANTIOCH

Apart from the apostle Paul, no other figure from the first two centuries of Christianity lays bare his soul as much as Ignatius of Antioch (died c.107–110). In the words of biblical scholar Bruce Metzger, Ignatius' letters, though somewhat staccato in style and punctuated with rhetorical embellishments, manifest "such strong faith and overwhelming love of Christ as to make them one of the finest literary expressions of Christianity during the second century."[40] Moreover, although we possess only seven authentic letters of Ignatius, they provide one of our richest resources for the understanding of Christianity in the era immediately following that of the Apostles.[41]

Ignatius, the bishop of the church in Antioch, had been arrested in this city somewhere between 107 and 110 and sent to Rome for trial.[42] There are no details of the persecution in which he was arrested, though Ignatius does mention others who were probably arrested during the same persecution and who had preceded him to Rome.[43] Thus, he was brought across the great roads of southern Asia Minor in the custody of ten Roman soldiers, whom he likens to "savage leopards."[44] He expects the end of the journey in Rome to have one certain outcome: death.

---

40 Cited John E. Lawyer, Jr., "Eucharist and Martyrdom in the Letters of Ignatius of Antioch," *Anglican Theological Review* 73 (1991): 281.

41 Rowan Williams, *Christian Spirituality* (Atlanta: John Knox Press, 1980), 14. On the transmission of the text of these letters, see the brief summary by Maxwell Staniforth in his trans., *Early Christian Writings: The Apostolic Fathers* (1968 ed.; reprint, Harmondsworth, Middlesex: Penguin Books, 1987), 55–56.

42 For the date, see Christine Trevett, *A Study of Ignatius of Antioch in Syria and Asia* (Lewiston/Queenston/Lampeter: Edwin Mellen Press, 1992), 3–9.

43 Ignatius, *Romans* 10.

44 Ignatius, *Romans* 5.

Among the concerns that were uppermost in Ignatius' mind as he wrote these letters was the heresy of Gnosticism, which was troubling a number of the churches to which he was writing and which maintained that the incarnation of Christ, and consequently his death and resurrection, did not really take place.[45] The divine status of Christ was not in debate, but on a number of occasions the letters show marked evidence of a very high Christology.[46]

In his letter to the Ephesian church, for example, Ignatius describes Christ as "God incarnate" and later in the letter reminds his readers that in Christ "God was revealing himself as a man."[47] Writing to the believers in Smyrna, Ignatius says that Christ is none other than "God the Word, the only-begotten Son."[48] At the very outset of his letter to the church at Rome, in which Ignatius sought to convince the church there not to attempt to free him from the Roman authorities but to allow him to fulfill his calling to be a martyr, he says of Jesus Christ that he is "our God."[49] Later in this letter, he says, "leave me to imitate the Passion of my God."[50] The one who died on the cross is none other than God. In referring to Christ as "God," Ignatius evidently expected the Christians to whom he was writing to be both familiar with such a view of Christ and comfortable with it.[51]

Reinforcing all of these texts is the statement in Ignatius' letter to the church at Magnesia-on-the-Meander that "Jesus Christ...was with the Father (*para patri*) from all eternity."[52] This clause is parallel to the

---

45 Lawyer, "Eucharist and Martyrdom," 281.

46 For a very brief overview of Ignatius' view of Christ as pre-existent deity, see McCready, *He Came Down from Heaven*, 210. For a detailed study of Ignatius' Christology, see Cullen I. K. Story, "The Christology of Ignatius of Antioch," *The Evangelical Quarterly* 56 (1984): 173–182; Charles Thomas Brown, *The Gospel and Ignatius of Antioch* (New York: Peter Lang, 2000), *passim*.

47 Ignatius, *Ephesians* 7 and 19. See also *Ephesians* 1, where Ignatius refers to the "blood of God." Williams (*The Da Vinci Code*, 23) cites the first of these texts as proof of post-apostolic Christian literature speaking of "Jesus plainly as God."

48 Ignatius, *Smyrnaeans* 1.

49 Ignatius, *Romans*, Salutation.

50 Ignatius, *Romans* 6.

51 Brown, *Gospel and Ignatius of Antioch*, 134.

52 Ignatius, *Magnesians* 6.

Johannine affirmation in John 1:1 that "the Word was with God (*pros ton theon*)." In *koinē* Greek at this time, the use of *para* with the dative to express the idea of "with someone" was receiving competition from *pros* with the accusative. In other words, Ignatius' statement that Jesus was "with the Father" and John's declaration that the Word "was with God" are making the same point: Jesus Christ/the Word has enjoyed an intimate, personal communion with the Father that is eternal in nature. But such a statement is ludicrous unless one believes in the deity of Christ.

THE *LETTER TO DIOGNETUS*

Easily overlooked among second-century Christian writings is the *Letter to Diognetus*, which has been well described by American author Avery Dulles as "the pearl of early Christian apologetics."[53] *In nuce*, this anonymous work is the joyous expression in Pauline terms of a man who stands utterly amazed at the gracious revelation of God's love in the death of his Son for sinners and who is seeking to persuade a Græco-Roman pagan by the name of Diognetus to make a similar commitment to the Christian faith. From the elegant Greek of the treatise it is probably correct to observe that the author had had a classical education and "possessed considerable literary skill and style."[54] Though the historical and geographical context of the work and audience is not known, it should probably be dated in the latter half of the second century.[55]

---

53 Avery Dulles, *A History of Apologetics* (New York: Corpus Instrumentorum/ Philadelphia: Westminster Press, 1971), 28.

54 L.W. Barnard, "The Enigma of the Epistle to Diognetus" in his *Studies in the Apostolic Fathers and Their Background* (New York: Shocken Books, 1966), 172. "[G]ood Hellenistic [Greek] with a marked approach to classical standards in vocabulary and diction" is the way H.G. Meecham describes the language of the letter ["The Theology of the Epistle to Diognetus," *The Expository Times* 54 (1942–1943): 97]. For a list of possible authors, see Barnard, "Epistle to Diognetus," 171–172.

55 For this dating, see Robert M. Grant, *Greek Apologists of the Second Century* (Philadelphia: Westminster Press, 1988), 178–179; Theofried Baumeister, "Zur Datierung der Schrift an Diognet," *Vigiliae Christianae* 42 (1988): 105–111. W.S. Walford, *Epistle to Diognetus* (London: James Nisbet & Co., 1908), 7–9 and Barnard, "Epistle to Diognetus," 172–173, would date it no later than 140.

Markus Bockmuehl has rightly noted that the theological centre of the *Letter to Diognetus* is found in chapters 7–9,[56] where, among other things, an answer is given to a question asked of the author by Diognetus, "Who is the God Christians believe in and worship?" The author formulates his answer to the question in terms of a high Christology. He begins by indicating that the Christian concept of God is not the product of human thought or philosophy.[57]

> [I]t is not an earthly discovery that has been passed on to them [i.e. Christians]. That which they think it worthwhile to guard so carefully is not a result of mortal thinking, nor is what has been entrusted to them a stewardship of merely human mysteries. On the contrary, the Almighty himself, the Creator of the universe and the invisible God, has from heaven planted the Truth, even the holy and incomprehensible Word, among men and fixed it firmly in their hearts.[58]

Here the author unequivocally affirms that Christian truth is ultimately not a matter of human reason or religious speculation. Rather, it is rooted in God's revelation of himself. Before he revealed himself to the world of paganism, God was unknown.

This revelation, the author of this treatise now maintains, was made through the incarnation of his Son. God has not, he writes,

> sent to humanity some servant, angel or ruler... Rather, [he has sent] the very Designer and Maker of the universe, by whom he made the heavens and confined the seas within their bounds; ... from whom the sun is assigned the limits of its daily course and

---

[56] *Revelation and Mystery in Ancient Judaism and Pauline Christianity* (Grand Rapids: Eerdmans, 1997), 219. Reference to the *Letter to Diognetus* is according to chapter and verse. I am following the chapter and verse divisions of H.G. Meecham, *The Epistle to Diognetus* (Manchester: Manchester University Press, 1949) and J.J. Thierry, ed., *The Epistle to Diognetus* (Leiden: E.J. Brill, 1964).

[57] For an earlier allusion in the letter to this fact, see *Diognetus* 5.3. The same point will be made yet a third time in *Diognetus* 8.1–5.

[58] *Diognetus* 7.1–2.

whom the moon obeys when he bids her to shine by night, and whom the stars obey as they follow the course of the moon. He is the One by whom all things have been set in order, determined, and placed in subjection—both the heavens and things in the heavens, the earth and things on the earth, the sea and the things in the sea, fire, air, abyss, the things in the heights and those in the depths and the realm between. Such was the One God sent to them. ...In gentleness and meekness he sent him, as a King sending his son who is a king. He sent him as God, he sent him as [man] to men, he sent him as Savior.[59]

Christianity, then, is ultimately not a human attempt to find God, be it by philosophical speculation or religious ritual. Rather, it is founded on God's revelation of himself, and that in a person, his Son. Although the personal name of the incarnate Son, Jesus, is not mentioned in this passage or even in the treatise as a whole,[60] there is no doubt that this is the person of whom the author here writes so eloquently.

Now, when many of the pagans in the Græco-Roman world stood outside of their homes on a cloudless night and looked up to the heavens they believed that the stars they could see were none other than divine beings. The long description of the Son's sovereignty over the entirety of creation clearly indicates that Christian theism does not believe in such a multiplicity of divine beings. Yet, it does believe in the deity of the Son. For the Son is depicted in terms that one can only regard as fully divine. He clearly does not belong to the order of creation. Who then is this One whom God has sent to reveal himself? Well, he is "a son." He is sent by God "as God." As L.B. Radford has commented: "He is God so truly that His coming can be described as the coming of God."[61]

---

59 *Diognetus* 7.2, 4.

60 On this fact, see Henri Irénée Marrou, *A Diognète* (Paris: Éditions du Cerf, 1951), 185–187.

61 *The Epistle to Diognetus* (London: Society for Promoting Christian Knowledge, 1908), 39.

A CONCLUDING WORD

More textual evidence from the second and the third centuries than what is adduced here could have been cited.[62] It would uniformly bear out what the texts we have looked at consistently assert: Jesus Christ was viewed as a divine being in both the New Testament era as well as in the two centuries that followed. As Bart Ehrman, himself no friend to orthodox Christianity, states: "Scholars who study the history of Christianity will find it bizarre, at best, to hear [Brown] claim that Christians before the Council of Nicæa did not consider Jesus to be divine."[63] What the creedal statement issued at this council declared, namely that Jesus is "true God of true God" and of "one being with the Father," had been the central conviction of the church in the years since the apostolic era. And this was the conviction of the church, for it ultimately derived from the church's foundational text, the New Testament itself.

---

62 For other second-century authors, see McCready, *He Came Down from Heaven*, 211–218.

63 Ehrman, *Truth and Fiction in The Da Vinci Code*, 15.

3

"The ground and pillar of our faith"

Irenaeus on the perfection and salvific impact of the Scriptures[1]

> All Scripture, which has been given to us by God, shall be found to be perfectly consistent...and there shall be heard one harmonious melody in us, praising in hymns that God who created all things.
> —IRENAEUS OF LYONS[2]

---

1 I am grateful to Joe Harrod and Dwayne Ewers, both of Louisville, Kentucky, for help received during the writing of what became this chapter. This chapter originally appeared as *"Fundamentum et Columnan Fidei Nostrae*: Irenaeus on the Perfect and Saving Nature of the Scriptures" in James K. Hoffmeier and Dennis R. Magary, ed., *Do Historical Matters Matter to Faith? A Critical Appraisal of Modern and Postmodern Approaches to Scripture* (Wheaton: Crossway, 2012), 135–147, and is reproduced here by kind permission of Crossway.

2 Irenaeus, *Against Heresies* 2.28.3.

The discovery of a cache of fifty or so Gnostic texts at Nag Hammadi in 1945 proved to be the major catalyst in the emergence in the twentieth century of the study of Gnosticism as a significant academic discipline. And as that discipline has matured over the years, these texts have confirmed in the minds of some scholars that the earliest communities of professing Christians were truly diverse bodies.[3] Yet, while an attentive reading of these texts does reveal some clear differences between the various Gnostic communities, such a reading also makes evident that they shared a number of commonalities over against their opponents in the ancient catholic church. The majority of the Gnostics were essentially committed to a radical dualism of immateriality and matter. The former was divine and wholly good, while the latter was irredeemably evil. They were essentially hostile to monotheism, since they postulated the existence of a variety of divine beings. Through an upheaval within the supreme divine being, which the various Gnostic systems explained by means of an atemporal myth, elements of the divine became trapped within material bodies. These material bodies and the entire material realm were the work of a lesser divinity (the demiurge), understood as either the God of the Old Testament or even Satan. Since awareness of the divine element's entrapment in the human body was not immediately known, knowledge of one's true state was needed, which, for most Gnostic systems, involved Jesus as the revealer, and hence his role as savior. Central to this entire quest was an eschatology that entailed escape from all materiality and temporality. [4]

Combating Gnosticism involved the finest of the earliest Christian thinkers, from Justin Martyr (c.100/110–c.165) to the great Alexandrian exegete Origen (c.185–254), but it is intriguing that what is probably the most significant reply to the leading heresiarchs of the

---

3 See, for example, David Brakke, *The Gnostics: Myth, Ritual, and Diversity in Early Christianity* (Cambridge: Harvard University Press, 2010).

4 For this mini-morphology of Gnosticism, I am indebted to Christoph Markschies, *Gnosis: An Introduction*, trans. John Bowden (London/New York: T&T Clark, 2003), 16–17; Robert A. Segal, "Religion: Karen L. King, What Is Gnosticism?," *Times Literary Supplement* (November 21, 2003), 31. For a selection of Gnostic texts, see Werner Foerster, ed., *Gnosis: A Selection of Gnostic Texts*, trans. R. McL. Wilson (Oxford: Clarendon Press, 1972 and 1974), 2 vols.

second century, Valentinus (*fl*.138–166)⁵ and Marcion (*fl*.150s–160s),⁶ came from a missionary theologian who complained about his ability to write theology. Although Greek was his mother tongue, he reckoned that he had spent far too much time among the Celts of Gaul speaking Gaulish, a Celtic language now extinct, and thus he believed he had lost any real facility he had had with his own language.⁷ Moreover, he claimed that he had never formally studied rhetoric and that he had neither the literary skills nor the "beauty of language" necessary for the task of a theologian.⁸ And yet many later students of his thought

---

5   According to Irenaeus, *Against Heresies* 3.4.3, Valentinus came to Rome during the episcopate of Hyginus (c.138–c.142) and was there till that of Anicetus (c.155–c.166). For Valentinus and his followers, see especially Markschies, *Gnosis*, 89–94; Einar Thomassen, *The Spiritual Seed: The Church of the 'Valentinians'* (Leiden/Boston: Brill, 2006); Ismo Dunderberg, *Beyond Gnosticism: Myth, Lifestyle, and Society in the School of Valentinus* (New York: Columbia University Press, 2008).

In an interesting venture into virtual history, Dunderberg has also written an article about what "Christianity" would have looked like if Valentinus' heresy had been successful in subverting orthodoxy. As with all virtual history, the further away in time Dunderberg's speculations are from Valentinus' actual lifetime, the more "sci-fi-ish" they get. See his "Valentinus and His School: What Might Have Been," *The Fourth R* 22, no.6 (November–December 2009): 3–10.

6   According to Irenaeus, *Against Heresies* 3.4.3, Marcion was principally active in Rome during the episcopate of Anicetus. For two recent overviews of Marcion's life and teaching, see Markschies, *Gnosis*, 86–89; Paul Foster, "Marcion: His Life, Works, Beliefs, and Impact," *The Expository Times* 121 (March 2010): 269–280. There were significant differences between Marcion and the Gnostics, and in many ways Marcion should not be classified as a Gnostic. On this, see the brief summary by Markschies, *Gnosis*, 88–89.

7   Irenaeus, *Against Heresies* 1.pref.3. For discussion of Irenaeus and Gaulish, see also C. Philip Slate, "Two Features of Irenaeus" Missiology," *Missiology* 23, no.4 (October 1995): 433–435.

8   Irenaeus, *Against Heresies* 1.pref.3. All translations from *Against Heresies* are by the author unless otherwise indicated. For the Greek and Latin text of *Against Heresies*, I have used Adelin Rousseau, et al., ed., *Irénée de Lyon: Contre les heresies*, 5 vols. (Sources chrétiennes, vols. 100.1–2, 152–153, 210–211, 263–264, 293–294; Paris: Les Éditions du Cerf, 1965 [vol.4], 1969 [vol.5], 1974 [vol.3], 1979 [vol.1], 1982 [vol.2]).

On Irenaeus' claim to have no knowledge of rhetoric, see Robert M. Grant, *Irenaeus of Lyons* (London: Routledge, 1997), 46–53; M.A. Donovan, *One Right Reading? A Guide to Irenaeus* (Collegeville, Minnesota: The Liturgical Press, 1997), 10–11; Eric Osborn, *Irenaeus of Lyons* (Cambridge: Cambridge University Press, 2001), 3–4.

rightly believe him to be a truly gifted expositor of what would become the core of orthodox Christianity.[9] The person in question is, of course, Irenaeus of Lyons (c.130/140–c.200), and there is a vigor and winsomeness about him that makes many students of his extant works wish that far more was known about his life than is available.[10]

SPARSE DETAILS OF A SIGNIFICANT LIFE

There seems to be no consensus in patristic scholarship about the place of Irenaeus' birth. There is a good likelihood that it was Smyrna (the modern Turkish city of Izmir), since he heard Polycarp of Smyrna (69/70–155/6) preach there when he was young, and Polycarp appears to have been something of a Christian mentor to him.[11] His date of birth is also obscure, with suggested dates ranging from 98 to 147.[12] Most

---

9 W. Brian Shelton, "Irenaeus" in Bradley G. Green, ed., *Shapers of Christian Orthodoxy: Engaging with Early and Medieval Theologians* (Downers Grove: InterVarsity Press, 2010), 15–16.

10 F.R. Montgomery Hitchcock, "Irenaeus of Lugdunum," *Expository Times* 44 (1932–1933): 167. Cyril C. Richardson was surely right when he stated, "The significance of Irenaeus cannot be overestimated" ["Introduction to Early Christian Literature and Its Setting" in his trans. and ed., *Early Christian Fathers* (The Library of Christian Classics, vol. 1; Philadelphia: The Westminster Press, 1953), 18]. It needs noting that there are some, however, who "find Irenaeus and what he stood for to be truly and genuinely unappealing" [C.E. Hill, *Who Chose the Gospels? Probing the Great Gospel Conspiracy* (Oxford: Oxford University Press, 2010), 52]. Hill details the dislike of certain contemporary scholars for Irenaeus and his thinking (*Who Chose the Gospels?*, 52–68).

For what follows in terms of a biographical sketch of Irenaeus, I have found the following sketches of his life helpful: Denis Minns, *Irenaeus* (Washington: Georgetown University Press, 1997), 1–9; Grant, *Irenaeus of Lyons*, 1–10; Donovan, *One Right Reading?*, 7–10; Osborn, *Irenaeus of Lyons*, 1–7; Shelton, "Irenaeus" in Green, ed., *Shapers of Christian Orthodoxy*, 17–24; D. Jeffrey Bingham, "Irenaeus of Lyons" in his ed., *The Routledge Companion to Early Christian Thought* (London/New York: Routledge, 2010), 137–139; Michael Todd Wilson, "Preaching Irenaeus: A Second-Century Pastor Speaks to a Twenty-First Century Church" (D.Min. thesis, Knox Theological Seminary, 2011), 60–76.

11 *The Martyrdom of Polycarp* 22.2 and "The Ending according to the Moscow Epilogue" 2; Irenaeus, *Letter to Florinus* (Eusebius, *Church History* 5.20.4–8); Irenaeus, *Against Heresies* 3.3.4.

12 Osborn, *Irenaeus of Lyons*, 2.

likely he was born between 130 and 140.[13] It is also quite possible that Irenaeus studied under Justin Martyr, either in Ephesus or later at Rome.[14] By the mid-150s, the time of Polycarp's martyrdom, Irenaeus was residing in Rome,[15] where he may have come with Polycarp on the latter's visit to Rome in 153 or 154, two years prior to his death.[16] It was during this time in Rome that Irenaeus had significant contact with the followers of Valentinus and Marcion, whose ideas Irenaeus would seek to refute in his *magnum opus*, *The Detection and Refutation of the Pseudo-Knowledge* (c.180), known today more simply as *Against Heresies*.[17]

From Rome, Irenaeus travelled to Lyons (Latin: Lugdunum) in southern Gaul as a missionary. This move would have taken place before the mid-160s, when Justin Martyr was put to death in Rome for his faith in Christ.[18] Situated at the confluence of the Rhône and Saône rivers, second-century Lyons was a miniature Rome in many ways. A bustling cosmopolitan centre of some seventy thousand or so in Irenaeus' day, it was the key port on the trade routes up and down the Rhône. It was also a provincial capital, the heart of the Roman road system for Gaul, and the seat of an important military garrison. Similar to Rome, its population contained a large Greek-speaking element, and it was among this element that Christianity had become firmly established in the city.[19] For example, in an account of the martyrdom of a large number of believers from Lyons and nearby Vienne in 177 there were two individuals who were identified as coming from Asia Minor and who would therefore have been Greek-speaking: Attalus,

---

13 Osborn, *Irenaeus of Lyons*, 2.
14 See Michael Slusser, "How Much Did Irenaeus Learn from Justin?" in F. Young, M. Edwards and P. Parvis, ed., *Studia Patristica* (Leuven/Paris/Dudley, Massachusetts: Peeters Press, 2006), 40:515–520.
15 *The Martyrdom of Polycarp*, "The Ending according to the Moscow Manuscript," 2.
16 Irenaeus, *Letter to Victor of Rome* (Eusebius, *Church History* 5.24.11–18).
17 The title of the treatise is based on the wording of 1 Timothy 6:20. On Irenaeus' encounter with disciples of Valentinus, see *Against Heresies* 1.pref.2. Irenaeus also had a collection of Gnostic works that he studied so as to better respond to his theological opponents. See *Against Heresies* 1.31.2.
18 Hitchcock, "Irenaeus of Lugdunum," 168.
19 For this overview about the city of Roman Lyons, I am indebted to Edward Rochie Hardy, "Introduction" to "Selections from the Work *Against Heresies* by Irenaeus, Bishop of Lyons" in Richardson, trans. and ed., *Early Christian Fathers*, 347–348.

whose family came from Pergamum, and a certain Alexander of Phrygia.[20]

Irenaeus was away in Rome during this brutal outburst of persecution. When he returned to the Rhône valley, he found the leadership in the churches of Lyons and Vienne decimated. He was subsequently appointed bishop of Lyons, as the previous bishop, Pothinus (c.87–177), had succumbed in prison after being beaten during the persecution.[21] Within a couple of years after his return to Lyons, Irenaeus was hard at work writing *Against Heresies*.[22] The final sight we catch of Irenaeus on the scene of history is a letter that he wrote to Victor I, bishop of Rome from about 189 to 198, seeking to defuse the Quartodeciman controversy. Differences between the church at Rome and various churches in Asia Minor regarding the dating of Easter had led the former to threaten excommunication of the latter if the eastern churches did not get into line with Roman practice. Irenaeus pled for tolerance and diversity of practice.[23]

This display of irenicism appears to have been typical of the second-century theologian. When it came to the Gnostics and their thinking, though, Irenaeus was fiercely antagonistic of what he saw as sheer error.[24] At the heart of this antagonism was Irenaeus' deeply held conviction about the perfection of the Scriptures and the fact that this perfection provided solid ground for saving belief in the meta-narrative of the Bible.

---

20 Eusebius, *Church History* 5.1.17, 49.

21 Eusebius, *Church History* 5.1.29–31.

22 For the date of *Against Heresies*, see Robert M. Grant, *Greek Apologists of the Second Century* (Philadelphia: Westminster Press, 1988), 182–183; Donovan, *One Right Reading?*, 9–10.

23 Eusebius, *Church History* 5.23–25. On Irenaeus' role in this controversy, see also Roch Kereszty, "The Unity of the Church in the Theology of Irenaeus," *The Second Century* 4 (1984): 215–216; Osborn, *Irenaeus of Lyons*, 5–6. According to a late, and unreliable, tradition, first mentioned by Gregory of Tours (d.594), Irenaeus died as a martyr (*The Glory of the Martyrs* 49). For a discussion of the claim that Irenaeus was martyred, see J. van der Straeten, "Saint Irénée fut-il martyr?" in *Les Martyrs de Lyon (177)* (Paris: Éditions du Centre national de la Recherche scientifique, 1978), 145–153.

24 It was Eusebius of Caesarea who first described Irenaeus as a peacemaker, making a play on the meaning of his name. See Eusebius, *Church History* 5.24.18.

SCRIPTURAE PERFECTAE

Norbert Brox has rightly noted that in "Irenaeus this principle stands at the beginning [of his thought]: that the Bible is in every respect perfect and sufficient."[25] Irenaeus' stress upon the perfection and sufficiency of the Scriptures is due in part to the strident affirmation by the Gnostics of the errancy of the Bible. When confronted with biblical arguments against their views, the Gnostics, according to Irenaeus, maintained that the Scriptures cannot be trusted. They rejected key aspects of the Old Testament out of hand, while they were adamant that the apostolic documents of the New Testament were penned by men who could be mistaken and thus introduced contradictions into their writings. What alone could be trusted was the teaching from the apostles that had been passed down to them by word of mouth (*per vivam vocem*). And for support of this secret oral tradition, they adduced Paul's words in 1 Corinthians 2:6 ("we speak wisdom among the perfect").[26]

Over against the Gnostic distortion of the Scriptures, Irenaeus reveals himself to be, as Reinhold Seeberg aptly put it, "the first great representative of biblicism."[27] The Scriptures are to be the normative source for the teaching of the Christian community. As Ellen Flesseman-van Leer noted, when "Irenaeus wants to prove the truth of a doctrine materially, he turns to Scripture."[28] They are the "Scriptures of the Lord" (*dominicis Scripturis*), and it would be absolute folly to abandon the words of the Lord, Moses and the other prophets, which set forth the truth, for the foolish opinions of Irenaeus' opponents.[29] Given the

---

25 Norbert Brox, "Irenaeus and the Bible. A Special Contribution" in Charles Kannengiesser, ed., *Handbook of Patristic Exegesis: The Bible in Ancient Christianity* (Leiden: E.J. Brill, 2004), 486. On Irenaeus' bibliology, see also D. Farkasfalvy, "Theology of Scripture in St. Irenaeus," *Revue Bénédictine* 68 (1968): 319–333.

26 Irenaeus, *Against Heresies* 3.2.1–2.

27 "Irenäus...ist der erste große Vertreter des Biblizismus" [*Lehrbuch der Dogmengeshcichte*, 2nd ed. (Leipzig: A. Deichert'sche Verlagsbuchhandlung Nachf., 1908), 290]. Though, note, the caution by Osborn, *Irenaeus of Lyons*, 172.

28 Ellen Flesseman-van Leer, *Tradition and Scripture in the Early Church* (Assen: Van Gorcum, 1953), 144.

29 Irenaeus, *Against Heresies* 2.30.6. For the translation of the phrase *dominicis Scripturis*, see John Lawson, *The Biblical Theology of Saint Irenaeus* (London: Epworth Press, 1948), 23–24, n.4.

Gnostic argument that the Scriptures had been falsified and the Gnostic propensity to fob off their writings as genuine revelation, Irenaeus rightly discerned that a discussion of the nature of Scripture was vital. Scholars disagree over the exact boundaries of Irenaeus' New Testament,[30] with some even asserting that Irenaeus was the creative genius behind the creation of the New Testament canon.[31] And there is also no essential agreement as to how Scripture relates to tradition in Irenaeus' thought.[32] But what is not disputable is his view of Scripture. The Bishop of Lyons was confident that the "Scriptures are indeed perfect (*perfectae*)" texts because they were spoken by the Word of God and his Spirit.[33] Referring specifically to the human authors of various books of the New Testament, Irenaeus asserted that they were given perfect knowledge by the Holy Spirit and thus were

---

30 For differing perspectives on Irenaeus' canon, see, for example, G. Nathanael Bonwetsch, *Die Theologie des Irenäus* (Gütersloh: C. Bertelsmann, 1925), 40; Osborn, *Irenaeus of Lyons*, 180–182; Brox, "Irenaeus and the Bible" in Kannengiesser, ed., *Handbook of Patristic Exegesis*, 484; M.C. Steenberg, "Irenaeus, Graphe, and the Status of Hermas," *St Vladimir's Theological Quarterly* 53 (2009): 29–66; Andreas Köstenberger and Michael J. Kruger, *The Heresy of Orthodoxy: How Contemporary Culture's Fascination with Diversity Has Reshaped Our Understanding of Early Christianity* (Wheaton: Crossway, 2010), 151–175.

31 For example, see Elaine Pagels, *Beyond Belief: The Secret Gospel of Thomas* (New York: Random House, 2003), 74–142, and Arthur Bellinzoni, "The Gospel of Luke in the Apostolic Fathers" in Andrew F. Gregory and Christopher M. Tuckett, ed., *Trajectories through the New Testament and the Apostolic Fathers* (Oxford: Oxford University Press, 2005), 49, n.17. According to Bellinzoni in this footnote: "Irenaeus...essentially created the core of the New Testament canon of Holy Scripture." But see the convincing riposte by Hill, *Who Chose the Gospels?*, 34–68.

32 See, for instance, Juan Ochagavía, *Visibile Patris Filius: A Study of Irenaeus' Teaching on Revelation and Tradition* (Rome: Pont. Institutum Orientalium Studiorum, 1964), especially 174–205; Dominic J. Unger and John J. Dillon, "Introduction" to *St. Irenaeus of Lyons: Against the Heresies*, trans. Dominic J. Unger and rev. John J. Dillon (New York: Newman Press, 1992), 8–11.

Also critical to note, but which I do not have space to deal with in this chapter, is Irenaeus' emphasis on the role of the church in the interpretation of Scripture. For this emphasis, see the helpful remarks of Brox, "Irenaeus and the Bible" in Kannengiesser, ed., *Handbook of Patristic Exegesis*, 495–499.

33 Irenaeus, *Against Heresies* 2.28.2. See also *Against Heresies* 4.33.8.

incapable of proclaiming error.³⁴ "Our Lord Jesus Christ," Irenaeus argued,

> is the Truth and there is no falsehood in him, even as David also said when he prophesied about his birth from a virgin and the resurrection from the dead, "Truth has sprung from the earth" (Ps. 85:11). And the Apostles, being disciples of the Truth, are free from all falsehood, for falsehood has no fellowship with the truth, just as darkness has no fellowship with the light, but the presence of the one drives away the other.³⁵

Here Irenaeus based the fidelity of the apostolic writings upon the absolute truthfulness of the Lord Jesus Christ and the conviction that truth and falsehood are polar opposites. From Irenaeus' standpoint, if Christ is the embodiment of truth, it is impossible to conceive of him ever uttering falsehood. By extension, the writings of his authorized representatives are also incapable of error. This quality of absolute truthfulness can also be predicated of the authors of the books of the Old Testament, since the Spirit who spoke through the apostles also spoke through the Old Testament writers.³⁶ Thus the Scriptures form a harmonious whole: "All Scripture, which has been given to us by God, shall be found to be perfectly consistent…and through the many diversified utterances (of Scripture) there shall be heard one harmonious melody in us, praising in hymns that God who created all things."³⁷

A second major emphasis in Irenaeus' bibliology is the unity of the testaments, and by extension, the unity of the history of God's salvific work. Marcion's denial of the revelatory value of the Old Testament led Irenaeus to affirm that the God who gave the law and the God who revealed the gospel is "one and the same." One piece of proof lay in the fact that in both the Old and New Testaments, the first and greatest

---

34 Irenaeus, *Against Heresies* 3.1.1.
35 Irenaeus, *Against Heresies* 3.5.1.
36 Irenaeus, *Against Heresies* 3.6.1, 5; 3.21.4; 4.20.8; *Demonstration of the Apostolic Preaching* 49. See also Bernard Sesboüé, "La preuve par les Ecritures chez S. Irénée; à propos d'un texte difficile du Livre III de l'Adversus Haereses," *Nouvelle Revue Théologique* 103 (1981): 872–887.
37 Irenaeus, *Against Heresies* 2.28.3. See also *Against Heresies* 1.8.1.

commandment was to love God with the entirety of one's being and then, to love one's neighbour as oneself.[38] Another line of evidence was the similar revelation of the holiness of God in both Testaments.[39] Irenaeus also urged his readers—which he hoped would include his Gnostic opponents—to "carefully read (*legite diligentius*)" both the Old Testament prophets and the apostolic writings of the New Testament, and they would find that the leading contours of Christ's ministry were predicted by the prophets of ancient Israel.[40] There is therefore a common theme that informs both Old Testament prophets and the New Testament apostles: Christ. He is that which binds together the covenants.[41] And this commonality speaks of one God behind both portions of Scripture. To reject the Old Testament is therefore tantamount to a failure to discern this Christological centre of the entirety of the Bible and to show oneself as not truly spiritual, a strong indictment of the Gnostics and their exegesis.[42]

FUNDAMENTUM ET COLUMNAM FIDEI NOSTRAE

Help in elucidating this unified history of salvation was especially found in the words of the apostle Paul, particularly those Pauline texts that had to do with the unity of the church.[43] Irenaeus viewed the Old

---

38 Irenaeus, *Against Heresies* 4.12.3.

39 Irenaeus, *Against Heresies* 4.27.4–28.1.

40 Irenaeus, *Against Heresies* 4.34.1. See also *Against Heresies* 4.7.1; 4.9.1; 4.11.4; 4.36.5.

41 Irenaeus, *Against Heresies* 4.9.1; 4.26.1. See in this regard Iain M. MacKenzie, *Irenaeus's Demonstration of the Apostolic Preaching. A Theological Commentary and Translation* (Aldershot: Ashgate, 2002), 60–62.

42 Irenaeus, *Against Heresies* 4.33.15. Irenaeus had been asked—possibly by a Gnostic—if the ministry of Christ had been announced and typified in the Old Testament, what then was truly new about his coming? Well, Irenaeus explained, the difference was this: What had been a matter of types and predictions was now reality, the Lord himself had come among them, and filled his servants with joy and freedom. See Irenaeus, *Against Heresies* 4.34.1.

43 John S. Coolidge, *The Pauline Basis of the Concept of Scriptural Form in Irenaeus* (Protocol of the colloquy of The Center for Hermeneutical Studies in Hellenistic and Modern Culture, no.8; Berkeley, California: The Center for Hermeneutical Studies in Hellenistic and Modern Culture, 1975), 1–3; Richard A. Norris, "Irenaeus' Use of Paul in His Polemic against the Gnostics" in William S. Babcock, ed., *Paul and the*

Testament prophets as having an essential unity with the New Testament since, in his mind, they were actually members of the body of Christ. As Irenaeus explained:

> Certainly the prophets, along with other things that they predicted, also foretold this, that on whomever the Spirit of God would rest, and who would obey the word of the Father, and serve him according to their strength, should suffer persecution, and be stoned and killed. For the prophets prefigured in themselves all these things, because of their love for God and because of his word. For since they themselves were members of Christ, each one of them in so far as he was a member...revealed the prophecy [assigned him]. All of them, although many, prefigured one, and proclaimed the things that belong to one. For just as the working of the whole body is disclosed by means of our [physical] members, yet the shape of the total man is not displayed by one member, but by all; so also did all the prophets prefigure the one [Christ], while every one of them, in so far as he was a member, did, in accordance with this, complete the [established] dispensation, and prefigured that work of Christ assigned to him as a member.[44]

The diverse predictive ministries of the Old Testament prophets were essentially part of the unity of the revelation of Christ. Irenaeus went on to borrow Pauline passages that spoke of the unity of the universal church in Ephesians 4 to describe the attentive reader's perception of the unity between the prophetic texts of the Old Testament and the texts that contain their New Testament fulfillment. In his words:

> If any one believes in the one God, who also made all things by the Word, just as both Moses says, "God said, 'Let there be light,' and there was light" [Genesis 1:3], and as we read in the Gospel,

---

Legacies of Paul (Dallas: Southern Methodist University Press, 1990), 91–92.

44 Irenaeus, *Against Heresies* 4.33.10, trans. Alexander Roberts and W.H. Rambaut in A. Cleveland Coxe, *The Apostolic Fathers with Justin Martyr and Irenaeus*, Ante-Nicene Fathers, Vol. 1 (1885 ed.; reprint, New York: Charles Scribner's Sons, 1903), 509, altered.

"All things were made by him, and nothing was made without him" [John 1:3], and similarly the Apostle Paul [says], "There is one Lord, one faith, one baptism, one God and Father, who is over all, and through all, and in us all" [Ephesians 4:5–6]—this man will first of all "hold the head, from which the whole body is firmly joined and united together, and which, through every joint according to the measure of the supply of each several part, causes the body to grow so that it builds itself up in love" [Ephesians 4:16]. Then afterwards shall every word also seem consistent to him, if he will carefully read the Scriptures among those who are presbyters in the Church, among whom is the apostolic doctrine, as I have shown.[45]

In another instance, Irenaeus applied 1 Corinthians 12:4–7, a passage that speaks of the diversity of the gifts in the body of Christ as being essential to the unity of the church, to the unity between the different prophetic ministries in the Old Testament and the saving work of Christ in the new covenant.[46] As John Coolidge has rightly pointed out, it appears that, for Irenaeus, perception of the unity between the Testaments is concomitant to participation in the communal unity of the church.[47]

It is surely this use of Pauline statements about ecclesial unity to affirm the unity of the Scriptures that explains Irenaeus' curious treatment of a phrase from 1 Timothy 3:15. The church, the Pauline verse declares, is the "pillar and ground of the truth." This striking statement becomes for Irenaeus an affirmation about the Scriptures. At the outset of Book 3 of *Against Heresies*, where Irenaeus explicitly rejected the claim by some of the Gnostics that the apostles compromised the truth in their transmission of it, the missionary theologian defended the integrity of the "plan of salvation (*dispositionem salutis*)" as it had come down to him in the written text of the Bible. The oral message of the

---

45 Irenaeus, *Against Heresies* 4.32.1. On Irenaeus' conviction of the vital importance of reading the Scriptures within the context of the church catholic, see also *Against Heresies* 3.24.1; 5.20.2.
46 Irenaeus, *Against Heresies* 4.20.6.
47 Coolidge, *Pauline Basis of the Concept of Scriptural Form*, 3.

apostles was identical to what was enshrined in the Scriptures and thus the latter could serve as "the ground and pillar (*fundamentum et columnam*) of our faith."[48] Again, when Irenaeus insisted that there had to be four gospels, and only four, because of the four corners of the earth and the earth's four winds—there being an aesthetic harmony between the four Gospels and creation[49]—he again stated that "the pillar and ground of the Church is the Gospel and the Spirit of life."[50] The inclusion of the Holy Spirit here is not accidental, for if Christ is the common theme of all of the Scriptures, the Spirit is the One who inspired all of the authors of the Bible to speak of the one Saviour.

IMMORTALITAS PANIS

In Irenaeus' mind what was at stake in this battle between the ancient church and her Gnostic opponents was nothing less than eternal salvation. The myth-making of the Gnostics subverted the biblical narrative of creation, fall, redemption and consummation. It attributed creation to the ignorant Demiurge and thus was constrained to find life's meaning outside of the created realm and history. The Gnostic denial of the biblical account of the fall of Adam and Eve into disobedience[51] had profound implications for understanding the enslavement of their progeny to the devil,[52] their progeny's enmity to God[53] and the reign of death on the earth.[54] The Gnostics further rejected the corporal nature of the incarnation and death of Christ, and thus undermined the core of biblical salvation, the main lineaments of which had been predicted by the Old Testament writers, and which was accomplished by Christ.[55] Finally, their failure to appreciate Christ's salvific work as

---

48 Irenaeus, *Against Heresies* 3.1.1.
49 Hill, *Who Chose the Gospels?*, 34–38.
50 Irenaeus, *Against Heresies* 3.11.8.
51 Irenaeus, *Against Heresies* 3.22.4; 3.23.1. On the creation of Adam, see *Against Heresies* 3.23.2; 4.14.1.
52 Irenaeus, *Against Heresies* 3.23.2.
53 Irenaeus, *Against Heresies* 5.17.1.
54 Irenaeus, *Against Heresies* 5.23.1–2.
55 Irenaeus, *Against Heresies* 1.10.1; 3.18.7; 5.1.1; 5.14.1–3. Irenaeus is the first to explicitly formulate what would become a cardinal tenet of Christianity, namely, in the words of Henry Chadwick, "any part of human nature, body, soul, or spirit, which

it relates to the whole human being also meant that they distorted the biblical understanding of the consummation.[56]

An excellent prism through which Irenaeus' conception of this meta-narrative of Christianity can be seen is his teaching regarding the work of the Holy Spirit.[57] The Spirit was intimately involved in the work of creation, for he and the Son are "the hands (*manus*)" of God the Father. By his Word and by his Spirit, the Father "makes, disposes, and governs all things, and gives existence to everything."[58] Thus, Irenaeus understood God's statement in Genesis 1:26, "let us make man," to be a discussion between the Father and his "hands," the Son and the Holy Spirit. In Irenaeus' words:

> The Scripture says, "And God formed man, taking dirt of the earth, and breathed into his face the breath of life" [Genesis 2:7]. Angels, therefore, did not make us nor did they form us, for angels were not able to make the image of God (*imaginem...Dei*), nor any other but the true God, nor any power far away from the Father of all things. For God did not need these [beings] to make

---

the Redeemer did not make his own is not saved" [Henry Chadwick, *The Church in Ancient Society: From Galilee to Gregory the Great* (Oxford: Oxford University Press, 2001), 102].

56 Irenaeus, *Against Heresies* 1.10.1; 5.8–17. For a helpful overview of Irenaeus' understanding of the entire Christian meta-narrative, see Shelton, "Irenaeus" in Green, ed., *Shapers of Christian Orthodoxy*, 44–50.

57 J.N.D. Kelly rightly observed that "Irenaeus's vision of the Godhead [is] the most complete and...most explicitly Trinitarian" of all the authors of second century except for the Latin-speaking North African Tertullian (*fl.*190–215) [*Early Christian Doctrines*, 4th ed. (London: Adam & Charles Black, 1968), 107]. Similarly Hitchcock, "Irenaeus of Lugdunum," 170. See also MacKenzie, *Irenaeus's Demonstration of the Apostolic Preaching*, 83, and the nuanced discussion of M.C. Steenberg, *Irenaeus on Creation: The Cosmic Christ and the Saga of Redemption* (Leiden: E.J. Brill, 2008), 62–64. Pace Brakke, *Gnostics*, 124, who argues that "Irenaeus did not simply believe in one God. Rather, he distinguished between the ultimate God, the Father,...and two clearly lower manifestations of God: the Word or Son...and the Spirit."

J. Armitage Robinson, trans., *St Irenaeus: The Demonstration of the Apostolic Preaching* (London: Society for Promoting Christian Knowledge, 1920), 24–68, is still a helpful summary of Irenaean pneumatology.

58 Irenaeus, *Against Heresies* 1.22.1.

what he had himself predetermined to make, as if he did not have his own hands. For always present with him were the Word and Wisdom, the Son and the Spirit, by whom and in whom, freely and independently, he made all things, to whom also he speaks, saying, "Let us make man according to our image and likeness" [Genesis 1:26].[59]

Far from being an image that subordinates the Spirit, this idea of the Spirit as being one of the Father's hands gives expression to a rich trinitarian view of God and his creative work.[60]

The Spirit not only created the first man and woman, Adam and Eve, but he rested on them in the garden, providing them with a "robe of sanctity (*sanctitatis stolam*)," which was lost at the Fall, as was the Spirit himself.[61] And without the Spirit of God, there was only death.[62] One of the great purposes, then, of the coming of Christ was the restoration of the Spirit to humanity. The Spirit descended on Christ, so that he could give the Spirit to fallen human beings, and lead them to communion with the Father and so make them spiritually fruitful in their lives.[63] By indwelling the human heart, the Spirit prepares men and women for the beatific vision, since he is "the bread of immortality."[64] And thus, in the end, "the fruit of the Spirit's work is the salvation of the flesh."[65]

---

59 Irenaeus, *Against Heresies* 4.20.1. See also *Against Heresies* 2.2.5; 4.pref.4; 5.1.3; 5.15.4; 5.28.4. On these texts, see Steenberg, *Irenaeus on Creation*, 62–84.

60 Lawson, *Biblical Theology of Saint Irenaeus*, 119–139; Steenberg, *Irenaeus on Creation*, 62–84.

61 Irenaeus, *Against Heresies* 3.23.5. For discussions on how to understand Irenaean anthropology, see Lawson, *Biblical Theology of Saint Irenaeus*, 199–251, *passim*; Mary Ann Donovan, "Alive to the Glory of God: A Key Insight in St. Irenaeus," *Theological Studies* 49 (1988): 283–297; Steenberg, *Irenaeus on Creation*, 101–193.

62 Irenaeus, *Against Heresies* 5.9.3.

63 Irenaeus, *Against Heresies* 3.9.3; 3.17.1–3; 5.1.1–2.

64 Irenaeus, *Against Heresies* 4.38.1. See also *Against Heresies* 5.8.1; 5.12.1–4.

65 Irenaeus, *Against Heresies* 5.12.4.

AN IRENAEAN PRAYER

Irenaeus was confident that a humble listening to and reading of the Word of God would produce a faith that was "firm, not fictitious, but solely true."[66] And one of his manifest goals in *Against Heresies* was to produce such a faith among his Gnostic opponents. Irenaeus' fierce opposition to Gnosticism did not arise from a hunger for power, as some recent scholars have argued, but out of a genuine love for truth and a sincere desire for the spiritual well-being of his fellow believers and their theological opponents.[67] This pastoral heart is well revealed as he prayed for the latter at the close of his third book of *Against Heresies*:

> And now we pray that these men may not remain in the pit that they have dug for themselves, but...being converted to the church of God, they may be legitimately begotten, and that Christ be formed in them, and that they may know the framer and maker of this universe, the only true God and Lord of all. This we pray for them, for we love them better than they think they love themselves. For our love, as it is true, is saving to them, if they will receive it. It is like a severe remedy, taking away the excessive and superfluous flesh that forms on a wound; for it puts an end to their exaltation and haughtiness. Therefore we shall not tire in endeavoring with all our might to stretch out [our] hand to them.[68]

A PERSONAL ADDENDUM

Thirty-five years ago, at the outset of my academic career, I wrote a small piece on the subject of this chapter in a popular format for a Canadian Baptist magazine —"Irenaeus and the Inerrancy of

---

66 Irenaeus, *Against Heresies* 3.21.3. On humility as an interpretative principle, see *Against Heresies* 2.28.2–3.

67 Irenaeus, *Against Heresies* 3.2.3; 3.6.4; 3.25.7. See also Marian Balwierz, *The Holy Spirit and the Church as a Subject of Evangelization According to St. Irenaeus* (Warsaw: Akademia Teologii Katolickiej, 1985), 50–57; Osborn, *Irenaeus of Lyons*, 5; Bingham, "Irenaeus of Lyons," in his ed., *Early Christian Thought*, 145.

68 Irenaeus, *Against Heresies* 3.25.7, trans. Roberts and Rambaut in Coxe, *The Apostolic Fathers with Justin Martyr and Irenaeus*, 460.

Scripture."[69] In large part that foray into this subject arose because of the battles among North American evangelicals over inerrancy in the 1970s and early 1980s. Now, it was personally rewarding in this chapter to return to Irenaeus and his view of the Bible in order to deal with it in a much more rigorous academic fashion. What is disturbing, though, is that the current scene is witnessing a renewal of those battles from thirty to thirty-five years ago.[70] Albeit there are some new emphases, but the end result is the same: a diminution of the authority of the Scriptures. It was helpful to listen to Irenaeus in the so-called "Battle for the Bible" thirty-five years ago, and, in the midst of these new challenges, it is still wisdom to heed, among other voices from the past, this second-century missionary theologian.

---

69 Michael A.G. Haykin, "Irenaeus and the Inerrancy of Scripture," *The Evangelical Baptist* 29, no.11 (October 1982): 8–9.

70 See, for example, Greg Beale, *The Erosion of Inerrancy in Evangelicalism: Responding to New Challenges to Biblical Authority* (Wheaton: Crossway, 2008).

4

"On the promises"
The millennium in the Greek patristic tradition[1]

> ...Such are the thoughts of men who believe indeed in Christ, but because they understand the divine Scriptures in a Judaistic sense, extract from them nothing that is worthy of the divine promises.
> —ORIGEN[2]

It has not been uncommon to find among various nineteenth- and twentieth-century evangelical communities the attitude that convictions

---

[1] This chapter originally appeared as "The Millennium in the Greek Patristic Tradition" in *The Christian and the Future. Papers given at the Fourth International Baptist Conference, October 17–21, 1988* (Toronto: Jarvis Street Baptist Church, 1988), 12–33. It has been slightly edited and brought up to date.

[2] Origen, *On First Principles* 2.11.2, trans. G.W. Butterworth, *Origen: On First Principles* (London: S.P.C.K., 1936), 148.

about the millennium are vital to determining whether or not a person was truly orthodox. In general, debates about the millennium among early Christians were never as intense as we have seen in the last two centuries, nevertheless, they were at times keenly pursued and could be as rancorous. In this chapter we will examine one major strand of these debates, that which occurred in the Greek-speaking Christian tradition between the late second and late fourth centuries.

When Joseph Mede (1586–1638), "the father of English millenarianism," began to advance the idea of a future millennium in the early 1600s, he turned to the writings of some of the earliest church fathers to buttress his exegesis of Revelation. According to Mede, the premillennial advent of Christ and the ensuing millennium were views held by those whom he called "the choycest of the learned" in the ancient church, authors such as Justin Martyr, Irenaeus of Lyons, Tertullian, Lactantius (c.240–320) and Methodius of Olympus (died c.311).[3] Although these significant patristic authors definitely embrace a premillennial position, Charles E. Hill has demonstrated in a groundbreaking study that alongside this eschatological tradition there is another tradition, just as ancient if not older, that would not have been at home within the premillennial camp.[4] In fact, this amillennial perspective, for so we may call it, became so influential in the patristic era that after the Council of Nicæa it is rare to find a Christian leader who opts for premillennialism.

Various reasons have been given to explain this triumph of the amillennial perspective, ranging from the replacement of Hebraic ways of thinking with Græco-Roman ones to the material success of Christianity associated with the accession of Constantine as emperor in 305. Anyone reading the patristic literature on this subject, however, cannot fail to be struck by the influence exercised by certain authors. In the Greek patristic tradition it is Origen, the influential Alexandrian theologian and exegete, and his one-time student Dionysius of Alexandria (died c.265), who played the pivotal role in turning the eastern

---

3 Bryan W. Ball, *A Great Expectation: Eschatological Thought in English Protestantism to 1660* (Leiden: E.J. Brill, 1975), 175.

4 Charles E. Hill, *Regnum Caelorum: Patterns of Future Hope in Early Christianity* (Oxford: Clarendon Press, 1992).

church against the doctrine of a literal millennium. In this chapter, we examine the thinking of four key authors in the Greek patristic tradition and elucidate their thought about the millennium: Irenaeus of Lyons, whom we have already met and who was the leading Greek premillennialist of the second and third centuries; Origen and Dionysius of Alexandria; Apollinaris of Laodicea (c.315–392), an important thinker about Christology who proved to be the last echo of premillennialism in the Greek Christian world; and his opponent, Basil of Caesarea (c.330–379), one of the most important theologians of the fourth century.

IRENAEUS OF LYONS

Irenaeus is not only the most important Greek-speaking theologian of the second century—we have seen something of his theology in the previous chapter—but his influence on the development of the church in its first three centuries was probably greater than that of any other teacher in the post-apostolic era.[5] Irenaeus' discussion of the millennial kingdom is concentrated in *Against Heresies* 5.32–36. It is noteworthy that efforts to suppress premillennial writings by the mediaeval church, which generally followed the amillennialism of the later church fathers, were so successful that these sections of Irenaeus' work were unknown to later generations till they were unearthed and published by F. Fauardent, a professor of theology at Paris, in 1575.[6] Indeed, a brief perusal of these sections of *Against Heresies* soon reveals what was so disturbing to the mediaeval scribes: "Irenaeus is robustly materialistic in his millennial expectations."[7]

Irenaeus begins his treatment of the millennium with the argument that there is a direct correspondence between the time taken to create

---

5 Franz Theodor Ritter von Zahn, "Irenaeus," *The New Schaff-Herzog Encyclopedia of Religious Knowledge* (New York: Funk and Wagnalls Co., 1910), VI, 31.

6 Marjorie O'Rourke Boyle, "Irenaeus [sic] Millennial Hope: A Polemical Weapon," *Recherches de Théologie Ancienne et Médiévale* 36 (1969): 6–7; Peter Toon, "Introduction" in his ed., *Puritans, the Millennium and the Future of Israel: Puritan Eschatology 1600 to 1660* (Cambridge: James Clarke & Co., 1970), 17.

7 Joel Cliff Gregory, "The Chiliastic Hermeneutic of Papias of Hierapolis and Justin Martyr compared with later Patristic Chiliasts" (Ph.D. thesis, Baylor University, 1983), 277.

the world and its history. Just as God took six days to create the world and then rested on the seventh (Genesis 1–2), so, Irenaeus reasons, history will last "six days" and conclude with a "seventh day" of rest. A length for the "days" of history is found by Irenaeus in 2 Peter 3:8 where it is stated that "with the Lord one day is as a thousand years" (NKJV). History will thus run its course for six thousand years and conclude with a millennium of rest.[8] This millennial period will commence when Christ returns in glory to destroy the rule of the antichrist:

> When the Antichrist has devastated everything in the world, reigned for three years and six months, and sat in the temple in Jerusalem, the Lord will come from heaven on the clouds in the glory of the Father. He will send the Antichrist and those who serve him into the lake of fire. But for the righteous he will inaugurate the times of the kingdom, that is, the rest, the seventh day which has been sanctified.[9]

During the millennium, this time of rest and tranquility, the created order will be under the rule of the righteous,[10] and will bring forth for them an abundance of all kinds of food.[11] The righteous, comprising both Old and New Testament saints, will reside at Jerusalem and eat of the earth's produce as they partake of the Messianic banquet with their Lord.[12] The animals likewise will feed solely on the fruit of the

---

8 Irenaeus, *Against Heresies* 5.28.3.

9 Irenaeus, *Against Heresies* 5.30.4. Gustaf Wingren [*Man and the Incarnation: A Study in the Biblical Theology of Irenaeus*, trans. Ross Mackenzie (Philadelphia: Muhlenberg Press, 1959), 190–192] notes that Irenaeus never explicitly describes the millennial period as a thousand years. But, as A. Skevington Wood ["The Eschatology of Irenaeus," *The Evangelical Quarterly* 41 (1969): 36, n.38] points out, in the above text Irenaeus does describe "the times of the kingdom" as "the seventh day which has been sanctified," and in *Against Heresies* 5.28.3 he equates one of the "days" of history with a thousand years. He thus implicitly regards "the times of the kingdom" as a thousand years.

10 Irenaeus, *Against Heresies* 5.32.1; 5.33.3.

11 Irenaeus, *Against Heresies* 5.33.3.

12 Irenaeus, *Against Heresies* 5.33.1–3; 5.34.1–4. For the presence of the Old Testament saints during the period of the millennium, see the discussion of Boyle, "Millennial Hope," 13–15; Wood, "Eschatology of Irenaeus," 35–36.

earth, living in peace and harmony with one another, and totally subject to man.[13] In this way God's original intent for his creation will be fulfilled. Proof for these assertions is found in prophetic texts such as Romans 8:19–21 and Isaiah 11:6–9, and promises like Matthew 26:29.

Irenaeus repeatedly warns against treating these biblical passages as allegories or attempting to spiritualize them away. Their realistic tone demands that they be taken literally. For instance, discussing the Lord's promise in Matthew 26:29, Irenaeus says,

> After [the Lord Jesus] had given thanks as he held the cup, and had drunk of it, and given it to the disciples, he said to them, "Drink from it, all of you. For this is my blood of the new covenant, which is poured out for many for the forgiveness of sins. For I tell you, I will not drink of the fruit of this vine until that day when I drink it new with you in my Father's kingdom."[14] ... He promised to drink from the fruit of the vine with his disciples, and thus he indicated...the physical resurrection of his disciples. For the new flesh that rises again is the same that has received the new cup. It is impossible to conceive of him being established on high with his disciples in a supra-celestial place, there drinking the fruit of the vine. Nor again are those who drink it without flesh; for the drink which is taken from the vine belongs to the realm of the flesh and not to that of the spirit.[15]

It was Irenaeus' Gnostic opponents who particularly sought to spiritualize such promises as this one recorded by Matthew—they envisioned a complete annihilation of matter in the world to come. From their perspective, the material world is intrinsically evil and thus irredeemable. Consequently, biblical texts that speak of a future for that world, especially those which assert a resurrection of the human

---

13 Irenaeus, *Against Heresies* 5.33.3–4.
14 Matthew 26:27–29.
15 Irenaeus, *Against Heresies* 5.33.1, trans. Edward Rochie Hardy in *Early Christian Fathers*, ed. and trans. Cyril C. Richardson with Eugene F. Fairweather, Edward Rochie Hardy and Massey Hamilton Shepherd (Philadelphia: The Westminster Press, 1953), 393, altered.

body, had to have another meaning, a spiritual one. Irenaeus, firmly convinced of "the integrity of matter"[16] and the resurrection of the flesh, will have none of this. The first half of the fifth book of *Against Heresies* is devoted to a passionate defense of the reality of the resurrection of the flesh. The discussion of the millennial kingdom in the last quarter of this book amplifies his argument against the Gnostics' disparagement of matter. The literal fulfillment of God's promises during the period of the millennium demonstrates that God is committed to his creation and that Christ's redemption extends to both the spiritual and physical realms.[17]

There is a second major theme that informs Irenaeus' millennial teaching. It is his belief that the millennium constitutes an indispensable stage of a process in which the Holy Spirit has been preparing men and women for a face-to-face vision of God in eternity. For an individual, this process begins when he or she receives the "earnest" of the Spirit.

> In the present we receive a certain portion of his Spirit, leading us towards perfection and preparing us for incorruption, by gradually making us accustomed to know and bear God. It is this that the Apostle calls "an earnest," ... as he says in Ephesians: "in him you also trusted, after you heard the word of truth, the gospel of your salvation; in whom also, having believed, you were sealed with the Holy Spirit of promise, who is the earnest of our inheritance."[18] Therefore, if this earnest dwells in us, it renders us spiritual even now and that which is mortal is swallowed up by immortality. For it says: "You are not in the flesh, but in the Spirit, if indeed the Spirit of God dwells in you."[19] But this does not happen through the discarding of the flesh, but through participation in the Spirit. For those to whom he was writing were not without flesh, but were people who had received the Spirit of God, "by

---

16 Boyle, "Millennial Hope," 8–13.
17 For further discussion, Boyle, "Millennial Hope," 8–13; D.H. Kromminga, *The Millennium in the Church: Studies in the History of Christian Chiliasm* (Grand Rapids: Eerdmans, 1945), 89–92.
18 Ephesians 1:13–14.
19 Romans 8:9.

whom we cry out, 'Abba, Father.'"[20] Therefore, if at this time we cry out "Abba, Father" due to the fact that we have the Spirit, what will it be when, being risen, we see him face to face, and when all the members burst out into an endless hymn of exultation, giving glory to the One who has raised them from the dead and who has given them eternal life? For if the earnest, by embracing man to himself, now makes him say, "Abba, Father," what will the entire grace of the Spirit bring to pass, which will be given to men by God? It will make us like him and accomplish the Father's will; for it will make man in the image and likeness of God.[21]

Irenaeus' rebuttal of Gnosticism is very much in evidence in this text as he seeks to show that spirituality and corporeality are not mutually exclusive. Central to his purpose in this regard is his exegesis of Ephesians 1:13–14, where Paul describes the Holy Spirit as an "earnest" or "first installment." Reception of the earnest of the Spirit is what renders a person spiritual, not the absence of a body, as the Gnostics maintained. Irenaeus rightly perceives that Paul's use of the term "earnest" in this text is an eschatological one. The indwelling and experience of the Spirit in this life is the first installment of a much greater experience in the life to come. From Irenaeus' vantage point, this initial installment prepares believers for that greater experience of the Spirit, one which will bestow on them incorruption and a deeper knowledge of God.

Now, the millennium serves as a crucial stage in this process of preparation. In Irenaeus' own words,

> The resurrection of the just and the [millennial] kingdom ... is the beginning of incorruption, by which kingdom those who are worthy will gradually be accustomed to know God... In [this time] the righteous will reign on the earth, growing through the sight of the Lord, and through him they will become accustomed to know the glory of God the Father.[22]

---

20 Romans 8:15.
21 Irenaeus, *Against Heresies* 5.8.1.
22 Irenaeus, *Against Heresies* 5.32.1, trans. Hardy in *Early Christian Fathers*, 391, altered; 5.35.1.

In the millennium the Spirit continues and perfects the work begun in this life. He gently forms within God's people the capacity for an open, unclouded vision of God: "our face shall see the face of God and rejoice with joy unspeakable."[23]

Irenaeus' defence of an earthly millennium is without a doubt the most eloquent of the patristic era, and he rightly merits A. Skevington Wood's description of him as the early church's "most distinguished and consistent exponent" of historic premillennialism.[24] Yet, it is striking that in his defence of the millennium Irenaeus does not draw heavily on the book of Revelation.[25] Whatever the reason for this, it certainly does not stem from a lack of esteem for this book, since Irenaeus regards John's Revelation as a genuine revelation from the Spirit of God.[26]

ORIGEN AND DIONYSIUS OF ALEXANDRIA

Although many of the leading Christian writers of Irenaeus' day shared his millennial vision, strong voices of dissent began to be raised in the following century. Two of the most persuasive were those of Origen and Dionysius of Alexandria.

Origen, born around 185, came from a Christian home in Alexandria, where he was the eldest of seven children.[27] His father, Leonides,

---

23 Irenaeus, *Against Heresies* 5.7.2. For the gentleness of the Spirit's work in preparing believers for the vision of God, see also *Against Heresies* 4.20.10. For further discussion of Irenaeus' understanding of the millennium as a time of spiritual preparation, see Alfred Bengsch, *Heilsgeschichte und Heilswissen. Eine Untersuchung zur Struktur und Entfaltung des theologischen Denkens im Werk 'Adversus Haeres' des hl. Irenäus von Lyon* (Leipzig: St. Benno-Verlag GMBH, 1957), 169–173; Boyle, "Millennial Hope", 15–16; Kromminga, *Millennium*, 94–98.

24 Skevington Wood, "Eschatology of Irenaeus," *The Evangelical Quarterly* 41: 41.

25 For a discussion of this fact, see Ned Bernard Stonehouse, *The Apocalypse in the Ancient Church. A Study in the History of the New Testament Canon* (Goes, Holland: Oosterbaan & Le Cointre, 1929), 80–81.

26 Irenaeus, *Against Heresies* 5.30.4. For a full discussion of Irenaeus' view of Revelation, see Stonehouse, *Apocalypse*, 71–81.

27 For Origen's life and thought, see especially Henri Crouzel, *Origen*, trans. A.S. Worrall (San Francisco: Harper & Row, 1989); Fred Norris, "Origen" in Philip F. Esler, ed., *The Early Christian World* (London: Routledge, 2000), II, 1005–1026. See also Michael A.G. Haykin, *Rediscovering the Church Fathers: Who They Were and How They*

gave him an excellent education in the Greek classics but also supervised his memorization of large portions of the Bible. Leonides was martyred when Origen was seventeen, and the young man never forgot that he was the son of a martyr.[28]

By 206, Origen had entered upon his life's work: teaching and catechizing in the Christian school at Alexandria. A converted Gnostic by the name of Ambrose became his patron, supported him financially, and so enabled him to compose Bible commentaries as well as treatises on a variety of theological topics. He became increasingly known as an exegete of Scripture, and he was frequently sought after as a theological expert.

Around 230, he left Alexandria for Caesarea in Palestine after a dispute with Demetrius (died 232), Bishop of Alexandria, over Origen's own ordination as an elder in the church at Caesarea. Here, he continued to pour out commentaries until his arrest in 249 during the persecution by the emperor Decius (r.249–251). Origen was tortured in an attempt to make him apostasize. But, he remained true to Christ and emerged from prison alive and triumphant, though broken physically. He appears to have died not long after.

Whatever faults can be found with his theology—and there are a number of them that stem from the fact that he was "a speculative theologian of unparalleled boldness and imagination"[29]—he had demonstrated that his devotion to Christ was far more than academic. Of his theological significance, Joseph T. Lienhard has persuasively argued that it was Origen's exegetical work and homilies on the Old Testament that helped ensure that it remained firmly part of the church's canon.[30]

Dionysius, on the other hand, was converted to Christianity from a pagan background.[31] He enrolled as a student at the catechetical school

---

Shaped the Church (Wheaton: Crossway, 2011), 69–90.
28 See his Origen, *Homilies on Ezekiel* 4.8.
29 Timothy D. Barnes, *Constantine and Eusebius* (Cambridge: Harvard University Press, 1981), 86. Origen speculated, for instance, about the shape of the resurrection body (He reasoned that it would be spherical in shape!) and that souls have eternally existed.
30 "Origen and the Crisis of the Old Testament in the Early Church," *Pro Ecclesia* 9, no.3 (2000): 355–366.
31 For a readable account of Dionysius' life, see E.R. Hardy, *Christian Egypt: Church*

in Alexandria, where Origen was the leading teacher. When Origen quit Alexandria for Caesarea, Dionysius was asked to assume leadership of this school. Here he remained till 247/248, when he was elected bishop of Alexandria, a position he filled with distinction until his death about 265. He was an important figure in the third-century church, taking an active role in the major dogmatic controversies of his day. Of his numerous works, however, only fragments survive, the majority of which may be found in the *Church History* of Eusebius of Caesarea (c.260–339).

Studying under Origen, Dionysius would have been exposed to Origen's forceful criticism of the premillennial position. What Origen appears to have found particularly distasteful about his premillennial contemporaries were their "carnal" visions of the future. In his systematic theology, *On First Principles*, written shortly before he left Alexandria for Palestine, Origen has this to say about those who look for an earthly millennium:

> Now some men, who reject the labour of thinking and seek after the outward and literal meaning of the law, or rather give way to their own desires and lusts, disciples of the mere letter, consider that the promises of the future are to be looked for in the form of pleasure and bodily luxury. And chiefly on this account they desire after the resurrection to have flesh of such a sort that they will never lack the power to eat and drink and to do all things that pertain to flesh and blood, not following the teaching of the apostle Paul about the resurrection of a "spiritual body."[32] Consequently they go on to say that even after the resurrection there will be engagements to marry and the procreation of children, for they picture to themselves the earthly city of Jerusalem about to be rebuilt with precious stones laid down for its foundations and its walls erected of jasper and its battlements adorned with crystal; ...and they consider that they are to receive the "wealth of nations" to live on and that they will have control over their

---

and People, *Christianity and Nationalism in the Patriarchate of Alexandria* (New York: Oxford University Press, 1952), 18–32.

32 1 Corinthians 15:44.

riches so that even the camels of Midian and Ephah will come and bring them "gold, incense and precious stones."[33] ...Such are the thoughts of men who believe indeed in Christ, but because they understand the divine Scriptures in a Judaistic sense, extract from them nothing that is worthy of the divine promises.[34]

For Origen the premillennial reading of Scripture is little different from the hopes of Jewish messianism, hence, the charge that the former "understand the Scriptures in a Judaistic sense." Despite the heavy defeats inflicted by the Romans on the Jewish nationalist cause during the Jewish War (66–73) and the Bar Kochba revolt (132–135), there is clear evidence that Jewish Messianic movements did not cease to hope that they would yet possess the land of Israel under the rule of the Messiah.[35]

In *On First Principles*, Origen seeks, among other things, "to establish a distinctively Christian reading of biblical prophecy."[36] This "distinctively Christian reading" is distinguished by a tendency to allegorize and psychologize the eschatology of the Scriptures. The prospect of an earthly millennium in which the saints will feast in a rebuilt Jerusalem is replaced with that of a heavenly rest in which the saints will nourish their souls "with the food of truth and wisdom."[37] Wherever predictions are made about the land of Judea and the city of Jerusalem, these are to be understood as signifying the heavenly Jerusalem.[38] At the resurrection individual believers will receive the same "form" of the body they bore on earth, that which remained unchanged through their earthly pilgrimage. However, the nature of the body will be different, since it will be a spiritual body, incorruptible,

---

33 Isaiah 60:5–6.
34 Origen, *On First Principles* 2.11.2, trans. Butterworth, *Origen: On First Principles*, 147–148, *passim*.
35 See Robert L. Wilken, "Early Christian Chiliasm, Jewish Messianism, and the Idea of the Holy Land" in George W. Nickelsburg and George E. MacRae, ed., *Christians among Jews and Gentiles* (Philadelphia: Fortress Press, 1986), 302–306.
36 Wilken, "Early Christian Chiliasm," 302.
37 Origen, *On First Principles* 2.11.3, 149.
38 Origen, *Against Celsus* 7.29.

free from any need of or desire for the material world.[39] In seeking to avoid the literalism of the premillennialists, Origen comes dangerously close to the worldview of dualistic Gnosticism that excluded matter from salvation.

Origen's treatment of the apocalyptic material in Matthew 24 illustrates the overall tendencies of his exegetical methodology. Joseph Trigg highlights some aspects of this treatment:

> When the Gospel predicts that Christ will come "on the clouds of heaven with power and great glory" (Matthew 24:30), it refers to his appearance to the perfect in their reading of the Bible. ... The trials and tribulations the world must endure before the second coming symbolize the difficulties the soul must overcome before it is worthy of union with the *Logos*. The imminence of the second coming refers to the imminent possibility, for each individual, of death. Perhaps more radically, the two men labouring in a field, one of whom is taken and the other left when the Messiah comes (Matthew 24:40), represent good and bad influences on a person's will, which fare differently when the *Logos* is revealed to that person. Although Origen did not openly deny the vivid apocalyptic expectations such passages originally expressed and still did for many Christians, he tended by psychologizing them to make them irrelevant.[40]

To what extent Dionysius of Alexandria followed Origen's "over-realized eschatology" is not clear. German scholar Wolfgang A. Bienert has scrutinized Dionysius' relationship as a churchman and theologian to Origen and argued persuasively that although Dionysius sat under Origen's teaching, he cannot be numbered among his followers.[41]

---

39 Origen, *On First Principles* 3.6.4–9. See also the discussion of François Altermath, *Du corps psychique au corps spirituel. Interprétation de I Cor 15, 35–49 par les auteurs chrétiens des quatre premiers siècles* (Tübingen: J.C.B. Mohr (Paul Siebeck), 1977), 104–124.

40 *Origen: The Bible and Philosophy in the Third-Century Church* (Atlanta: John Knox Press, 1983), 212–213.

41 Wolfgang A. Bienert, *Dionysius von Alexandrien: Zur Frage des Origenismus im dritten Jahrhundert* (New York: Walter de Gruyter, 1978).

Nonetheless, Dionysius was influenced by Origen in the formulation of his position on the millennium for, like Origen, he is firmly set against premillennialism.

Now, it was during Dionysius' time as bishop of Alexandria that his eschatological views were put to the test when he became a central figure in a public debate on the nature of the millennium.[42] Our only source for the details of this debate comes from Eusebius of Caesarea, who was an ardent admirer of Origen and hardly a lover of premillennial doctrine.[43] Preserved in his *Church History* are a number of lengthy fragments from a book by Dionysius entitled *On the Promises*, which the Alexandrian bishop wrote in response to the premillennial views of a certain Nepos of Arsinoë in Egypt, who was a contemporary of Origen.[44]

Nepos had written a tract against Origen entitled *Refutation of the Allegorists*, which is no longer extant. But according to Eusebius, Nepos maintained that the "promises which had been made to the saints in the divine Scriptures should be interpreted after a more Jewish fashion, and...that there will be a kind of millennium on this earth devoted to bodily indulgence."[45] Eusebius also adds that Nepos employed the

---

42 Bienert suggests that the debate took place sometime between 253 and 257 (Bienert, *Dionysius von Alexandrien*, 193–194).

43 On Eusebius' admiration for Origen, see Barnes, *Constantine and Eusebius*, 94–105. For Eusebius' dislike of premillennialism, see also his *Church History* 3.28.1–5; 3.29.11–13. For a study of Eusebius' eschatology, see Frank S. Thielman, "Another Look at the Eschatology of Eusebius of Caesarea," *Vigiliae Christianae*, 41 (1987): 226–237.

44 These fragments are preserved in Eusebius of Caesarea, *Church History* 7.24–25. Of Nepos we know nothing beyond what is recorded by Eusebius. In the first fragment of Dionysius' *On the Promises* which Eusebius cites, Dionysius states that he has great admiration for Nepos' faith, his devotion to hard work, his industry in studying God's Word and his love of psalmody (Eusebius, *Church History* 7.24.41). On Nepos, see also Gerhard Maier, *Die Johannesoffenbarung und die Kirche* (Tübingen: J.C.B. Mohr (Paul Siebeck), 1981), 87–94; Philip Rousseau, *Pachomius: The Making of a Community in Fourth-Century Egypt* (Berkeley: University of California Press, 1985), 32.

45 Eusebius, *Church History* 7.24.1, J.E.L. Oulton and H.J. Lawlor, ed., *Eusebius: The Ecclesiastical History*, trans. J.E.L. Oulton (Cambridge: Harvard University Press, 1932), 191. Maier, *Die Johannesoffenbarung und die Kirche*, 93 n.406, dates this tract around 245–248.

Revelation of John to establish his position.[46] Nepos appears to have relied on a literal exegesis of Revelation 20:1–6 to argue for an earthly rule of the saints with Christ for a thousand years. In this respect his views were probably much like those of earlier premillennialists like Irenaeus. Eusebius' own eschatological commitments may be detected in his remark that Nepos interpreted the Scriptures after a "Jewish fashion." This was a common charge made by those who were influenced by Origen in their eschatology.[47]

By the time that Dionysius arrived on the scene, Nepos was dead, but his views were very much alive. In fact, according to one of the fragments preserved from Dionysius' *On the Promises*, some teachers at Arsinoë were regarding Nepos' *Against the Allegorists* as having greater value than the Scriptures![48] Moreover, disagreement over eschatology at Arsinoë and in the surrounding area was making havoc of the churches: a number of churches had been split and others reportedly had fallen away from the faith.[49]

In seeking to remedy this situation Dionysius called together the elders and teachers of the area to openly discuss the issue. According to his account of this discussion,

> When they brought me this book [of Nepos] as some invincible weapon and rampart, I sat with them and for three successive days from morn till night attempted to correct what had been written. On that occasion I conceived the greatest admiration for the brethren, their firmness, love of truth, facility in following an argument, and intelligence, as we propounded in order and with forbearance the questions, the difficulties raised and the points of agreement; on the one hand refusing to cling obstinately and at all costs (even though they were manifestly wrong) to opinions once held; and on the other hand not shirking the counter-arguments, but as far as possible attempting to grapple with the questions in hand and master them. Nor, if convinced

---

46 Eusebius, *Church History* 7.24.2.
47 Bienert, *Dionysius von Alexandrien*, 194 n.6.
48 Eusebius, *Church History* 7.24.5.
49 Eusebius, *Church History* 7.24.6.

by reason, were we ashamed to change our opinions and give our assent; but conscientiously and unfeignedly and with hearts laid open to God we accepted whatever was established by the proofs and teachings of the holy Scriptures. And in the end the leader and introducer of this teaching, Coracion, as he was called, in the hearing of all the brethren present, assented, and testified to us that he would no longer adhere to it, nor discourse upon it, nor mention nor teach it, since he had been sufficiently convinced by the contrary arguments. And as to the rest of the brethren, some rejoiced at the joint conference, and the mutual deference and unanimity which all displayed.[50]

This cameo is of great value since "it is one of the only ancient sources showing a typical dialogue between chiliasts and their opponents."[51] Furthermore, the dialogue reflects well on all involved. There is no indication that either side attempted to force their position on the other. Instead, there is on the part of both sides a desire that scriptural truth prevail and a willingness to listen to contrary views. In the end, Coracion, the leading advocate of Nepos' millenarianism, admitted himself wholly convinced by Dionysius' argumentation. The understanding that was finally reached between the two sides clearly contained elements of compromise, for Dionysius himself admits that in a few points he changed his mind.[52]

When Dionysius returned to Alexandria he set to work on what would eventually be the book *On the Promises*, of which only fragments are extant. According to Eusebius the work consisted of two volumes: in the first volume Dionysius outlined his own position on the millennium and in the second he took up the question of the canonicity and authorship of John's Revelation.[53] As mentioned above, Nepos rested his case largely upon Revelation and appealed to its apostolic author-

---

[50] Eusebius, *Church History*, Vol II, 7.24.8–9, trans. Oulton in his and Lawlor, ed., *Eusebius: The Ecclesiastical History*, II, 195, 197.
[51] Gregory, "Chiliastic Hermeneutic of Papias of Hierapolis and Justin Martyr," 26–27.
[52] Bienert, *Dionysius von Alexandrien*, 196.
[53] Eusebius, *Church History* 7.24.3.

ship as clinching proof for the rectitude of his own position. In order to better refute Nepos' millennial views, Dionysius appears to have felt constrained to shake this confidence in the apostolic authorship of Revelation. Unlike Origen, who accepted Revelation as a work by the apostle John,[54] Dionysius argued that its author was not John, the son of Zebedee, but another Christian of the same name.[55] Although Dionysius rejects the apostolic authorship of Revelation, he does not wish to jettison it from the New Testament canon:

> I dare not reject the book, since many brethren held it in high esteem; but, assuming that my understanding is inadequate to form an opinion concerning it, I hold that there is some hidden and more wonderful interpretation in each passage. For, even if I do not understand it, yet I suspect that some deeper meaning underlies the words. For I do not measure and judge these things by my own reasoning, but, assigning greater importance to faith, I have come to the conclusion that they are too high for my comprehension, and I do not reject what I have not understood, but I rather wonder that I did not even see them.[56]

This is an amazing admission for one who had been thoroughly trained under Origen's allegorical exegesis, and it may well indicate that Dionysius was not really at home with Origen's method of exposition. Be this as it may, Dionysius' confession displays a definite reluctance to interpret Revelation in a thoroughly literal fashion. He is at a loss to know how to interpret the book. Of one thing, though, he appears certain: a literal interpretation of Revelation 20, as found in Nepos' tract, is not an option either for him or for the church.

Dionysius' views regarding the authorship of Revelation enjoyed only limited success. However, his reasoned rejection of premillennialism, combined with the eschatological perspective of Origen,

---

54 See the texts cited by Stonehouse, *Apocalypse*, 117–121.

55 For the arguments that he presented to support his position, see Eusebius, *Church History* 7.25.6–27. For a critical discussion of the arguments, see Stonehouse, *Apocalypse*, 125–128.

56 Eusebius, *Church History*, Vol. II, 7.24.4–5, 197, 199, altered.

came to exercise a decisive influence on the Greek patristic tradition.[57] The extent of this influence may be gauged by the fact that only one post-Nicene author of significance in the Greek Christian world was prepared to defend a premillennial position: Apollinaris of Laodicea.

APOLLINARIS OF LAODICEA AND BASIL OF CAESAREA

In the words of J.N.D. Kelly, a leading twentieth-century historian of the early church, Apollinaris "was one of the most accomplished and keen-sighted Greek exegetes of his time." As an exegete he habitually shunned the allegorical method of interpretation favoured among the followers of Origen, but instead sought to bring out the literal, historical meaning of a Scriptural passage.[58] Although this exegetical methodology was practised by exegetes of his day, notably those of the so-called Antiochene school—for example, Diodore of Tarsus (died c.390) and John Chrysostom (c.347–407)—only Apollinaris seems to have applied it to the millennium. All that we know of his millennial teaching comes from his opponents. Jerome, the famous translator of the Bible into the Latin Vulgate, who actually studied under Apollinaris in Antioch during the 370s, states that Apollinaris wrote two books against Dionysius of Alexandria in defence of an earthly millennium.[59] Dionysius' *On the Promises* may well have become something of a standard refutation of premillennialism among Greek-speaking Christians, and thus the key book for a premillennialist to answer. According to Epiphanius of Salamis (c.315–403), the author of a massive catalogue of heresies in the ancient church, Apollinaris maintained that the millennial kingdom will be an earthly paradise in which the Old Testament law would once again be observed.[60]

A third witness for Apollinaris' premillennialism is Basil of Caesarea.[61] Basil had been born into a prominent Christian family of Cappadocia, in what is now modern Turkey, but it was not until 356 that he became

---

57 Bienert, *Dionysius von Alexandrien*, 200; Maier, *Johannesoffenbarung*, 105–106.
58 J.N.D. Kelly, *Jerome: His Life, Writings, and Controversies* (London: Gerald Duckworth & Co. Ltd., 1975), 59–60.
59 Jerome, *Commentary on Isaiah 18*, prologue. See also Jerome, *Famous Men 18*.
60 Hans Bietenhard, "The Millennial Hope of the Early Church," trans. G.W. Bromiley, *Scottish Journal of Theology* 6 (1953): 23.
61 For more on his life, see Chapters 7 and 8.

a Christian. For a number of years, Basil and a close friend, Gregory of Nazianzus (c.330–389), devoted themselves to poring over the Scriptures, to prayer and fasting and to the compiling of a book of extracts from the writings of Origen. While Basil was undoubtedly influenced by Origen, he was discriminating in what he took from the Alexandrian theologian. In 370, he was elected bishop of Caesarea. Prominent during his time as bishop was his struggle against the Pneumatomachi, who denied the deity of the Holy Spirit. Indeed, Basil's chief theological work, *On the Holy Spirit* (375), marked a decisive step toward the resolution of this controversy and the confession of the Spirit's deity in the creedal statement issued by the Council of Constantinople in 381.[62]

Two years prior to his death in 379, Basil wrote a letter to the bishops in the western Roman Empire, in which he states the following about Apollinaris' eschatology:

> His theological works are constructed not with Scriptural proofs, but with human arguments. And he has also written books about the resurrection, composed in the manner of myths, or rather in the manner of the Jews, in which he tells us that we shall return again to the worship prescribed by the Law: to again be circumcised, keep the Sabbath, abstain from meats, offer sacrifices to God, worship in the Temple at Jerusalem, and in short, to become Jews instead of Christians. Could anything be more ridiculous, or more foreign to the doctrine of the gospel than these statements? Then too his statements about the incarnation have caused such confusion among the brethren, that now few of those who have read them preserve the character of the true religion. The majority, intent on innovations, have been turned aside to inquiries and contentious investigations of these unprofitable words.[63]

It was Apollinaris' Christological errors that would eventually lead to his condemnation as a heretic. His zealous concern for the unity of the person of Christ and Christ's impeccability led him to argue that

---

62 See Chapter 8 for the discussion of this controversy.
63 *Letter* 263.4, *Saint Basil: The Letters*, trans. Roy J. Deferrari (Cambridge, Mass.: Harvard University Press/London: William Heinemann Ltd., 1934), IV, 99, altered.

there was only one nature in Christ: the divine Word took the place of Christ's human mind and spirit. But it is interesting that Basil appears just as concerned about Apollinaris' millennial views as about his Christological position. He repeats the standard charge from Origen that premillennialism is a "Jewish" way of viewing the future, and adds that this eschatological position is folly and utterly foreign to the gospel. The overall purpose of the letter from which this extract is taken was to persuade the western bishops to issue a public and official statement regarding their fellowship with Apollinaris and his followers: if they persist in their views, then the Western church will have to separate from them.[64]

In another letter written in the same year to three Egyptian bishops, Basil expanded on his statements about Apollinaris' eschatology. He began by indicating the awful distress he felt about Apollinaris' errors, since he had always considered him a friend and ally.[65] It should be noted that at the height of the Arian controversy, Apollinaris had stood alongside others such as Athanasius (c.299–373), the staunch defender of the full deity of Christ. Moreover, in the 350s and 360s Basil had had occasion to write to him for theological advice.[66] Basil goes on to mention Apollinaris' fostering of schism among local congregations and his confusion regarding the nature of the incarnation.[67]

Finally, he devotes a lengthy passage to detailing Apollinaris' eschatological errors. The length of the passage is an indication of the depth of Basil's concern about this issue.

> On the subject of the promises, who has so obscured and darkened it as the myth-making of this man? He has dared to explain the blessed hope, that is laid up for those who have lived their lives according to the gospel of Christ, in so base and poor a

---

64 Paul Jonathan Fedwick, *The Church and the Charisma of Leadership in Basil of Caesarea* (Toronto: Pontifical Institute of Mediaeval Studies, 1979), 111–112.
65 Letter 265.2.
66 See Basil, *Letters*, 361–364.
67 Basil also states that he has seen documents which are purportedly from the pen of Apollinaris and which contain statements defending modalism. Basil has a slight suspicion that these documents may have been doctored by Apollinaris' enemies. He suspected rightly.

manner that it has been turned into old wives' fables and Jewish stories![68] He proclaims anew the restoration of the Temple; the observance of worship according to the law; a figurative high priest after the true High Priest, and a sacrifice for sins after the Lamb of God who takes away the sins of the world[69]; partial baptisms after the one baptism; a heifer's ashes sprinkling the Church which, through faith in Christ, does not have spot or wrinkle or any such thing[70]; cleansing of leprosy after being made incapable of suffering by the resurrection; and offering of jealousy when they neither marry nor are given in marriage[71]; shewbread after the Bread from heaven[72]; burning lamps after the true light[73]; and, in short, if the law of commandments has now been abolished in our doctrines, clearly then the doctrines of Christ will some day be made void by the precepts of the law.

Because of these things shame and humiliation have covered our faces and a deep grief has filled our hearts. Therefore, we exhort you, as skilled physicians and men who have been trained to instruct your opponents in gentleness, to try to lead him back to the good order of the church...and to place firmly before him the doctrines of orthodoxy, that his amendment may become evident and his repentance made known to the brethren.[74]

Unless Basil has greatly distorted Apollinaris' teaching, it does appear that Basil has some justification for charging Apollinaris with looking forward to a restoration of life under the old covenant. Apollinaris seems to have failed to recognize the extent to which Christ has fulfilled the ceremonial aspects of the law. This failure simply provided opponents such as Basil with more ammunition to attack Apollinaris'

---

68 Cf. 1 Timothy 4:7.
69 John 1:29.
70 See Ephesians 5:25–27.
71 See Matthew 22:30.
72 See John 6:32.
73 See John 1:9.
74 *Letter* 265.2, *Saint Basil: The Letters*, trans. Deferrari, IV, 113, 115, altered.

overall position.⁷⁵ Moreover, it is instructive to note the depth of revulsion which Basil has for Apollinaris' vision of the millennium. To Basil, the Bishop of Laodicea is conjuring up myths and "Jewish stories," which can in no way be considered sound doctrine. Basil feels that Paul's advice in 1 Timothy 4:7 is apropos: "reject [such] profane and old wives' fables." Basil does, however, conclude on a positive note, expressing the hope that Apollinaris, once he has been shown his errors, will repent and thus be restored.

Apollinaris does not appear to have done so. He was condemned for doctrinal error at a synod in Rome in 377, not long after the Western bishops received Basil's letter. He was subsequently condemned at Antioch in 379, and then again at the Council of Constantinople in 381. In 383, the emperor Theodosius (r.379–395) declared Apollinarianism to be illegal, and in 388, under pressure from Basil's friend Gregory of Nazianzus, he actually launched measures to repress the teachings of Apollinaris.⁷⁶ The major reason for this treatment of Apollinaris was his Christological error. Apollinaris' premillennialism is never actually cited as a reason for his being declared heretical. But, as the texts from Basil reveal, Apollinaris' premillennialism was regarded as both bizarre and unhealthy as concerns sound doctrine.⁷⁷

Basil's strong aversion to Apollinaris' teachings on the millennium comes as no surprise when his own eschatology is laid bare, for it bears the imprint of Origen.⁷⁸ At the resurrection, Basil believes, the body of the believer will be transformed by the Spirit into a spiritual body.⁷⁹ Unlike Origen, however, Basil is extremely wary of trying to explain the nature of this spiritual body. That the dualistic perspective of

---

75 Bietenhard, "Millennial Hope," 23. For a reconstruction of the possible theological basis of Apollinaris' millennial doctrine, see Georg Günter Blum, "Chiliasmus. II. Alte Kirche," *Theologische Realenzyklopädie* 7 (1981), 731.

76 Charles E. Raven, *Apollinarianism* (Cambridge: Cambridge University Press, 1923), 144–147.

77 Compare with the remarks of Jaroslav Pelikan, *The Emergence of the Catholic Tradition (100–600)* (Chicago: University of Chicago Press, 1971), 129.

78 For a study of Basil's eschatology, see M.A. Orphanos, *Creation and Salvation According to St. Basil of Caesarea* (Athens: n.p., 1975), 135–157. For the following remarks on Basil's eschatology, I am indebted to this fine study.

79 *On the Holy Spirit* 19.49; 28.69.

Origen has influenced him is beyond dispute, but Basil is content to affirm "sown a natural body, raised a spiritual body."[80] Consonant with this body the believer will enter a realm in which,

> there is no night, in which there is no sleep, the image of death, in which there is no eating, no drinking, the supports of our weakness; in which there is no disease, no pains, no remedies, no courts of justice, no businesses, no arts, no money, the beginning of evil, the excuse for wars, the root of hatred; but a country of the living, who...live the true life in Christ Jesus.[81]

Again, Basil can state that in the world to come, "one must not expect the special features of this world to continue after the resurrection, but must know that life in the world to come is angelic and in need of nothing."[82] Given this perspective on the world to come, Basil's opposition to Apollinaris' millennialism is readily understandable. It is inconceivable to Basil that the spiritual body of a risen saint would once again engage in activates intrinsically linked to a material environment, such as marriage.

It is not without significance that the Book of Revelation had little influence in the Cappadocian church in the last half of the fourth century. In all of his extant works Basil cites it but once and then in a somewhat vague manner.[83] Furthermore, in two listings of New Testament books, one by Basil's close friend, Gregory of Nazianzus, and the other by Gregory's cousin, Amphilochius of Iconium (c.340–395), the book of Revelation is omitted. Amphilochius goes so far as to make the following comment on this book: "The Revelation of John some indeed accept, but most will say that it is spurious."[84] Dionysius" rejec-

---

80 1 Corinthians 15:44.
81 *Homily 22* [on Psalm 114:5], *Saint Basil: Exegetic Homilies*, trans. Agnes Clare Way (Washington: The Catholic University of America Press, 1963), 358–359.
82 Morals 68.1, *The Ascetic Works of Saint Basil*, trans W.K.L. Clarke (London: S.P.C.K., 1925), 119.
83 See the discussion by Jean Gribomont, "La Tradition johannique chez saint Basile" in his *Saint Basile: Évangile et Église*, ed. Enzo Bianchi (Bégrolles-en-Mauges [Maine-&-Loire]: Abbaye de Bellefontaine, 1984), 225–226.
84 *Iambics for Seleucus* 316–319. See also Stonehouse, *Apocalypse*, 134.

tion of the apostolic authorship of Revelation is certainly the impetus behind this denial of its canonicity. Moreover, it should not be forgotten that Amphilochius was the protégé and spiritual son of Basil.[85] Consequently, it is not improbable that Basil's hostility to premillennialism would have been heightened by the fact that it employed, as one of its mainstays, a book whose canonical status was, in his opinion, at best a matter of dispute and at worst to be rejected.

CONCLUSION

Greek-speaking Christian thought about the millennium underwent enormous changes from the second to the fourth centuries. What Irenaeus had regarded as orthodoxy was by the time of Basil viewed as an "old wives' fable." It is clear that Origen and his spiritualizing method of exegesis played a key role through men like Dionysius of Alexandria and Eusebius of Caesarea in bringing about this transformation of perspective. Regrettably it also brought into question the canonicity of the book of Revelation.

And yet, for all the differences in outlook on this topic between, for example, Irenaeus and Basil, there are some central items that they hold in common. Both of them, for instance, share the hope that the first installment of the Spirit that they had experienced would one day give way to fullness and the Spirit would exercise full sovereignty in their lives. It is a hope which is fundamentally Pauline and which lies at the heart of the gospel. While Basil and Irenaeus would have disagreed on some of the details whereby that hope would be fulfilled, as the following text from his treatise on the Spirit reveals, Basil could express this hope in terms that recall both Irenaeus and the apostle Paul:

> Through the Holy Spirit comes...our restoration to paradise, our ascent into the kingdom of heaven, our return to be adopted as sons, our confidence to call God our Father, our being made partakers of the grace of Christ, our being called children of light,

---

85 Basil's treatise on the Spirit was initially sent to Amphilochius, who had asked Basil to compose such a treatise. See *On the Holy Spirit* 1.1; *Letter* 231. Amphilochius frequently sought theological advice from Basil. See Basil, *Letters* 188, 199, 217, 233–236.

our sharing in eternal glory. ...If such is the earnest, how great will its perfection be and if such is the firstfruits, how great its complete fulfillment?[86]

Finally, it must be admitted that millennial convictions were not as vital an issue as these early debaters about eschatology thought. They needed to be more humble about their perspectives and more forbearing with differing opinions. Contrary to what some thought in the fourth century, premillennialism was not a heresy. In the more recent days of the twentieth and twenty-first centuries, evangelicals have come through similar divisions over eschatology. All too frequently distinct boundary lines of fellowship with regard to this issue have been drawn and needless division has taken place. These disagreements, though, are not the essence of the faith. And while eschatology is not an unimportant issue, such debates about what the Scriptures teach on this issue need to be shaped by humility, open minds, and ultimately, a willingness to agree to disagree.

---

86 *On the Holy Spirit* 15.36.

5

"The *imperium* of the Holy Spirit"
The Holy Spirit in Cyprian's *To Donatus*[1]

> Just as the sun shines of its own accord, the day gives it light, the fountain waters, the shower its light rain, so the celestial Spirit outpours himself.
> —CYPRIAN[2]

---

1 For help with the acquisition of some of the secondary sources used in the preparation of this paper, I am indebted to Drs. Joe Harrod, Paul Roberts and Fred Zaspel. This paper was originally presented at the annual meeting of the Evangelical Theological Society in November 2010 and appeared as "The Holy Spirit in Cyprian's *To Donatus*," *Evangelical Quarterly* 83, no.4 (2011): 321–329. It appears here by permission.

2 *To Donatus* 14–15, in *St Cyprian of Carthage, On the Church: Select Treatises*, trans. Allen Brent (Crestwood: St Vladimir's Seminary Press, 2006), 65, altered. Subsequent quotations from *To Donatus* will be taken from either this translation—cited simply as Brent with the page number—or that of Saint Cyprian, *Treatises*, trans. Roy J. Deferrari (Washington: Catholic University of America Press, 1958), 7–21—cited simply as

In the midst of the chaos that plagued the Roman *imperium* during the third century—the rapid and violent turnover of emperors, the constant warfare against the Sassanians in the east and the Germanic tribes to the north, the collapse of key aspects of the monetary system, the political eclipse of the Senate, and the significant decline in fresh architectural projects[3]—a North African rhetor from the curial class, Caecilius Cyprianus qui et Thascius (c.200–258),[4] better known as simply Cyprian of Carthage, suggested a radical solution to the anxieties and fears of the day: conversion to the one true God who had revealed himself in Jesus Christ. This was the "one sure means to peace and to calm," Cyprian affirmed in a tract written for a Christian friend named Donatus,[5] the only "genuine and steadfast place of security" amidst "the storms of this restless age."[6] This tract, *To Donatus*, is the earliest of the authentic writings of the North African theologian and appears to have been written in the autumn of 246, not long after Cyprian's conversion and baptism.[7] Both Michael Sage, in his detailed theological biography of Cyprian, and Allen Brent, a translator of this work, have argued that it is intended to be an evangelistic tract that would lead Cyprian's pagan contemporaries in Roman North Africa to

---

Deferrari with the page number. The Latin, when referenced, is from Cyprien de Carthage, *A Donat et La vertu de patience* (texte latin), trans. Jean Molager (Paris: Les Éditions du Cerf), 74–116.

3 For a succinct summary of these military, political and social ills, see Averil Cameron, *The Later Roman Empire* AD 284–430 (Cambridge: Harvard University Press, 1993), 1–12.

4 For Cyprian's social status, see Michael M. Sage, *Cyprian* (Philadelphia: The Philadelphia Patristic Foundation, 1975), 98–100 and 105–110. As Maurice Wiles has noted, Cyprian "was a man of wealth with a considerable personal fortune." See "The Theological Legacy of St Cyprian" in Maurice Wiles, *Working Papers in Doctrine* (London: SCM Press, 1976), 68. On his name, see W.D. Niven, "Leaders of the Ancient Church. V. Cyprian of Carthage," *The Expository Times* 44 (1932–1933): 363; Sage, *Cyprian*, 98–100.

5 For the difficulty in identifying this individual, see Molager, trans., *A Donat et La Vertue de Patience*, 9 n.2.

6 *To Donatus* 14 (Brent, 64).

7 Sage, *Cyprian*, 110, 118, 380, 383; Molager, trans., *A Donat et La Vertue de Patience*, 12. On the time of year, see *To Donatus* 1. Cyprian alludes to the relatively brief time he had been a Christian in *To Donatus* 2.

see the folly and vanity of their entire culture, and so turn to Christ.[8] In point of fact, both the military and political turmoil and the massive moral declension, which Cyprian scathingly details in *To Donatus* 6–13, may well have played a role in Cyprian's own conversion.[9]

Now, what is so striking about Cyprian's salvific solution to the problems of his day is his insistence that it was ultimately not attainable by human energy—it was a free gift of God by means of the Holy Spirit. Prior to launching into his overview of the breakdown of Roman society and moral order, Cyprian argues this point through an account of his own encounter with the message of Christianity. When Cyprian first heard the gospel he was a man in the meridian of life, a patron with numerous clients and laden with the public honours that his social status brought. He was used to extravagance in food and dress, and, in a word, so immersed in the privileges and pleasures of the Roman world that, although he disliked the way he was and the way he lived, he could not envision how his lifestyle could ever be changed.[10] And for a period of time after hearing the Christian message, Cyprian despaired of ever changing his life. He thus plunged back into his personal maelstrom of sin.[11] But during this time he was befriended by one of the elders in the Carthaginian church, Caecilianus, who persuaded him to study the Scriptures,[12] and in due course, he became a Christian.

"WHEN I DRANK IN THE SPIRIT"

As Sage has noted, Cyprian's account of his conversion highlights the fact that "the major propulsion" toward the Christian "way of life came from God."[13] In Cyprian's own words: "everything we are able to do is

---

8 Sage, *Cyprian*, 128; Brent, *St Cyprian of Carthage: On the Church*, 47.

9 Sage, *Cyprian*, 126–127.

10 For these details, see *To Donatus* 3, which I am taking to be a somewhat autobiographical reflection. Support for this interpretation can be found in the first sentence of *To Donatus* 4, where Cyprian notes that what he describes in the previous sentences "often applied to me" [*To Donatus* 4 (Brent, 52)]. See also Sage, *Cyprian*, 111.

11 *To Donatus* 4.

12 Pontius, *The Life of Cyprian* 4, 2.

13 Sage, *Cyprian*, 129.

of God. From him we live, by him we are empowered."[14] In particular, Cyprian emphasizes the role played by the Holy Spirit:

> When I drank in the Spirit from heaven a second birth made me into a new man. Immediately in a marvelous manner what was doubtful was confirmed, what was closed opened, what was shadowy shone with light, what before seemed difficult I was granted the means to do, [and] it was possible to practice what I had thought impossible.[15]

Maurice Wiles has argued that this conversion account does not bespeak "a deep transformation of personal life or moral ideals." It is that of a man who wishes to make a clean break with his past, but who did not have the capacity to "make that break effective at the deeper levels of his thinking." The result is that Cyprian cannot really be reckoned as a "profound Christian theologian."[16] While Wiles definitely has a point regarding the depth of Cyprian as a Christian thinker, a close reading of the text cited above, alongside Cyprian's earlier statements about his pagan past, actually conveys quite a different impression about his conversion. The change wrought by the Spirit in Cyprian's life gave him a deep sense of the truth of the Christian faith. It illuminated key aspects of that faith that had hitherto been totally unclear. And, most significantly, it gave him a real measure of moral victory over his sins. Before, it seemed as if his sins and bent to sinning were insuperable. God's power, as experienced through the Holy Spirit, proved otherwise. As Rowan A. Greer has rightly pointed out, Cyprian's experience of deliverance, which gave him the "power to live in hope and freedom" and enabled him to have a life of true virtue, was actually an experience "central to early Christianity."[17]

Cyprian also linked this powerful encounter with the Holy Spirit to baptism. Immediately before the passage cited above, Cyprian

---

14 *To Donatus* 4 (Brent, 53). See also *To Donatus* 14.
15 *To Donatus* 4 (Brent, 52, altered).
16 Wiles, "Theological Legacy of St Cyprian," 69–70.
17 Rowan A. Greer, *Broken Lights and Mended Lives: Theology and Common Life in the Early Church* (University Park: Pennsylvania State University Press, 1986), 22–23.

observed that "when the stain of my past life had been washed away by the aid of the water of regeneration, a light from above poured itself upon my chastened and pure heart."[18] This is not the first mention of baptism in *To Donatus*. Cyprian had already referred to it as "the bath/ washing of the saving water" (*lavacro aquae salutaris*) when he had been detailing the sins of his pagan days.[19] What is the relationship in Cyprian's mind between the gift of the Spirit and baptism? The very fact that he can use the adjective "saving" (*salutaris*) about baptism here indicates that he sees water baptism as a vital part of the experience of salvation. It is part of the salvific "package." On the other hand, when Cyprian tells the pagan Demetrian in 252, six years after he wrote *To Donatus*, what salvation entails, he simply tells him, "we have been recreated in the Spirit, having laid aside our earthly birth, and have been reborn."[20] Ultimately, the all-important element in conversion is the person of the Holy Spirit and his saving power: without him there is no rebirth.

In later writings, Cyprian would refine his thinking about the relationship between water baptism, the laying-on-of-hands that normally immediately followed baptism in the North African church's rite of initiation and the gift of the Spirit.[21] Much of this refinement came as a result of the bitter controversy between Cyprian and Stephen of Rome (died 257) over whether heretics and schismatics who returned to the catholic church were to be baptized or not.[22] This controversy

---

18 *To Donatus* 4 (Deferrari, 9).

19 *To Donatus* 3. For this way of referring to baptism, see also Cyprian, *The Dress of Virgins* 23.

20 *To Demetrian* 20 (Brent, 89).

21 See especially Cyprian, *Letters* 63, 69–74. See also the extensive treatment by Everett Ferguson, *Baptism in the Early Church: History, Theology, and Liturgy in the First Five Centuries* (Grand Rapids: Eerdmans, 2009), 351–361, 388–392. For the history of this controversy, see Sage, *Cyprian*, 295–335. There were two other post-baptismal aspects of the rite of initiation in the North African church: unction and signation (Ferguson, *Baptism in the Early Church*, 353).

22 For example, Stephen's last word about Cyprian, cited by Firmilian in *Letter* 75.25.4 was that he was "a bogus Christ, a bogus apostle, and a crooked dealer" [*The Letters of St. Cyprian of Carthage*, trans. G.W. Clarke (New York: Newman Press, 1989), IV, 94].

is usually described as a controversy about rebaptism, though, in many ways, the real issue at stake had to do not so much with baptism as with the Spirit.[23] Was the Spirit present within heretical or schismatic assemblies? If not, then, as Cyprian argued, the only valid baptism that the Spirit would honour as a true baptism is that given within the church that he indwelt.[24] In the way that Cyprian developed his later thought about the Holy Spirit, he thus effectively "locked the sanctifying power of the Holy Spirit into the one Catholic communion," which he identified as that body that was bound together by the bishops who were the successors of the apostolic college.[25]

But when he wrote *To Donatus*, Cyprian was not a bishop and the issues of his future controversy with Stephen were not at all in his immediate purview. The central focus of his reflections in this treatise is very much the Spirit's powerful work of conversion and its concomitant fruit.

"THE ENCAMPMENT OF THE SPIRIT"

With regard to this fruit, Cyprian first of all focuses on the Spirit's power. The North African author is insistent that the power which the Spirit gives to believers is first of all power to live a life of virtue.

> If you keep to the path of innocence, of righteousness, with the firmness of your footsteps unfaltering—if, consecrated to God with all your strength and with all your heart, you become merely that which you have begun to be, [and] you will be granted freedom of action according to the measure in which spiritual grace increases. For there is neither measure nor limit in grasping God's favour, as is the custom in earthly benefactions. When the Spirit bountifully flows forth, it is suppressed by no boundaries…

---

23 Michel Réveillaud, "Note pour une Pneumatologie Cyprienne" in F.L. Cross, ed., *Studia Patristica* (Texte und Untersuchungen, Vol. 81; Berlin: Akademie-Verlag, 1962), 6:181–182.

24 Brent, *St Cyprian of Carthage: On the Church*, 32–33.

25 J. Patout Burns and Gerald M. Fagin, *The Holy Spirit*, Message of the Fathers of the Church, Vol.3 (Wilmington: Michael Glazier, 1984), 80, 88. For a similar conclusion, see F. LeRon Shults and Andrew Hollingsworth, *The Holy Spirit* (Grand Rapids: Eerdmans, 2008), 23–24.

He flows forth continually, he bursts forth abundantly to the extent that our heart thirsts for him and is open to him.[26]

Key to understanding this passage is the pneumatological affirmation that there is no limit to the Spirit's sovereign and free presence.[27] He is not hemmed in by boundaries. As such, the believer, if he or she wishes to flourish and mature as a Christian, must increasingly draw upon the Spirit's sovereign power. In Cyprian's words, there must be a thirst for it, an openness to it.

At the close of this treatise, Cyprian returns to this theme of the life of holiness. Speaking about the freeness of salvation, the escape from this world of misery and sin, he is led to reflect on the nature of the Christian life. He writes:

[This salvation] is the gift of God, given for naught and willingly. Just as the sun shines of its own accord, the day gives it light, the fountain waters, the shower its light rain, so the celestial Spirit outpours himself.... You, however, whom the heavenly warfare has marked for the encampment of the Spirit (*spiritalibus castris*), hold fast the imperishable, hold fast the sober discipline in religious virtues. May your prayer or reading (*oratio...lectio*) be often. At one time you speak with God, at another God with you.[28]

To experience the free outpouring of the Spirit of God is to become a soldier in the Spirit's army, where, like the imperial legions, there is discipline. In this case, the disciplines of prayer and the reading of Scripture are mentioned. While Cyprian would have affirmed that prayer should be a part of every Christian's spiritual regimen, his mention of reading (*lectio*) should not be so interpreted, since literacy levels in Roman North Africa, like the rest of the empire, would not have been much higher than ten to fifteen per cent.[29] This instruction must therefore be understood as being recipient-specific, namely, addressed primarily to Donatus.

---

26 *To Donatus* 5 (Brent, 53, altered).
27 Réveillaud, "Note pour une Pneumatologie Cyprienne," 182.
28 *To Donatus* 14–15 (Brent, 65, altered).
29 W.V. Harris, *Ancient Literacy* (Cambridge: Harvard University Press, 1989).

Cyprian now shifts his imagery from the military camp to the villas of the wealthy, places he knew well. They have "paneled ceilings embellished with gold" and are "decorated with slabs of costly marble."[30] Such places might once have seemed quite desirable, but now they will seem of little true value to the Christian who is

> to be adorned and decorated better than this. You are instead to be God's dwelling place, occupied by the Lord in place of a temple, in which the Holy Spirit has commenced his habitation. Let us paint this house with the colors of integrity (*innocentiae*), let us enlighten it with the light of righteousness (*iustitiae*). This house will never fall into ruin over the long course of old age, nor will the color or gold of the wall deteriorate and be marred.[31]

Drawing upon his memory of how the wealthy adorned their houses and employing the Pauline imagery of the believer as the temple of the Holy Spirit (1 Corinthians 6:19), Cyprian admonishes his reader that the Spirit's indwelling of the Christian must be honoured with a life of integrity and righteousness, a life that will endure and whose "splendour [is] permanent."[32]

THE *IMPERIUM* OF THE HOLY SPIRIT

According to Cyprian, the power that the Spirit gives to believers is not restricted to the moral realm. It can "cleanse the defects of foolish souls by restoring their health" and "command those reacting with hostility" to Christians "to be at peace, to be quiet instead of violent, gentle instead of savage."[33] From the surrounding context, it appears that the restoration of health that Cyprian has in mind relates to physical healing.[34] The second clause refers to individuals indwelt by demonic

---

30 *To Donatus* 15 (Brent, 65–66, altered).

31 *To Donatus* 15 (Brent, 66, altered).

32 *To Donatus* 15 (Brent, 66). Cp. Cyprian, *Letter* 55.27.2: "evil deeds do not proceed from the Holy Spirit" [trans. G.W. Clarke, *The Letters of St. Cyprian of Carthage*, Ancient Christian Writers, no.46 (New York/Ramsey, New Jersey: Newman Press, 1986), III, 50].

33 *To Donatus* 5 (Brent, 53).

34 Earlier in the passage, Cyprian states that Spirit-indwelt Christians who are living

powers, for Cyprian immediately goes on to talk about the Spirit's empowering of Christians to exorcise "unclean and erring spirits, who have plunged themselves into human beings."[35]

Cyprian spends some time describing the way that Christians can defeat such spirits, and then reiterates that the power Christians have received is not

> simply that our human spirit can withdraw itself from destructive contacts with the world, so that anyone who has received atonement and purification sustains no damage from the attacking enemy. Rather, our human spirit is made greater and stronger in its powers so that it has dominion by an imperial right over every attack of a raging adversary.[36]

CYPRIAN'S PNEUMATOLOGY: AN OVERVIEW

After the Scriptures, the most important influence on Cyprian's life and thinking were the works of Tertullian,[37] and it was Cyprian's daily habit to peruse one or more of the works of his fellow North African. According to a report by the fourth-century Latin translator and polemicist Jerome (c.347–419/420), Cyprian would tell his secretary, "Hand me the master," by which he meant Tertullian.[38] The influence of Tertullian on Cyprian is indeed unmistakable in a number of key areas,[39] but a quick reading of the Cyprianic corpus—his eighty or so letters, the three volumes of the *Testimonia*, and his eleven treatises[40]—

---

holy lives are able "to provide curing medicine for the sick." *To Donatus* 5 (Brent, 53).

35 *To Donatus* 5 (Brent, 53).
36 *To Donatus* 5 (Brent, 54).
37 "Theological Legacy of St Cyprian," 69–70.
38 Jerome, *On Illustrious Men* 53. For Jerome's mini–biography of Cyprian, see his *On Illustrious Men* 67.
39 Wiles, "Theological Legacy of St Cyprian," 69–70; Rex D. Butler, *The New Prophecy & "New Visions": Evidence of Montanism in The Passion of Perpetua and Felicitas* (Washington: The Catholic University of America Press, 2006), 104. For some details, see Molager, trans., *A Donat et La Vertue de Patience*, 140–155; J. Patout Burns, *Cyprian the Bishop* (London/New York: Routledge, 2002), 102; 157 and 229, n.66; 176.
40 For details about this corpus and the individual dates of each of the items, see Sage, *Cyprian*, 377–383.

appears to reveal that very little of Tertullian's ardent interest in pneumatology has rubbed off on the younger North African. Tertullian has extensive discussions of the Spirit especially in his Montanist treatises as well as in his *Against Praxeas*, which is a vital work in the historical development of the doctrine of the Trinity.[41] Compared to Tertullian's pneumatological passion, some scholars have argued that there is a distinct decline of interest in the Spirit in Cyprian. Adhemar d'Alès, for example, maintained that in Cyprian's writings "le Saint-Esprit n'apparaît presque pas,"[42] while Manlio Simonetti sees Cyprian as one example of a "regresso" in third-century pneumatology.[43] On the other hand, as Michel Réveillaud has noted, these judgments fail to take note of how frequently Cyprian does mention the Holy Spirit.[44]

Cyprian habitually thinks of the Holy Spirit as the prophetic Spirit, the inspirer of the Scriptures. So, for example, in *To Demetrian* 20, Cyprian states that the Spirit speaks through the Old Testament prophet Habakkuk. The soul of the believer is filled with joy and is "always free from anxiety, even as the Holy Spirit says and exhorts through the prophet, strengthening the sure foundation of our hope and faith with his heavenly voice," and Cyprian then cites Habakkuk 3:17–18.[45] Or again, in 253/254, just prior to Cyprian's controversy with Stephen, he can state in *Letter* 69:

[T]he Church is declared one by the Holy Spirit in the Song of Songs, speaking in the person of Christ: "My dove, my perfect one, is but one; she is the only one of her mother, the favourite of her who bore her" [Cant. 6:9]. And the Spirit again says of her:

---

41 For Tertullian's pneumatology, see especially Claire Ann Bradley Stegman, "The Development of Tertullian's Doctrine of 'Spiritus Sanctus' " (Ph.D. thesis, Southern Methodist University, 1978). For the importance of *Against Praxeas*, see, for example, the lucid discussion of Benjamin B. Warfield, *Studies in Tertullian and Augustine*, vol. 3 of *The Works of Benjamin B. Warfield* (1930; reprint, Grand Rapids: Baker Book House, 1991), 3–109.

42 Adhemar d'Alès, *La théologie de Saint Cyprien* (Paris: G. Beauchesne, 1922), 11.

43 Manlio Simonetti, "Il regresso della teologia dello Spirito santo in Occidente dopo Tertulliano," *Augustinianum* 20 (1980), 655–669, *passim*.

44 Réveillaud, "Note pour une Pneumatologie Cyprienne," 181.

45 *To Demetrian* 20 (Brent, 89).

"An enclosed garden is my sister, my bride, a sealed fountain, a well of living water" [Cant. 4:12].[46]

The Spirit also frequently appears as the One who strengthens the martyrs in their time of trial and speaks through their lips a powerful witness for Christ.[47] Then, there is the extensive appeal to the Spirit as the One who indwells the church and so makes her the one true spouse of Christ, which the section cited above from *Letter* 69 is seeking to argue from the Song of Songs and which has been discussed briefly above.

There are also a few references in Cyprian's writings to the triunity of God that are usually made by means of the citation of the baptismal command from Matthew 28.[48] The most famous of these is the statement in *On the unity of the Catholic Church* that "it is written concerning Father, Son, and Holy Spirit: 'And the three are one'," the latter quote being a citation of 1 John 5:8.[49] This gloss on 1 John 5:8 is almost definitely the origin of the *Comma Johanneum*.

Unique among Cyprian's discussions of the Spirit, though, is what we have examined in *To Donatus*, which, from one perspective, is an extended meditation on his personal experience of the empowering Spirit, and from another perspective, given the evangelistic purpose of the document, a call to his fellow Romans to experience the same. Réveillaud has rightly observed that the importance of this document for understanding the shape of Cyprian's theology as a whole should not be underestimated.[50]

THE SPIRIT OF MARTYRDOM

Just as the Spirit figured prominently at the outset of Cyprian's Christian life, so he also appeared at the close. In August 258, the Roman emperor Valerian (r.253–260) initiated the bloodiest persecution of

---

46 *Letter* 69.2.1, trans. Clarke, *Letters of St. Cyprian of Carthage*, IV, 33. The instances of Cyprian"s depiction of the Spirit as the prophetic Spirit are too numerous to list in this context.
47 See, for example, Cyprian, *Letter* 6.2.1; 10.4.1; 57.4.2; 58.5.2; 66.7.2.
48 See, for example, *Letter* 27.3.3; 73.5.2; 73.18.1;
49 *On the Unity of the Catholic Church* 6 (Brent, 157).
50 Réveillaud, "Note pour une Pneumatologie Cyprienne," 181.

the church prior to that of Diocletian (r.284–305).⁵¹ His goal was to decimate the leadership of the church throughout the Empire in the hope that the Christian movement would soon fall apart. Cyprian was living in exile not far from Carthage, where he had been for the previous year for refusing to worship the Roman gods. Toward the end of August, he was summoned back to Carthage to face trial. Just before he left for his home city, he wrote a letter to his congregation, in which he informed them that "whatever a confessor-bishop speaks at the very moment he confesses his faith, he speaks under inspiration of God."⁵² As G.W. Clarke has noted, Cyprian is clearly thinking of Matthew 10:19–20, one of Cyprian's favourite verses, which encourages Christians not to be anxious about what they will say during times of persecution for they will be given the words to speak, for "the Spirit of [their] Father" will speak through them.⁵³ Within two weeks of writing these words, on the morning of September 14, 258, Cyprian was beheaded on the *ager Sexti* on the outskirts of Carthage after he had refused to worship the Roman gods at the behest of the proconsul Galerius Maximus. To the end of his Christian life, Cyprian sought to be a Spirit-filled man.

---

51 For the details of what follows, see Sage, *Cyprian*, 337–353.
52 *Letter* 81.1.2, trans. Clarke, *Letters of St. Cyprian of Carthage*, IV, 105.
53 Clarke, *Letters of St. Cyprian of Carthage*, IV, 316. On Cyprian as a prophetic figure, see Adolf von Harnack, "Cyprian als Enthusiast," *Zeitschrift für die neutestamentliche Wissenschaft* 3 (1902): 177–191.

6

"A disciple of the holy God"

Constantine and his revolution[1]

> I confess that I honour this God with never-dying remembrance, this God in the height of his glory I delight to contemplate with a pure and simple heart.
> —CONSTANTINE[2]

Among the most striking reactions to the news that Rome had been sacked by Alaric (d.410) and his Visigothic hordes in 410 was that of Jerome, best remembered for his production of the Latin Vulgate Bible.

---

1 This chapter had its origins in a lecture given at The Fellowship for Reformation and Pastoral Studies in Toronto on February 8, 1999.

2 Eusebius of Caesarea, *Life of Constantine* 4.9, trans. Paul Keresztes, "Constantine: Called by Divine Providence" in Elizabeth A. Livingstone, ed. *Tudia Patristica* (Kalamazoo: Cistercian Publications, 1985), 52.

At the time Jerome was living in a monastery in Bethlehem. "A terrible rumour," he wrote to a correspondent,

> has arrived from the West. Rome is besieged; the lives of the citizens have been redeemed by gold. Despoiled, they are again encircled, and are losing their lives after they have lost their riches. My voice cannot continue, sobs interrupt my dictation. The City is taken which took the whole world.... "O God, the heathen have come into thy inheritance, they have defiled thy holy temple. They have made of Jerusalem a shed for an orchard keeper. They have given the bodies of thy servants as food for the birds of the air, the flesh of thy saints to the beasts of the earth; they have poured out their blood as water round about Jerusalem, and there was no man to bury them" [Psalm 79:1–3].[3]

What is especially noteworthy about this text is not so much Jerome's personal reaction to one of the most important events in the history of the West, but the biblical passage that he cites in relation to it. Jerome compares the fall of Rome to the destruction of Jerusalem by Babylonian troops in the sixth century B.C. Just as Jerusalem was marked out as the holy city of God's people, so, Jerome implies, Rome has a like status.

Two centuries earlier, though, the city to which Christians were most likely to have compared Rome was not Jerusalem, but Jerusalem's mortal enemy, Babylon. In the second- and third-century Christian mind, Rome was best likened to Babylon, because both were notorious centres of immorality and godlessness, and, in the words of Tertullian, Rome "like Babylon is great, and proud of empire and at war against the saints of God."[4] Why the change in perception? In a word: Constantine (c.285–337). His acclamation at York as emperor in 306 and

---

3 *Letter* 127.12 in J.N. Hillgarth, ed., *The Conversion of Western Europe, 350–750* (Englewood Cliffs: Prentice-Hall, 1969), 67. For other reactions, see R.P.C. Hanson, "The Reaction of the Church to the Collapse of the Western Roman Empire in the Fifth Century," *Vigiliae Christianae* 26 (1972): 272–287.

4 Tertullian, *Against Marcion* 3.13 in Tertullian, *Adversus Marcionem*, ed. and trans. Ernest Evans (Oxford: Clarendon Press, 1972), 211.

Constantine the Great
(c.285–337; r.306–337)

his subsequent reign of thirty-one years was one of the most decisive moments in the history of Christianity. It radically altered the entire context and community in which Christians lived out their faith.

Now, evangelical authors vary in their view of Constantine and his "revolution." Jonathan Edwards (1703–1758), in *A History of the Work of Redemption*, was convinced that Constantine's "great revolution" was "like Christ's appearing in the clouds of heaven to save his people and judge the world." It was, in Edwards' fulsome words,

> the greatest revolution and change in the face of things on the face of the earth that ever came to pass in the world since the flood. Satan, the prince of darkness, that king and god of the heathen world, was cast out; the roaring lion was conquered by the Lamb of God in the strongest dominion that ever he had, even the Roman empire.[5]

More typical, though, of mainstream evangelical historiography are the following remarks of John Wesley (1703–1791). In a sermon he first preached in 1756 entitled "The Mystery of Iniquity," Wesley averred that the greatest blow ever struck at the root of genuine Christianity

> was struck in the fourth century by Constantine the Great, when he called himself a Christian, and poured in a flood of riches, honours, and power upon the Christians, more especially upon the clergy.... Then the mystery of iniquity was no more hid, but stalked abroad in the face of the sun. Then, not the golden, but the iron age of the church commenced.[6]

For Wesley, as for many other evangelical authors, Constantine was merely an astute politician, an opportunist who used the church to help save classical culture and the Roman way of life. As a result an

---

5 Jonathan Edwards, *A History of the Work of Redemption*, transcribed and ed. John F. Wilson (New Haven: Yale University Press, 1989), 394, 396.

6 *The Works of John Wesley*, ed. Albert C. Outler (Nashville: Abingdon Press, 1985), 2:462–463.

alliance between church and state ensued which ultimately wrought spiritual havoc in the church.[7]

How then is Constantine to be viewed, as a friend of the church or its foe? To answer this question we must first look at Constantine himself, his achievements and his convictions about himself. Only then is it appropriate to look at the long-term results of his reign. The latter, though, should never be used as the criterion by which we determine the sincerity of Constantine's motives.

THE ROMAN EMPIRE

Historians have long debated why the Roman Empire did not fall in the third century. From the 240s to the 270s there were massive assaults by Germanic tribes along the entire length of the frontier of the empire in Europe. The Franks, Alemanni and Juthungi, Vandals and Sarmatians, and the Goths defeated and decimated numerous Roman legions and sent raiding parties deep within the empire. In the east, there was a disastrous war with the resurgent Sassanid kingdom of Persia which culminated with the capture of the Roman emperor Valerian at Edessa in 260. More than a few Roman legions mutinied and for a number of years some of the provinces in the west and the east broke away from the empire to set up their own domains.

Between the reigns of Caracalla (r.211–217) and Diocletian, who ascended to the imperial purple in 284, there were roughly twenty emperors and all but two died violently. Accompanying all of this military and political turmoil, there was rampant inflation and economic instability, famine and plague. The North African bishop Cyprian, whom we looked at in the previous chapter, captured the chaos of the times when he wrote to Donatus, a fellow believer: "Observe the roads blocked by robbers, the seas beset by pirates, wars spread everywhere with the bloody horrors of camps. The world is soaked with mutual blood."[8]

---

[7] For further discussion of this historiographical perspective, see Daniel H. Williams, "Constantine, Nicaea and the 'Fall' of the Church" in Lewis Ayres and Gareth Jones, eds., *Christian Origins: Theology, Rhetoric and Community* (London: Routledge, 1998), 117–136.

[8] *To Donatus* 6 (Deferrari, 12).

The restoration of order was largely the work of Diocletian, a brilliant Illyrian army officer. The army was beefed up and came to number as many as 400,000 men. Frontier defences were strengthened. Imperial security was tightened, making assassination of the emperor more difficult. A series of monetary reforms that stabilized the economy were pushed through. The most radical changes had to do with the position of the emperor. Recognizing that the empire had grown far too unwieldy to govern, Diocletian first created a dual emperorship with two emperors, one in the west and one in the east, both of whom went by the title "Augustus." And, because the peaceful transfer of power from one emperor to another had been a major problem in the third century, Diocletian later established an arrangement whereby the Augustus could hand over the reins of power to a "junior emperor," denoted by the term "Caesar." This division of power, called the Tetrarchy, had important consequences for the political future of the empire. It formally divided the empire into two, which eventually led to a point in the fifth century where there were really two separate regimes.[9]

Diocletian ruled as Augustus in the east, and appointed as the Augustus of the west the loyal Maximian (r.286–305). As Caesar of the east, Diocletian chose Galerius (died 311), a fanatical pagan with an inveterate hatred of Christians and their faith. Maximian took Flavius Valerius Constantius (died 306), commonly called Chlorus ("Pale Face"), for his Caesar. Constantius, the father of Constantine, was assigned the responsibility of administering Gaul and Britain.

The nature of Constantius' religious convictions is far from clear. There is numismatic evidence that proclaims a devotion to Mars, Jupiter and Hercules. During the so-called Great Persecution, which commenced in 303, he refused to kill any Christians in his realm, though he does appear to have destroyed a number of buildings that were being used as churches.[10] Yet, his youngest daughter, born no later than 300, was named Anastasia, which seems to betray a

---

9 Chris Scarre, *The Penguin Historical Atlas of Ancient Rome* (London: Penguin Books, 1995), 114–116.

10 Mark D. Smith, "Eusebius and the Religion of Constantius I" in Elizabeth A. Livingstone, ed., *Studia Patristica* (Louvain: Peeters Publishers, 1997), 29:133–140.

predilection for Christianity.[11] And Eusebius of Caesarea maintains in his *Ecclesiastical History* that Constantius never actually demolished any churches.[12] Historians will continue to argue over Constantius' precise religious predilections. There is, however, little doubt about those of his son. As soon as Constantine is made Caesar in 306 and comes into the limelight of history, he has a marked favouritism for the Christian faith.

Two years before Constantine's appointment to the imperial college, Galerius pressured Diocletian into adding religious renewal to his long list of reforms. He convinced Diocletian that Christianity posed a significant threat to the official ideology underlying the government of the Tetrarchy.[13] The first edict against Christians was issued on February 23, 303, and declared assembly for Christian worship illegal. To enforce the ruling, Diocletian ordered the destruction of all churches and private homes where Christian worship took place.

Intellectual support for this concerted attack on the church was drawn from a number of articulate pagan voices, the most notable being the Neoplatonist philosopher Porphyry (c.233–c.303). In his fifteen-volume *Against the Christians*, Porphyry maintained that the Christian faith was inimical to civilization. He thus denounced Christians "as barbarians, as apostates from ancestral religion, as atheists who deserved punishment." And Porphyry had no doubts about what that punishment should be: execution.[14]

Other edicts soon followed in the east: one in the spring or summer of 303 ordered the arrest of all involved in Christian leadership. If they refused to sacrifice to the Roman gods, they were executed. Another in 304 required all inhabitants under the rule of Diocletian and Galerius to sacrifice and offer libations to the Roman gods. Christians who refused were martyred and their bodies mutilated and tortured beyond recognition. Eusebius of Caesarea, who was an eyewitness of

---

11 Timothy D. Barnes, *Constantine and Eusebius* (Cambridge: Harvard University Press, 1981), 3–4.

12 *Ecclesiastical History* 8.13.13. See also Smith, "Eusebius and the Religion of Constantius I," 133–140.

13 For Galerius' key role in the Great Persecution, see Barnes, *Constantine and Eusebius*, 15–27.

14 Barnes, *Constantine and Eusebius*, 21–22.

the persecution at its most savage in Palestine and Egypt, talks of ten, twenty, even sixty or a hundred believers being martyred every day for months on end.[15]

Now, by this point in time, there were some six million believers in the empire, around ten percent of the total population.[16] In some areas of the empire, the percentage was much higher. For instance, Robert S. Bagnall conducted a study of Egyptian papyri that sought to identify those with definite Christian names and so trace a curve of Christianization in Egypt. His research yielded a figure of eighteen percent of Egypt being professedly Christian around 313.[17] Even before this time, there were villages in Palestine and Phrygia that were totally Christian. And, in many of the towns in the eastern Roman empire, Christians formed a majority or influential minority of the population.[18] The number of martyrs then was by no means insignificant.

At the height of the persecution in 305, Diocletian voluntarily abdicated, the only Roman emperor ever to do so. Too old and too sick to carry on shouldering the heavy load of imperial duties, he turned the government over to his Caesar, Galerius. He subsequently retired to a huge fortress villa at Split on the shores of the Adriatic, where he spent his final years in such domestic pursuits as growing turnips and cabbages. At the same time in Milan, Maximian also stepped down and Constantius became the senior emperor of the west.

A BRIEF SKETCH OF CONSTANTINE'S CAREER

Just over a year after he became senior emperor in the Tetrarchy, Constantius died at York on July 25, 306, with Constantine at his side. Although there was a Caesar, one Severus, in Milan, who according to the Diocletianic arrangement, should now have become Augustus, Constantius' legions saluted Constantine as Augustus in his father's stead. Galerius, the Augustus in the east, had absolutely no desire to have

---

15 *Ecclesiastical History* 8.9.3. His account of the persecution makes for sobering reading: see *Ecclesiastical History* 8.2.1–13.8.
16 Rodney Stark, *The Rise of Christianity. A Sociologist Reconsiders History* (Princeton: Princeton University Press, 1996), 4–13.
17 See Stark, *Rise of Christianity*, 12–13.
18 Barnes, *Constantine and Eusebius*, 191.

Constantine as a colleague. But he was not prepared to tangle with Constantine. In an astute move, he declared his recognition of Constantine as Caesar, the junior of Severus. Long groomed for power and the possessor of political sagacity, Constantine accepted the appointment, thereby silencing any who would question the legitimacy of his reign.[19]

Constantine's first actions as emperor reveal both his religious sympathies as well as his political savvy. He totally halted the persecution of the church—in the east it would rage on for another six years. Furthermore, he gave full restitution to those believers under his direct rule in Spain, Gaul and Britain, who had suffered the loss of land and possessions. This strategic move not only marked him out as a champion of the Christian cause; it also asserted his right to legislate for those under his jurisdiction and was thus an open declaration that he was indeed a legitimate ruler in the west.[20]

Summing up Constantine's political character, Timothy D. Barnes has characterized him as "implacably ambitious," determined from the beginning of his reign to become the sole ruler of a unified Roman Empire.[21] For the six years following Galerius' recognition of him in 306, Constantine strategized toward control of the west. The decisive moment to act came in 312 when Constantine marched on Rome. On October 28, just outside of Rome, at the Milvian Bridge, he confronted his last major opponent in the west, a pagan by the name of Maxentius (r.306–312). His victory in the brief battle that ensued made him the undisputed master of the western Roman Empire. A dozen years later, in 324, he realized his dream of ruling over a united empire when he defeated his co-ruler in the east, Licinus (r.308–324), in a couple of key battles. It is, however, the events surrounding the Battle of the Milvian Bridge that have captured the primary attention of historians down through the years.

"A DISCIPLE OF THE HOLY GOD"

As his troops went into battle on that autumn day in 312 they bore on their standards not the usual pagan emblems, but a distinctively

---

19 Barnes, *Constantine and Eusebius*, 28–29.
20 Barnes, *Constantine and Eusebius*, 28.
21 Barnes, *Constantine and Eusebius*, 29.

Christian sign, probably a variant of an ancient Christian symbol, the Chi-Rho (☧), produced by the intertwining of the first two letters of Christ's name in Greek.[22] Many years later, according to an interview Eusebius of Caesarea had with Constantine, the emperor would tell the church historian that he placed this sign on the standards of his army in obedience to a direct command he received from Christ in a vision.[23] Whatever one makes of the vision, there is no gainsaying the fact that Constantine's army went into battle as identifiably on the side of Christianity.

In the years immediately following his victory over Maxentius, Constantine followed up this open avowal of Christianity with legislation and actions that left no doubt as to his convictions.[24] The so-called Edict of Milan, issued in 313 in both Constantine's name and that of his pagan co-emperor Licinius, recognized Christianity as a legal religion throughout the Empire. Constantine proceeded to donate funds to erect a splendid basilica in Rome that would accommodate up to 4,000 worshippers and would serve as the principal place of worship for believers in the city. He also gave monetary aid to support the poverty-stricken, orphans and widows. Christian bishops and pastors became exempt from taxation, a remarkable innovation in the history of the empire. Courts in which bishops presided as judges were legally established. This meant that where the litigants in a lawsuit were both Christians, they could have their case tried in a court presided over by a bishop, instead of in a civil court where the judge might well be a pagan.

Roman law and culture also began to be remoulded. Crucifixion was abolished as a legal punishment. The gladiatorial games, a staple of Roman entertainment for more than four centuries, were totally forbidden in 325, though it took some years for this cruel blood sport

---

22 For a picture of this symbol as it probably appeared that day, see Matthew Black, "The Chi-Rho Sign—Christogram and/or Staurogram" in W. Ward Gasque and Ralph P. Martin, ed., *Apostolic History and the Gospel: Biblical and Historical Essays presented to F. F. Bruce on his 60th Birthday* (Grand Rapids: Wm. B. Eerdmans Publ. Co., 1970), 322–323.

23 Eusebius of Caesarea, *Life of Constantine* 1.28–31.

24 For the following account of this legislation, I am indebted to Barnes, *Constantine and Eusebius*, 48–53.

to be totally replaced with chariot racing. The observance of Sunday as a holy day was made mandatory for all.[25] In accordance with Constantine's reading of Christian moral standards, divorce and re-marriage were made far more difficult: a woman could divorce her husband only if he were a murderer, poisoner or tomb violator, while a man could divorce his spouse only if she were guilty of adultery, poisoning or running a brothel. And in one key area he abandonned a long-standing Roman tradition, the imposition of legal disabilities on the unmarried. Some Christians chose to be celibate for the sake of the kingdom of God, and Constantine felt that such should be admired, not penalized.

Places where some historians have seen evidence of what they regard as Constantine's religious syncretism—for instance, the continued usage of the pagan Sol Invictus image on his coins for a number of years after his victory at the Milvian Bridge—actually reveal a shrewd politician. In the years between the Battle of the Milvian Bridge and his defeat of the pagan Licinus, Constantine well knew that a direct attack on the public aspects of pagan religion was not feasible. After his conquest of the entire empire, however, the erection of idols, the consultation of pagan oracles, the use of divination and sacrificing to the gods, central aspects of traditional Roman religion, were all proscribed and made illegal.[26]

Documentary evidence confirms the convictions lying behind all of this legislation which sought to remould Roman society and culture along the lines of Christianity. In a public decree that he issued in 324, after his victory over Licinus, Constantine declared:

> To acknowledge...in solemn terms the beneficence of the Supreme Being is by no means boasting. He searched for and chose my service to carry out his purpose. Starting...at the faraway Britannic sea and the regions where the sun...sets, by the help of the Supreme Power, I drove out and scattered all the prevailing evil things, in order that the human race, reared with my assistance, might call upon the service of the holy law.[27]

---

25 Eusebius of Caesarea, *Life of Constantine* 4.18.
26 Barnes, *Constantine and Eusebius*, 210.
27 Eusebius of Caesarea, *Life of Constantine* 2.28, trans. Paul Keresztes, "Constantine: Called by Divine Providence" in Elizabeth A. Livingstone, ed., *Studia Patristica* (Kala-

Constantine here recalls his march of triumph from his elevation to the purple at York in 306 to his then-recent defeat of Licinus. He is conscious of being an instrument in the hand of the One he calls the Supreme Being, to whom he gives full credit for his victorious career. He is the one whom God entrusted with a divine mission to educate the Romans to acknowledge the true God and instil in them reverence.[28] In the same public document, he was quite prepared to acknowledge all that he owed to God: "I am firmly convinced that I owe my life and every breath...to the Supreme God."[29]

In a second text, issued by Constantine in 325, Constantine stated his abhorrence of the memory of those emperors who "persecuted the true doctrine during the whole period of their reign." But these persecutors had met their rightful end in an eternal hell. The only recent emperor who meant anything to Constantine was his father, Constantius, because he was not a persecutor like the others. Constantine was willing to extend freedom of conscience to the devotees of Roman paganism, those who "delight in error" at "their shrines of falsehood," but they had to realize that Christianity was now the emperor's religion. "Your name," he said to God, "I truly love, while I regard with reverence that power of which you have given abundant proofs to the confirmation and increase of my faith."[30]

One final document that reveals the depth of his religious convictions and his belief in God's providential ordering of his life is a letter that he sent to King Shapur II (309–379) of Persia. The Persians were Rome's traditional enemy, and there were numerous Christians in the Persian kingdom. Constantine told the Persian king that if he harmed these Christians he would have to answer to Constantine. To give added weight to this threat he told Shapur that God had given him victory in all of his campaigns.

---

mazoo, Michigan: Cistercian Publications, 1985), XVIII/1, 47, altered. For a commentary on this text, see Keresztes, "Constantine: Called by Divine Providence," 47, and Barnes, *Constantine and Eusebius*, 208–209.

28 Barnes, *Constantine and Eusebius*, 43. See also Hermann Doerries, *Constantine the Great*, trans. Roland H. Bainton (New York: Harper Row Publications, 1972), 61–67.

29 Eusebius of Caesarea, *Life of Constantine* 2.29, trans. Keresztes, "Constantine: Called by Divine Providence," 47.

30 Eusebius of Caesarea, *Life of Constantine* 2.49, 54–56.

I profess the most holy religion. I confess that as a disciple of the Holy God I observe this worship. With the power of this God on my side to help me, beginning at the boundaries of the Ocean, I have gathered every nation, one after another, throughout the world, to the certain hope of salvation.... This God I worship and my army is dedicated to him and wears his sign on their shoulders, marching directly wherever the cause of justice summons them. I confess that I honour this God with never-dying remembrance, this God in the height of his glory I delight to contemplate with a pure and simple heart.[31]

These three texts (and more could be cited) reveal a man who was sincerely convinced that he had been given a divine mission to inculcate virtue in his subjects and persuade them to worship the true God proclaimed in the Christian faith. Yes, this conviction was wedded to an intense ambition for personal power, but that does not diminish its sincerity.

CONSTANTINE—FRIEND OR FOE?

When Constantine died in 337 there was scarcely any facet of the public life of the empire that had not been impacted by his policy of official Christianization. In acting thus, Constantine had sincerely perceived himself as a friend to the church. Yet, his legacy was by no means all good.

The incredible turn of events that accompanied the reign of Constantine, the way in which almost overnight Christians went from being a persecuted minority to being the power brokers in the new order, all but seduced some believers into thinking that the state and the church could work together to establish the kingdom of God. A major figure who articulated this view was Eusebius of Caesarea.

On July 25, 336, the year before Constantine's death, Eusebius was asked to preach at the celebration of the thirtieth anniversary of Constantine's accession to power. The main theme of his sermon is that the empire of Constantine is a visible image of the heavenly kingdom,

---

31 Eusebius of Caesarea, *Life of Constantine* 4.9, trans. Keresztes, "Constantine: Called by Divine Providence," 51–52, altered.

"the manifestation on earth of that ideal monarchy which exists in the heavenly realm." Eusebius went on to affirm that Constantine governs it in accordance with the divine archetype, ever keeping his eyes on heaven to find the pattern for his government. In other words, what Eusebius enunciated here is a sacralization of the state.[32]

It was an idea that bore bitter fruit seventy-five years or so later when the western portion of this Christian Roman Empire fell before the onslaught of various Germanic tribes and the question was raised of why God would allow his "holy state" to suffer in this way. This sacralization of the state thus contributed in no small way to the tears of Jerome. It was left to Augustine of Hippo (354–430) to argue at length in his monumental *City of God* (413–426) that no earthly kingdom can be identified with the kingdom of God and that no earthly kingdom, even a Christian state, is essential to the outworking of God's purposes in history.[33]

A related question is, What happens if the emperor or ruler happens to disagree with your theological views? If the state is vital to the advance of the kingdom of God, then religious nonconformity runs the risk of persecution. As Basil of Caesarea, later wrote:

> When he [i.e. the Devil] saw that by the persecution of our enemies the Church was increasing and thriving the more, [he] changed his plan. He no longer makes war openly, but places hidden snares for us, concealing his treachery by the means of the name which his followers bear, in order that we may endure the same sufferings as our fathers, and yet not seem to suffer for Christ, since our persecutors have the name of Christian.[34]

The stage was set for the mediæval era when the church would regularly use the arm of the state to enforce "orthodoxy."

Finally, as Christianity became the government's preferred option, many were tempted to join the church simply because it provided a

---

32 Eusebius of Caesarea, *Oration in Praise of Constantine* 3.5; Barnes, *Constantine and Eusebius*, 254.
33 See Chapter 10.
34 *Letter* 139.1.

way to get ahead in society. In other words, during the fourth and fifth centuries, nominal believers entered the church in significantly large numbers to help bring about an identity crisis within the church. In essence that crisis can be boiled down to this question: "What does it mean to be a Christian in a 'Christian' society?"

In the second and third centuries the lines between the church and pagan society were sharply drawn, but not so after Constantine. The answer to this crisis that the church came up with was the renewal movement that we call monasticism. In the long run, this movement created as many problems as it set out to solve. But in the fourth century, in the hands of such capable exponents as Athanasius and Basil of Caesarea, it did indeed function as a vehicle of renewal. Indeed, it played an essential role in the survival of Christianity after the fall of the western Roman empire. It was in the monastic sodalities formed by this renewal movement, for instance, that the Christian Scriptures were preserved and handed on.

Having described three ways in which Constantine's revolution introduced elements of radical change into the life of the church, it is important to recognize that there were also significant elements of continuity between the pre- and post-Constantinian church. Post-Constantinian Nicene orthodoxy, for example, that is summed up in the Nicene and Niceno-Constantinopolitan creeds of 325 and 381 respectively, and that affirms the full deity of Christ and his Spirit, is by no means a drastic shift from the theological perspective of the Christianity of earlier centuries.[35] If this is so, there must then have been significant forces of theological integrity and spirituality in the period after Constantine to produce such documents. In other words, there is positive value in the history of the church in the period immediately after Constantine, and things are not as gloomy as Wesley and other evangelicals of his persuasion have supposed.[36]

---

35 See Chapter 8.
36 Williams, "Constantine, Nicaea and the 'Fall' of the Church," 130–131.

7

"Restoration... [and] repentance"
Basil of Caesarea and those who commit abortion[1]

> ...among us there is no fine distinction between a completely formed and unformed [embryo].
> —BASIL OF CAESAREA[2]

Central to the early Christian community was an ethic which, on the one hand, condemned violence and bloodshed, and on the other, vigorously upheld the sanctity of life. Such an ethic had, and still has, manifold ramifications. In the case of the early Christians, it led them

---

[1] This chapter originally appeared as "Benefiting from the Fathers—A Test Case: Basil of Caesarea on Abortion," *Eusebeia* 8 (Fall 2007): 11–18. Used by permission.

[2] *Letter* 188.2, trans. Michael A.G. Haykin.

not only to shun the violent pastimes of the Roman arena but also to eschew participation in the militarism of the Roman state. And, of great import with regard to our contemporary scene, this ethic led the early church to articulate a clear position concerning the treatment of the unborn. In this chapter, the treatment of abortion by a key figure in the early church, namely Basil of Caesarea, is examined in the hope that it may help to set the current discussion of this issue in historical perspective.

THE PATRISTIC BACKGROUND
The New Testament nowhere explicitly condemns the practice of abortion, which is somewhat surprising in view of the fact that abortion was not at all uncommon in the Græco-Roman world.[3] Whatever the reason for this explicit silence, early Christian authors outside of the New Testament consistently saw, in the frequent recourse to abortion by women in the Græco-Roman world, a violation of the scriptural prohibition against murder. For instance, the second-century apologist, Athenagoras (133–190), answering the pagan accusation that Christians practiced cannibalism (a charge that was rooted in a misunderstanding of the Lord's Supper) could declare:

> What sense does it make to think of us as murderers when we say that women who practice abortion are murderers and will render account to God for abortion? The same man cannot regard that which is in the womb as a living being and for that reason an object of God's concern and then murder it when it has come into the light.[4]

---

3   For the Græco-Roman view of abortion, see Richard Harrow Fein, "Abortion and Exposure in Ancient Greece: Assessing the Status of the Fetus and 'Newborn' from Classical Sources" in William B. Bondeson, et al. ed., *Abortion and the Status of the Fetus* (Dordrecht/Boston/Lancaster: D. Reidel, 1983), 283–300; Michael J. Gorman, *Abortion and the Early Church* (Downers Grove: InterVarsity Press, 1982), 13–32. For a discussion of the implicit evidence of the New Testament with regard to abortion, see Gorman, *Abortion*, 48. Gorman's book remains the best book-length study of this issue.

4   *Plea on behalf of the Christians* 35.6, in *Athenagoras: Legatio and De Resurrectione*, trans. William R. Schoedel (Oxford: Clarendon Press, 1972), 85. For a discussion of this text from Athenagoras, see Gorman, *Abortion*, 53–54.

Substantially, this was to be the position with regard to abortion that the church would maintain throughout this early period.

BASIL OF CAESAREA—A SKETCH OF HIS LIFE

Basil was born in Caesarea, then the capital of Cappadocia (now in central Turkey), around the year 330.[5] His parents, Basil and Emmelia, were Christians, as were his grandparents. One of his grandmothers, the Elder Macrina, had been converted through the remarkable ministry of a man named Gregory Thaumaturgus (c.210–c.270)—the Wonderworker—an avid church-planter in the region of Pontus, while two of his brothers—Gregory of Nyssa (c.335–c.394) and Peter of Sebaste (c.340–391)—were to go on to become bishops like Basil.

After Basil had received a first-class education at various schools in Caesarea, Constantinople and Athens, he returned to Caesarea in Cappadocia in 355. He had grandiose plans to become a teacher of rhetoric, but God had other plans for his life. His elder sister Macrina (c.327–380)—named after their grandmother—confronted him with the way that he was wasting his life upon the wisdom of this world. He came to realize, as he would later say, that "human wisdom is illusory, for it is a meagre and lowly thing and not a great and pre-eminent good."[6] Macrina's words and her passionate devotion to Christ had an enormous impact upon Basil. He was converted and baptized in 356 and turned to a life of simplicity, Christian obedience and good works. In 360, he was ordained as a reader in his local church in Caesarea. Given the low level of literacy in that era, to be able to read and write was of such great value to the church that people were often appointed as "reader." Two years later he became an elder, and finally in 370 he was elected bishop of Caesarea.

Today, Basil is probably best known for the key role that he played in the articulation of the orthodox doctrine of the Trinity. His chief theological work, *On the Holy Spirit* (written in 375), marked a decisive

---

5 For an excellent study of Basil, see Paul Jonathan Fedwick, *The Church and the Charisma of Leadership in Basil of Caesarea* (Toronto: Pontifical Institute of Mediaeval Studies, 1979); Stephen M. Hildebrand, *Basil of Caesarea* (Grand Rapids: Baker Academic, 2014).

6 Homily 20, in *Saint Basil: Ascetical Works*, trans. M.M. Wagner (New York: Fathers of the Church, 1950), 478.

step toward the resolution of the fourth-century controversy over the deity of the Spirit. Yet, he was also vitally interested in ethical questions, and his statement on the issue of abortion has been well described by Michael J. Gorman as "one of the most profound theological and ethical statements on abortion" that has come down to us from the early church.[7]

BASIL ON ABORTION—GENERAL REMARKS

In a letter to Amphilochius of Iconium, written in either 374 or 375, Basil is responding to a number of questions that Amphilochius had raised with regard to a variety of topics. To a question apparently about abortion, Basil makes this reply:

> The woman who has deliberately destroyed [her fetus] is subject to the penalty for murder. And among us there is no fine distinction between a completely formed and unformed [embryo]. For here justice is not only to be procured for the woman, who conspired [to kill] herself, because the women who attempt such things often die afterwards. Moreover, added to this is the destruction of the embryo, another murder, at least according to the intention of those who dare such things. Yet, it is not necessary to extend this penitence until their death, but one should accept a period of ten years' [penitence]. Moreover, their restoration (*therapeian*) should be determined not by time, but by the manner of their repentance (*metanoias*).[8]

Basil begins by reiterating the position of Athenagoras: abortion is murder. In fact, Basil notes, it often results in two murders, since the woman seeking to have an abortion often dies in the endeavour.[9]

---

    7 Gorman, *Abortion*, 66.
    8 *Letter* 188.2, trans. Michael A.G. Haykin. The Greek text upon which this translation is based is contained in the most recent critical edition, that of Yves Courtonne, *Saint Basile: Lettres*, trans. Yves Courtonne (Paris: Société d'Édition, 1961), II, 124. The words in parentheses are not part of the original Greek text but are added to bring out Basil's meaning.
    9 As Beverly Wildung Harrison observes: "until recently, any act of abortion always endangered the life of the mother every bit as much as it imperiled the prenatal life

Moreover, he rejects any arbitrary attempt to distinguish between stages of fetal development. Basil clearly believes that a human soul is present in a developing fetus from the moment of conception,[10] and he is thus concerned that the deliberate killing of *any* unborn be regarded as murder. As Gorman puts it, Basil "dismisses as irrelevant all casuistic distinctions between the formed and unformed fetus. For him...all life...is sacred."[11]

BASIL'S TREATMENT OF EXODUS 21:22–24 (LXX)

That Basil would take such a position is fascinating in view of the fact that the Greek translation of the Old Testament which he used, namely the Septuagint, contained a text which did, in fact, make a distinction between a completely formed fetus (one which possesses a human soul) and an unformed one (one which does not yet possess a human soul). The passage in question is Exodus 21:22–24. The Hebrew text of this passage as translated by the King James Version reads as follows:

> If men strive, and hurt a woman with child, so that her fruit depart from her, and yet no mischief follow: he shall surely be punished, according as the woman's husband will lay upon him; and he shall pay as the judges determine. And if any mischief follow, then thou shalt give life for life, eye for eye, tooth for tooth, hand for hand, foot for foot.[12]

---

in her womb" [Beverly Wildung Harrison, *Our Right to Choose: Toward a New Ethic of Abortion* (Boston: Beacon Press, 1983), 124]. Further on in the same letter, Basil will turn his attention to those who help women to procure abortions and roundly condemn them as murderers as well: "Women who give drugs which cause abortions are as much murderesses as those who take the poisions which kill the fetus" [*Letter* 188.8 (Courtonne, trans., *Lettres*, II, 128)].

10 See Joseph F. Donceel, "Immediate Animation and Delayed Hominization," *Theological Studies* 31 (1970): 77; Enzo Nardi, *Procurato aborto nel mondo greco romano* (Milan: Dott. A. Giuffrè Editore, 1971), 513 n.72; 580.

11 Gorman, *Abortion*, 67.

12 For a discussion of this text and its interpretation, see Harold O. J. Brown, "What the Supreme Court Didn't Know: Ancient and Early Christian Views on Abortion," *Human Life Review* 1, no. 2 (Spring 1975): 8–11; idem, *Death before Birth* (Nashville: Thomas Nelson, 1977), 124–126; John M. Frame, "Abortion from a Biblical Perspective" in R.L. Ganz, ed., *Thou Shalt Not Kill* (New Rochelle: Arlington House, 1978), 50–57;

The rendition of this verse in the Septuagint, however, differs significantly from the Hebrew text. For it renders this verse thus:

> If two men fight and they strike a woman who is pregnant, and her child comes out while not yet fully formed, the one liable to punishment will be fined; whatever the woman's husband imposes, he will give as is fitting. But if it is fully formed, he will give life for life.[13]

The distinction made here between a formed and unformed fetus probably reflects the position of the Greek philosopher Aristotle (384–322 B.C.), who sought to distinguish between lawful and unlawful abortions on the basis of whether or not the human embryo was fully formed or not.[14] Although the Greek translation of this text from Exodus does not have in view the *intentional* killing of an unborn child, there were some in Basil's day who used this passage from the Septuagint to argue that abortion in the early stages of fetal development is not equivalent to murder.[15] Basil implicitly rejects this argument by refusing to countenance the distinction drawn from Exodus 21:22–24 as it was translated in the Septuagint.[16] Since Basil was committed to the inerrancy of the Scriptures, it may well be the case that he discerned that this inerrancy should not be extended to a translation.

Gorman, Abortion, 33–45, *passim*; Meredith G. Kline, "*Lex Talionis* and The Human Fetus," *Journal of The Evangelical Theological Society* 20 (1977): 193–201.

13 Trans. Gorman, *Abortion*, 35.

14 Gorman, *Abortion*, 21–22, 35. Compare Feen, "Abortion and Exposure," 292–295.

15 See Franz Joseph Dölger, "Das Lebensrecht des ungeborenen Kindes und die Fruchtabtreibung in der Bewertung der heidnischen und christlichen Antike" in his *Antike und Christentum*, 2nd ed. (Münster: Verlag Aschendorff, 1975), IV, 56–58; Nardi, *Procurato aborto nel mondo greco romano*, 178 n.80; 516–517. At one point, the great North African theologian Augustine held to such a view, but as his thought matured, he came to "emphasize the value of all life, whether actual or potential" (Gorman, *Abortion*, 72).

16 Brown, "What the Supreme Court Didn't Know," 17–18; John T. Noonan, Jr., "An Almost Absolute Value in History" in his ed., *The Morality of Abortion* (Cambridge: Harvard University Press, 1972), 17.

ABORTION AND THE PASTORAL CONTEXT

Basil's discussion of abortion is set firmly in a pastoral context, for he now proceeds to give advice on how to deal with those who have had abortions but are now repentant. He makes it clear that, while abortion is indeed a serious sin, it is not one that is unforgiveable when there is repentance. He thus rejects the harsh ruling of the Spanish Council of Elvira (305/306) that the woman who had procured an abortion could never be received back into the full fellowship of the church while she was alive.[17] Instead, he accepts the later ruling from the Council of Ancyra (314), which was composed of church leaders from the Roman provinces of Asia Minor and Syria. This council prescribed a period of ten years before a woman who had had an abortion and was now repentant could be restored to communion.[18]

Basil, though, goes beyond this somewhat legalistic approach to the sin of abortion. What is important for him is not the amount of time spent in sorrowing for the sin committed, but the depth and sincerity of repentance. Once again, to cite Gorman, Basil "views sincere repentance as a valid sign of God's grace and forgiveness."[19] Moreover, unlike the rulings issued by the Councils of Elvira and Ancyra, Basil makes no mention of sexual sin in his condemnation of abortion.[20] Basil regards abortion as a sin due to the fact that it involves the destruction of human life, not because it was often employed to conceal illicit sexual activity.[21]

Basil's advice with regard to abortion strikes a good balance between truth and mercy. He recognizes the heinousness of this sin in the eyes of God, but at the same time, he is cognizant that this sin is not beyond the pale of God's forgiveness. In fact, his advice is only part of a much larger attitude toward the physically weak and infirm. Whereas the pagan Græco-Roman world was extremely callous with regard to the

---

17 Brown, "What the Supreme Court Didn't Know", 17; Gorman, *Abortion*, 64–65.
18 Brown, "What the Supreme Court Didn't Know", 17; Gorman, *Abortion*, 65–66.
19 Gorman, *Abortion*, 67.
20 Noonan, "Absolute Value," 17.
21 *Pace* Harrison, *Our Right to Choose*, 119–141, who argues that the early Christians' condemnation of abortion was necessarily linked to their denunciation of illicit sex and contraception. For an effective reply to this argument, see Gorman, *Abortion*, 78–82.

value of human life, Basil—indeed the early Christian community as a whole—sought to demonstrate the compassion of the Lord Jesus for the weak and defenceless.[22] For instance, only a couple of years prior to the composition of his letter to Amphilochius, Basil had been instrumental in the founding of what would become the most famous hospital in the ancient world.[23]

The conception of this hospital appears to have been the direct result of Basil's active involvement in a programme of relief for the victims of a very severe famine and drought during the winter of 368-369.[24] From the pen of Gregory of Nazianzus, another of Basil's close friends, comes the following description of Basil's activity during this period of famine and drought:

> He gathered together the victims of the famine...men and women, children, old people, sufferers of every age. Then he collected contributions of food of all sorts, anything that could be eaten. He provided great pots of pea soup and salted meat, the sort poor folk eat, and he imitated the service Christ gave when he girded himself with a towel and humbly washed his disciples' feet. Working with his own servants as their equal, he served the poor both as to their bodies and their souls.[25]

The stance taken by Basil with regard to abortion is yet another facet of the compassion and concern he exhibited on this occasion and at other times during his life. This stance emanated from a genuine concern for the life of the unborn child and remains both a model and a challenge for the church at the beginning of the twenty-first century.

---

22 It is noteworthy that one of the major reasons for the successful expansion of the church throughout the Roman empire was the practical expression of love shown by Christians for one another and for unbelievers. See Henry Chadwick, *The Early Church*, rev. ed. (London: Penguin Books, 1993), 56-58.

23 George E. Gask and John Todd, "The Origin of Hospitals" in E. Ashworth Underwood, ed., *Science, Medicine and History* (London: Oxford University Press, 1953), I, 127-128.

24 See Fedwick, *Church and the Charisma of Leadership*, 38.

25 From Gregory of Nazianzus' funeral oration for Basil, *Oration* 43.35, cited in *St. Basil the Great*, trans. James Hanrahan (Toronto: The Basilian Press, 1979), 97.

8

"To give glory to Father, Son and Holy Spirit"
Biblical exegesis in fourth-century Trinitarian debates[1]

> We have been taught that the Spirit of truth proceeds from the Father, and we confess him to be of God without creation. —BASIL OF CAESAREA[2]

In his masterful study of the unfolding of early Christian thought, Jaroslav Pelikan notes that the "climax of the doctrinal development of the early church was the dogma of the Trinity."[3] And the textual

---

1   This chapter was presented as a paper at a conference on the Trinity hosted by Reformed Theological Seminary in Houston, Texas, on November 12, 2016.
2   Basil, *Letter* 125.3, trans. Michael A.G. Haykin.
3   Jaroslav Pelikan, *The Christian Tradition: Vol. 1: The Emergence of the Catholic Tradition (100–600)* (Chicago: The University of Chicago Press, 1971), 172.

expression of that climax is undoubtedly the Niceno-Constantinopolitan Creed that was issued at the Council of Constantinople in 381, in which Jesus Christ is unequivocally declared to be "true God" and "of one being (*homoousios*) with the Father" and the Holy Spirit is said to be the "Lord and Giver of life," who "together with the Father and the Son is worshipped and glorified." The original Nicene Creed, issued by the Council of Nicæa in 325, had made a similar statement about the Son and his deity, but nothing had been said about the Holy Spirit beyond the statement, "[We believe] in the Holy Spirit." When the deity of the Spirit was subsequently questioned in the 360s and 370s, it was necessary to expand the Nicene Creed to include a statement about the deity of the Holy Spirit. In the end, this expansion involved the drafting of a new creedal statement at the Council of Constantinople.[4] In short, this creedal settlement understood God to be one being (*ousia*) who exists in three co-eternal persons (*hypostaseis*): Father, Son and Holy Spirit.[5]

Some historians have argued that these fourth-century creedal statements represent the apex of the Hellenization of the church's teaching, in which fourth-century Christianity traded the vitality of the New Testament church's experience of God for a cold, abstract philosophical formula. The great German historian Adolf von Harnack (1851–1930), for instance, famously declared that the doctrine of the Trinity was "a work of the Greek spirit on the soil of the Gospel."[6] But nothing could be further from the truth.[7] The Nicene and Niceno-

---

4 For the text of these two creeds, see J.N.D. Kelly, *Early Christian Creeds*, 2nd ed. (London: Longmans, Green and Co., 1960), 215–216, 297–298. See also Johannes Roldanus, *The Church in the Age of Constantine: The Theological Challenges* (Abingdon: Routledge, 2006), 123–126.

5 Joseph T. Lienhard, "Basil of Caesarea, Marcellus of Ancyra, and 'Sabellius'," *Church History* 58 (1989): 159.

6 Adolf von Harnack, *Lehrbuch der Dogmengeschichte*, 4th ed. (1909, reprint; Darmstadt: Wissenschaftliche Buchgesellschaft, 1965), I, 20. See Stephen M. Hildebrand, *The Trinitarian Theology of Basil of Caesarea: A Synthesis of Greek Thought and Biblical Truth* (Washington: Catholic University of America Press, 2007), 7. Hildebrand also identifies Edwin Hatch as another scholar who argued along this line.

7 As noted by Lewis Ayres, *Nicaea and Its Legacy: An Approach to Fourth-Century Trinitarian Theology* (Oxford: Oxford University Press, 2004).

Constantinopolitan Creeds helped to sum up a long process of reflection that had its origin in the texts of the New Testament. As Douglas F. Ottati, long-time professor of theology at Union Seminary in Richmond, Virginia, once put it, "Trinitarian theology continues a biblically initiated exploration."[8] Or, in the words of the early twentieth-century theologian, the American Presbyterian Benjamin B. Warfield: the "doctrine of the Trinity lies in Scripture in solution; when it is crystallized from its solvent it does not cease to be Scriptural, but only comes into clearer view."[9]

PRE-NICENE TRINITARIANISM

A Trinitarian understanding of God had shaped the life of the church from the very beginning of the Christian faith. Consider, for example, the portion of a third-century hymn discovered in the 1920s at Oxyrhynchus, about 100 miles southwest of Cairo and a few miles west of the Nile.

> May none of God's wonderful works
>   keep silence, night or morning.
> Bright stars, high mountains, the depths of the seas,
>   sources of rushing rivers:
>   may all these break into song as we sing
>   to Father, Son and Holy Spirit.
> May all the angels in the heavens reply.
>   Amen! Amen! Amen!
> Power, praise, honour, eternal glory to God,
>   the only Giver of grace.
> Amen! Amen! Amen![10]

---

8   Douglas F. Ottati, "Being trinitarian: The shape of saving faith," *The Christian Century* 112, no. 32 (November 8, 1995): 1045.

9   "The Biblical Doctrine of the Trinity" in Benjamin B. Warfield, *Biblical and Theological Studies*, ed. Samuel G. Craig (Philadelphia: The Presbyterian and Reformed Publishing Co., 1952), 22.

10 Cited Mark A. Noll, *Turning Points: Decisive Moments in the History of Christianity* (Grand Rapids: Baker Books, 1997), 47.

This hymn of worship clearly implies what the fourth-century councils of Nicæa and Constantinople would affirm to be the nature of God, namely, his triunity.

In the previous century, when Irenaeus of Lyons debated with Valentinian Gnostics and Marcionites in the Rhône valley about the nature of God, his vision of the Godhead was one that has been rightly described as "explicitly Trinitarian."[11] He called the Son "our Lord and God."[12] And he employed the adjective "eternal," drawn from Hebrews 9:14, to describe the Holy Spirit, thereby implying the Spirit's deity.[13] Over against Gnostic speculation that this world and its inhabitants came into existence through the work of a being who was not the true God, Irenaeus asserted that God made all things without the assistance of anyone outside of himself. And yet he did have help, namely, what Irenaeus calls "the hands of the Father," namely, "the Son and the Holy Spirit," a metaphor that implies their deity.[14]

Another important theological debate of this era, this time with modalism, forced the North African theologian Tertullian to demonstrate, in the words of the French historian Jean Daniélou, that there can be number in God without jeopardizing the unity of the divine substance."[15] Tertullian was forthright in the dual affirmation that "Father and Son and Spirit are unseparated from one another," and that "the Father is one [person (*persona*)], and the Son another, and the Spirit another."[16] Among other texts, Tertullian argued from Genesis 1:26, where God says, "Let us make man after our image and likeness" to prove that the Father was "speaking with the Son who was to assume

---

11 J.N.D. Kelly, *Early Christian Doctrines*, 4th ed. (London: Adam & Charles Black, 1968), 107.

12 Irenaeus, *Against Heresies* 1.10.1.

13 Irenaeus, *Against Heresies* 5.12.2.

14 Irenaeus, *Against Heresies* 4.preface.4; 5.6.1; 5.28.4. Cf. also Irenaeus, *Against Heresies* 2.30.9; 4.20.4. On the phrase "the hands of the Father," see also Joseph Haroutunian, "The Church, the Spirit, and the Hands of God," *Journal of Religion* 54 (1974): 154–165; D. Jeffrey Bingham, "Himself within Himself: The Father and His Hands in Early Christianity," *Southwestern Journal of Theology* 47 (2005): 137–151.

15 Jean Daniélou, *The Origins of Latin Christianity*, ed. and trans. D. Smith and J.A. Baker (Philadelphia: The Westminster Press, 1977), 363.

16 Tertullian, *Against Praxeas* 9.

manhood, and the Spirit who was to sanctify man."[17] On the basis of this prosopological exegesis—reasoning from the fact that the persons (*prosōpa/personae*) within the Godhead address one another—Tertullian argued that there must be three within the one Godhead. "'Two gods' or 'two lords' we never let issue from our mouth," the African theologian asserted, for "both the Father is God and the Son is God and the Holy Spirit is God, and each several one [of them] is God."[18] The God who has revealed himself in the Scriptures must be understood as *Trinitas*, a word that Tertullian appears to have coined in the context of his battle with modalism.[19]

CHALLENGING TRINITARIANISM AND THE RESPONSE OF NICÆA

At the beginning of the fourth century, though, there emerged a studied rejection of the full deity of the Son and the Spirit. Through the teaching of Arius (c.250/256–336), an elder and popular preacher in the Church of the Baucalis near the harbour in eastern Alexandria, Christian communities throughout the Roman empire, especially in the eastern regions, were plunged into a lengthy, bitter controversy about the person of Christ and his Spirit that dominated much of the fourth century.[20]

Arius' career before 318, when his views became controversial, is shadowy. It was in that year that he publicly claimed that only the Father was truly God. As he wrote in a letter to Alexander (d.328), the

---

17 Tertullian, *Against Praxeas* 12.
18 Tertullian, *Against Praxeas* 13.
19 For example, see Tertullian, *Against Praxeas* 11–12.
20 For studies of this controversy, see especially Pelikan, *Christian Tradition*, 1:172–225; R.P.C. Hanson, *The Search for the Christian Doctrine of God: The Arian Controversy, 318–381*, 1988 ed. (reprint; Grand Rapids: Baker, 2005); John Behr, *The Formation of Christian Theology, Vol. 2: The Nicene Faith* (Crestwood: St. Vladimir's Press, 2004), 2 vols. On Arius, see Rowan Williams, *Arius: Heresy and Tradition*, 2nd. ed. (London: SCM Press, 2001) and Behr, *The Nicene Faith*, 1:130–149. For a succinct statement of the philosophical and theological roots of Arianism, see Roldanus, *Church in the Age of Constantine*, 74–77, and for an excellent sketch of the entire controversy, see Michel René Barnes, "The Fourth Century as Trinitarian Canon" in Lewis Ayres and Gareth Jones, ed., *Christian Origins: Theology, Rhetoric and Community* (London: Routledge, 1998), 47–67.

bishop of Alexandria, God the Father alone, "the cause of all, is without beginning." The Son was created by the Father as "an immutable and unchangeable perfect creature," and thus cannot be "everlasting or co-everlasting with the Father."[21] The Son, must therefore have had a beginning, while God is without beginning.[22] And since there was a time when the Son did not exist, there must have been a time when it was inappropriate to call God "Father." In fact, Arius was so committed to the transcendence of the Father that he was prepared to assert that the "Father remains ineffable to the Son, and the Son can neither see nor know the Father perfectly or accurately."[23] As for the Holy Spirit, by Arius' reckoning, he was even less divine than the Son, for he was the first of the creatures made by the Son and thus did not share the being of either the Father or the Son.[24]

Arius claimed to be following Scripture, and it is important to note that this is where the key battle had to be fought. As Rowan Williams has rightly noted, the history of theology in this patristic era is a history of exegesis.[25] To articulate his position, Arius cited texts like Proverbs 8:22, where Wisdom is cited as saying in the Septuagint, "the Lord created me"; John 14:28, "my Father is greater than I"; or Colossians 1:15, where Christ is called "the image of the invisible God" and the "firstborn of every creature."[26] Arius was also deeply fearful of modalism or Sabellianism—so-named after Sabellius (*fl*.215), a third-century errorist, whose views had been condemned for all but eliminating any distinction between the persons of the Godhead. In seeking to avoid the heresy of Sabellianism, though, Arius fell into the equally pernicious error of denying the full deity of the Son and the Spirit.

---

21 Arius, *Letter to Alexander of Alexandria*, translation in William G. Rusch, *The Trinitarian Controversy* (Philadelphia: Fortress Press, 1980), 31–32.

22 Arius, *Letter to Eusebius of Nicomedia*, trans. Rusch, *Trinitarian Controversy*, 29–30.

23 Cited Athanasius, *Encyclical Letter to the Bishops of Egypt and Libya* 2.12. For a discussion of this assertion, see Williams, *Arius*, 105–107.

24 Cited Athanasius, *Orations against the Arians* 1.6; Hanson, *The Search for the Christian Doctrine of God*, 103.

25 Williams, *Arius*, 108.

26 Hanson, *The Search for the Christian Doctrine of God*, 102–103; J. Warren Smith, "The Trinity in the Fourth-Century Fathers" in *The Oxford Handbook of the Trinity*, ed. Gilles Emery and Matthew Levering (Oxford: Oxford University Press, 2011), 118.

Alexander's initial response was to emphasize that the Son was indeed as eternal as God the Father. According to Arius, Alexander taught, "Always God always Son," namely that the Son is co-eternal with the Father.²⁷ Thus there never was a time when the Father was without his Son. As such, he must be fully God.²⁸ Alexander summoned Arius to a meeting of all the church leaders of Alexandria and urged him to reconsider his views. When Arius refused, an open breach became unavoidable. In 321, Alexander convened a council of about 100 elders from Egypt and Libya, which drew up a creed that repudiated Arius' novel views. When Arius and those who supported him refused to accept this document, the council had no choice but to excommunicate them. But Arius had no intention of letting things rest. He began to correspond with other church leaders outside of North Africa and thus took the definitive step that spread the conflict to the rest of the church in the eastern Roman empire.

What was especially difficult about this conflict was the "slippery" nature of Arius' views and, of course, his appeal to the Bible. For instance, he could call Jesus "God." But what he and his partisans understood by this term was very different from what Alexander and his friends meant by the term. For Arius, Jesus was "God" but not fully God like the Father, for he did not share all of the attributes of the Father. In Arius' theology, the Son is ontologically subordinate to the Father and is really a creature, albeit the highest of all creatures.²⁹

Eventually, in the summer of 325, a council was called to provide definitive closure to the issue. Around 220 bishops and elders met at Nicæa, most of them from churches in the eastern Roman empire. The creedal statement that they issued, known to history as the Nicene Creed, was designed to end the dispute with its unequivocal declaration that the Lord Jesus Christ is "true God of true God, begotten (*gennēthenta*) not made, of one being (*homoousios*) with the Father." As "true God," the Son is confessed to be as truly God in whatever sense the Father is God. Whatever belongs to and characterizes God

---

27 Arius, *Letter to Eusebius of Nicomedia*, trans. Rusch, *Trinitarian Controversy*, 29–30.
28 For a concise summary of Alexander's views, see Roldanus, *Church in the Age of Constantine*, 77.
29 Smith, "Trinity in the Fourth-Century Fathers," 110.

the Father belongs to and characterizes the Son. A key phrase in this creed is undoubtedly the statement that the Son is "of one being (*homoousios*) with the Father."[30] Here, the full deity of the Son is asserted, the term *homoousios* emphasizing the fact that the Son shares the very being of the Father. He is therefore not a creature, contrary to the view of Arius and his fellow supporters. As a refutation of Arius' theology, the language of this text is "intended to be a strong statement of divine unity" between the Father and the Son.[31]

But what of avoiding the danger of modalism, the danger from the previous century that third-century theologians like Tertullian had battled and that fourth-century preachers like Arius feared? Well, the term "begotten" serves to differentiate the Son from the Father, but that term alone was not sufficient to avoid deep-seated concerns about the defenders of Nicæa being crypto-modalists. It should be noted also that the creed said nothing about the Spirit being divine. This was due to the fact that the heart of the controversy lay with regard to the nature of the Son. Clearly something explicit needed to be confessed about the Spirit's deity, but that confession would not come without further controversy.

THE ATTACK ON MARCELLUS OF ANCYRA FOR MODALISM

In spite of the hopes of those who drafted this confessional text, the Nicene Creed did not end the controversy. Eusebius of Nicomedia (died c.342), an *habitué* of the imperial court and supporter of Arius, had the ear of the professing Christian emperor, Constantine, and he was able to convince Constantine that the condemnation of Arius was far too harsh. In fact, so prominent a role did Eusebius play in the rehabilitation of Arius, that recent scholars have argued that the anti-Nicene party is better denominated "the Eusebians" rather than the Arians. Various Arian leaders, and even Arius himself, were brought back into favour from 327 onward and the leading enthusiasts for Nicæa dismissed.[32] Among the latter were Athanasius of Alexandria and

---

30 For some fourth-century concerns about the term homoousios, see Barnes, "Fourth Century as Trinitarian Canon," 49.

31 Barnes, "Fourth Century as Trinitarian Canon," 51.

32 Roldanus, *Church in the Age of Constantine*, 82–84; Joseph T. Lienhard, *Contra*

Marcellus of Ancyra (c.285–374). Athanasius had succeeded Alexander as bishop of Alexandria in 328.[33] A native Egyptian, Athanasius was a theological genius and, until his death in 373, the most formidable opponent of Arianism in the Roman empire. Marcellus, on the other hand, is usually remembered in histories of the ancient church simply for the statement in the Niceno-Constantinopolitan Creed that Christ's "kingdom will have no end," which is generally thought to be a refutation of his interpretation of 1 Corinthians 15:28. But Marcellus and his theological defence of Nicæa are of much greater import and merit far more attention.

A decade after the Council of Nicæa, Athanasius was deposed at the Synod of Tyre (335). Marcellus responded to this deposition with a treatise against a prominent member of the Arian party, the Cappadocian Asterius the Sophist (d.341), who had defended Eusebius of Nicomedia.[34] Marcellus presented this work, now known as *Against Asterius*, to the Emperor Constantine, but it was not well received, and in 336, Marcellus was also deposed as a heretic by a synod at Constantinople. This was the first of a number of condemnations of Marcellus that, in the words of Michel Barnes, appeared "almost annually and... [stretched] into the early 350s."[35] Probably the high-water mark of these denunciations was at the Synod of Philippopolis (343), where Marcellus was denounced as "the most detestable of all heretics."[36] And his heresy? Modalism. The fears of the Arians or anti-Nicene party that the Nicene Creed was indeed a modalist statement seemed to be confirmed in one of its leading defenders.

What exactly Marcellus did believe is not easy to determine, as virtually none of his writings have survived. One of his main oppo-

---

Marcellum: Marcellus of Ancyra and Fourth-Century Theology (Washington: Catholic University of America Press, 1999), 2–4.

33 On the career and thought of Athanasius, see especially Alvyn Petersen, *Athanasius* (Ridgefield: Morehouse Publishing, 1995); Khaled Anatolios, *Athanasius: The Coherence of His Thought* (New York: Routledge, 1998); Behr, *The Nicene Faith*, 1:163–259; and Peter J. Leithart, *Athanasius* (Grand Rapids: Baker Academic, 2011).

34 For Asterius' thought, see Hanson, *Search for the Christian Doctrine of God*, 32–41. For the chronology of Marcellus' life, I am following Lienhard, *Contra Marcellum*, 1–9.

35 Barnes, "Fourth Century as Trinitarian Canon," 51.

36 Lienhard, *Contra Marcellum*, 6.

nents, the historian Eusebius of Caesarea, did cite passages from Marcellus' *Against Asterius* which he then refuted. From these, it is clear that Marcellus "propounded a radical monotheism" that spoke of God as one being (*ousia*) and one person (*hypostasis*). While Marcellus regarded the Son (whom he consistently called the Word in accord with John 1) and Spirit (and he did not have a developed ontology of the Spirit) as eternal, his emphasis on the unity of God hampered his ability to speak about what is triadic in God.[37] In other words, to authors like Eusebius of Caesarea, Marcellus certainly appeared to be a modalist.

ATHANASIUS' TRINITARIANISM

If Marcellus was quick to seize upon the *homoousios* of the Nicene Creed as the *sine qua non* of orthodoxy—though, as noted, he interpreted it in a modalistic direction—his friend Athanasius, who never formally broke with him,[38] took the best part of thirty years to realize the importance of this phrase.[39] It was not until the 350s that Athanasius began to use the term *homoousios* frequently, a fact well seen in some letters that he wrote to a friend, Serapion of Thmuis (died after 362), in 358 and 359, while on the run from persecution by the Arian emperor Constantius II (317–361). From John 16:15, Jesus' statement that "all that belongs to the Father is mine," and John 17:10, Jesus' words to the Father, "all you have is mine," Athanasius reasoned that the Son shares all of the divine attributes of the Father. "The Father is light," he wrote, "the Son is radiance and true light. The Father is true God; the Son is true God."[40] John 16:15, Athanasius further noted,

---

37 For Marcellus' early theology, see Lienhard, *Contra Marcellum*, 47–68; Joseph T. Lienhard, "Two Friends of Athanasius: Marcellus of Ancyra and Apollinaris of Laodicea," *Zeitschrift für Antikes Christentum* 10 (2006): 60–61; Christopher A. Beeley, "Eusebius' Contra Marcellum. Anti-Modalist Doctrine and Orthodox Christology," *Zeitschrift für Antikes Christentum* 12 (2009): 435–437. See also Sara Parvis, *Marcellus of Ancyra and the Lost Years of the Arian Controversy 325–345* (Oxford: Oxford University Press, 2006), 30–37.

38 Barnes, "Fourth Century as Trinitarian Canon," 56; Lienhard, "Two Friends of Athanasius," 58–61.

39 Barnes, "Fourth Century as Trinitarian Canon," 53–59, *passim*.

40 Athanasius, *Letter to Serapion* 2.2, trans. CRB. Shapland, *The Letters of Saint Athanasius Concerning the Holy Spirit* (London: Epworth Press, 1951), 153.

could never have been said by a creature, no matter how highly exalted. It is only appropriate from the mouth of one who is "one in being with (*homoousios*) the Father." Thus Athanasius summed up: "of that which the Father has, there is nothing which does not belong to the Son." It is thus "impious" to say that "the Son is a creature."[41] Shaping Athanasius' overall Trinitarian exegesis of the Bible was his determination to find the overall "meaning" or "purport" (*skopos*) of what the Bible taught about God.[42]

These letters also reveal that the divinity of the Holy Spirit was becoming a topic of intense theological conflict, for Serapion informed Athanasius that there were individuals in his community of Thmuis who confessed the Son's deity but who were maintaining that the Holy Spirit is a creature, albeit of angelic nature.[43] In his response, Athanasius insisted that the Holy Spirit cannot be a creature, since creatures come from nothing, and there must have been a point when they came into being. Athanasius found evidence for this in Genesis 1:1.[44] By contrast, according to 1 Corinthians 2:12, the Holy Spirit is said to be from God:

> What kinship could there be...between the Spirit and the creatures? For the creatures were not; but God is being, and the Spirit is from him. That which is from God could not be from that which is not, nor could it be a creature, lest, by their judgment, he also from whom the Spirit is should be considered a creature.[45]

Athanasius' intent in this passage is to point to the gulf that lies between the Holy Spirit and the creatures. The created realm comes "from nothing," but 1 Corinthians 2:12 indicates that the Spirit is "from

---

41 Athanasius, *Letter to Serapion* 2.2–3, trans. Shapland, *Letters of Saint Athanasius Concerning the Holy Spirit*, 153–154.
42 See M.B. Handspicker, "Athanasius on Tradition and Scripture," *Andover Newton Quarterly*, n.s., 3 (1962): 13–29; James D. Ernest, "Athanasius of Alexandria: The Scope of Scripture in Polemical and Pastoral Context," *Vigiliae Christianae* 47 (1993): 341–361. Also see James D. Ernest, *The Bible in Athanasius of Alexandria* (Leiden: Brill, 2004)
43 Athanasius, *Letter to Serapion* 1.1.
44 Athanasius, *Letter to Serapion* 1.22.
45 Athanasius, *Letter to Serapion* 1.22, trans. Shapland, *Letters*, 121, revised.

God," who is uncreated being, and as such, the Spirit must also be uncreated. Again, the Alexandrian bishop argued:

> The creatures come from nothing and their existence has a beginning; for "in the beginning God made the heaven and the earth" [Genesis 1:1], and what is in them. The Holy Spirit is, and is said to be, from God, so said the Apostle. But if the Son cannot be a creature because he does not come from nothing but from God, then of necessity the Spirit is not a creature, for we have confessed that he comes from God. It is creatures that come from nothing.[46]

Here the phrase "from God" is applied to both the Spirit and the Son: if they are both from God, neither of them can be created. Since the opponents of the Spirit's deity in Thmuis confess the full divinity of the Son, and this, in part, because he was from God, Athanasius was hopeful that they would see the parallel with the Spirit: he too must be divine because he is from God. Athanasius' exegesis of 1 Corinthians 2:12 ensured that the Spirit has an uncreated nature, and so has a right to be worshipped alongside the Father and the Son.[47]

Athanasius' defence of the Spirit's divinity in the letters to Serapion helped him realize that the creedal formulation of Nicæa needed to be supplemented by a statement about the Spirit. Thus at the Council of Alexandria, held in 362 and over which Athanasius presided, it was declared:

> All who desire peace with us [ought]...to anathematize the Arian heresy, to confess the faith that was confessed by the Holy Fathers at Nicæa, and also to anathematize those who say the Holy Spirit is a creature and separate him from the being of Christ. For a true departure from the loathsome heresy of the Arians is this: [a refusal] to divide the Holy Trinity, or to say that any member of it is a creature. For those who pretend to profess the faith con-

---

46 Athanasius, *Letter to Serapion* 3.2, trans. Shapland, *Letters*, 171.
47 For a fuller discussion of Athanasius' exegesis of this passage, see Michael A.G. Haykin, *The Spirit of God: The Exegesis of 1 and 2 Corinthians in the Pneumatomachian Controversy of the Fourth Century* (Leiden: E.J. Brill, 1994), 78–83.

fessed at Nicæa, but who dare to blaspheme against the Holy Spirit, do nothing more than deny the Arian heresy in words, while they hold it fast in thought.[48]

However, it was only after the death of Athanasius in 373, that a definitive exposition of the Spirit's deity was published by a theologian whom Athanasius once described as "the pride of the Church,"[49] namely, the Cappadocian theologian Basil of Caesarea.

BASIL OF CAESAREA AND HIS PNEUMATOLOGICAL JOURNEY

In many respects, Basil's main contribution to the history of dogma is his pneumatological thought.[50] Basil's own conversion in 356 had come in the context of the early monastic movement that introduced him to an environment in which there was a heightened interest in the Holy Spirit as the sanctifier of God's people. Basil's experience of the Spirit in the monastic life was definitely a key factor in his growing interest in the question of the Holy Spirit's nature and person. This personal interest coincided with a rapid increase in the 360s and 370s of ontological questions about the being of the Spirit, of which Athanasius' dispute with the individuals in Thmuis in the late 350s appears to have been a forerunner. Those who opposed an expansion of the Nicene Creed to include a confession of the Spirit's deity during this era became known as Pneumatomachi—"fighters against the Spirit"—a coinage based on Acts 5:39.

---

48 Athanasius, *Tome to the Antiochenes* 3, trans. Michael A.G. Haykin.

49 Athanasius, *Letter to Palladius*.

50 For an excellent study of Basil's life and thought, see, Paul Jonathan Fedwick, *The Church and the Charisma of Leadership in Basil of Caesarea* (Toronto: Pontifical Institute of Mediaeval Studies, 1979), 133–155. The work by Philip Rousseau, *Basil of Caesarea* (Berkeley: University of California Press, 1998) needs to be used with care. For a complete bibliography of works on Basil, see Paul Jonathan Fedwick, *Bibliotheca Basiliana Universalis. A Study of the Manuscript Tradition, Translations and Editions of the Works of Basil of Caesarea. Vol. V: Studies of the Basil of Caesarea and His World: An Annotated Bio-Bibliography* (Turnhout: Brepols, 2004). For the historical details that follow in this sub-section, see Haykin, *Spirit of God*, 24–50.

For example, after the death of Silvanus, the bishop of Tarsus, in 369, certain Pneumatomachi emerged in the Christian community there, ardent advocates for the creaturehood of the Spirit. The rest of the community was polarized into two groups: "zealots," who wanted to disfellowship anyone who could not unequivocally declare the Spirit to be God and "moderates," who were uncertain about what to say about the Spirit's being. In an attempt to prevent a schism between these two latter groups, Basil wrote to the former and told them:

> The present circumstances hold a great propensity for the destruction of the churches, of which I have been aware for some time now. Edification of the Church and correction of error, sympathy towards the weak and protection of those brethren who are sound are all non-existent. Moreover, there is no remedy available either to heal this sickness which plagues us or to prevent that which threatens. All in all the condition of the Church is like that of an old coat (to use an unambiguous example, even if it appears somewhat trite), which is easily torn by the slightest occasion of use and which cannot be restored to its original condition. Consequently, in such circumstances, there is a need for great zeal and much diligence, so that the churches might receive some benefit. This benefit, in a word, is the unification of those parts which have long been separated.
>
> Now union would occur if we were willing to accommodate ourselves to those who are weaker, where we can do so without harm to souls. Therefore, since many voices have been raised against the Holy Spirit and many tongues have been whetted to blasphemy against him, I ask you, in so far as you can, to reduce the blasphemers to a small number and receive into communion those who do not say that the Holy Spirit is a creature. Thus, the blasphemers may be left alone, and either become ashamed and return to the truth or remain in their sin and become discredited because of their small number. Hence, let us seek nothing more beyond proposing the faith of Nicæa to those brothers who wish to join us. And if they accept that, then let us demand also that they must not call the Holy Spirit a creature and that those who do so should not be received into communion. But I do not think

it is appropriate to ask for anything beyond these requirements. For I am convinced that if something more needs to be added for clarification, the Lord, who in all things works for the good of those who love him [Romans 8:28], will grant it through the continued sharing of the same way of life and through peaceful discussions.[51]

Basil concurred with the opinion of the orthodox zealots of Tarsus that zeal is good, but, he stressed, only so long as it is directed toward a worthy goal. Due to the dissension and disregard for other believers which already characterized far too much of the church in the eastern Mediterranean, Basil was convinced that a worthy goal was to avoid further fragmentation, which would be the case if Basil's addressees had their way. Rather, the efforts of the latter should be directed toward the unification of all who were not clearly heretical. But this unification could only come about if those to whom Basil was writing, and others of similar zeal, were willing to accommodate themselves to those whose beliefs were not as settled. Basil then proceeded to indicate how this principle was to be put into practice. Basil's addressees should receive into communion all who confessed the Nicene Creed and who refused to describe the Spirit as a creature. In this way those who were openly blaspheming the Spirit through their description of him as a creature would be discredited due to their small number.

The irenicism of the closing sentence in this letter, with its reference to "peaceful discussions," continued for a couple of years to be Basil's approach to discussions about the Spirit's divinity. But Basil was not to escape conflict. It came through his mentor in the monastic life and an old friend, Eustathius of Sebaste (c.300–c.377), who came under suspicion due to the theological ambiguity of his pneumatological position.[52] Eustathius had been the leading figure in the monastic

---

51 Basil of Caesarea, *Letter* 113, trans. Michael A.G. Haykin.
52 On Eustathius and his pneumatology, see especially Wolf-Dieter Hauschild, "Eustathius von Sebaste," *Theologische Realenczyklopädie* 10 (1982): 548–549 and Haykin, *The Spirit of God*, 27 n.86. On Eustathius' career, see also Jean Gribomont, "Eustathe de Sébaste," *Dictionnaire de Spiritualité* IV/2 (1961): 1708–1712; C.A. Frazee, "Anatolian Asceticism in the Fourth Century: Eustathios of Sebastea and Basil of Caesarea," *The Catholic Historical Review* 66 (1980): 16–33.

movement in Asia Minor at the time of Basil's conversion and Basil was deeply indebted to him. However, although they held much in common with regard to the ascetic life, there were large differences when it came to Trinitarian doctrine. Eustathius was largely unconcerned about questions of dogma such as the nature and status of Spirit, and it was undoubtedly because he was not a theologian that no written works of his have been transmitted. As Wolf-Dieter Hauschild has described the keynote of his pneumatology: "the Holy Spirit was... a charismatic reality primarily to be experienced."[53] He appears to have been quite happy to affirm the Nicene Creed as it stood, but he had a deep aversion to expanding it to include a dogmatic assertion with regard to the Spirit. He was, for lack of a better term, committed to a Binitarianism that was hostile to any conglorification of the Spirit with the Father and the Son. Eustathius' refusal to clearly take a position as the Spirit's deity is well captured by a remark he reputedly uttered at a synod in 364, when the question of the Spirit's ontological status was raised: "I neither choose to name the Holy Spirit God nor dare to call him a creature."[54]

Basil, though, retained his friendship with Eustathius, clearly with the hope of bringing his old friend around to a position of full orthodoxy. But Basil's irenicism made his own orthodoxy suspect to some. In late 372 and early 373, Theodotus of Nicopolis (d.375), a leading bishop in northern Asia Minor and an orthodox zealot, began to bring pressure on Basil to clarify his own position on the Spirit and also his relationship with Eustathius. Meletius of Antioch (d.381), another leading supporter of the Nicene Creed, shared Theodotus' view. Basil, by associating with a suspected heretic, was himself dogmatically suspect! Basil found himself in an unenviable position. On the one hand, he was beginning to be criticized by Eustathius' followers for doctrinal convictions regarding the Spirit that were increasingly unacceptable to many of Eustathius' Pneumatomachian partisans. On the other hand, his close ties to Eustathius were making him dogmatically suspect to a number of his episcopal colleagues and some of his monastic friends.[55]

---

53 Hauschild, "Eustathius von Sebaste," 548–549.
54 Socrates, *Church History* 2.45.
55 Haykin, *Spirit of God*, 31–36.

Biblical exegesis in fourth-century Trinitarian debates   113

So, Basil arranged to meet with Eustathius in June 373. In a two-day colloquy, Basil and Eustathius appeared to have come to an agreement on pneumatological issues. In order to satisfy Theodotus, Meletius and the other bishops, Basil convinced Eustathius to sign a statement that has been transmitted as *Letter* 125 in the Basilian corpus. The key part of this text runs thus:

> [We] must anathematize all who call the Holy Spirit a creature, and all who so think; all who do not confess that he is holy by nature, as the Father is holy by nature and the Son is holy by nature, and refuse him his place in the blessed divine nature. Our not separating him from Father and Son is a proof of our right of mind. For we are bound to be baptized in the terms we have received and to profess belief in the terms in which we are baptized, and as we have professed belief in, so to give glory to Father, Son and Holy Spirit. Thus we must hold aloof from the communion of all who call him creature, as from open blasphemers. One point must be regarded as settled; the remark is necessary because of our slanderers. We do not speak of the Holy Spirit as unbegotten, for we recognise one Unbegotten and one Origin of all things, the Father of our Lord Jesus Christ. Nor do we speak of the Holy Spirit as begotten, for by the tradition of the faith we have been taught one Only-begotten. We have been taught that the Spirit of truth proceeds from the Father, and we confess him to be of God without creation.[56]

This statement is probably modelled on Athanasius' *Tome to the Antiochenes*. However, whereas Athanasius' focus was on the inseparable nature of the triune God, Basil's emphasis was placed on the natural holiness of the Spirit. Since the Spirit is holy without qualification, he cannot be a creature and must be indivisibly one with the divine nature. The confession of this unity was both the criterion of orthodoxy and the basis upon which communion could be terminated with those who affirmed that the Spirit was a creature. As to the details of the Spirit's origin, the phrase "without creation" was considered

---

56 Basil, *Letter* 125.3, trans. Michael A.G. Haykin.

sufficient. As well as supplying an effective defence against the Pneumatomachian assertion that the Spirit must be a creature because he is neither unbegotten nor begotten, it provides a non-speculative statement on the mode of the Spirit's existence. This pneumatological position thus defined the precise limits beyond which Basil was not prepared to venture, even for a friend such as Eustathius.[57] Finally, the baptismal formula of Matthew 28:19 clearly played a key role in shaping Basil's thinking: to be baptized into "the name of the Father and of the Son and of the Holy Spirit" implies faith in the three persons of the Godhead and also determines doxological ultimacy—the Father along with the Son and the Holy Spirit are to receive equal honour and worship.

At the meeting where this document was drawn up and initially agreed to by both Basil and Eustathius, another meeting was planned later that year when this document would be formally ratified in the presence of Theodotus and Meletius. But Eustathius never came to that meeting. Instead, he renounced his signature on the statement and, at a series of Pneumatomachian synods, denounced what he described as the doctrinal innovations of Basil. And for the next two years he openly slandered Basil as a Sabellian and consequently a heretic. Basil was so stunned by this turn of events and what amounted to the betrayal by a close friend that he kept silence until the winter of 374–375. Eventually, when he was convinced that some reply to Eustathius and his Pneumatomachian party had to be made, he responded with a series of letters and his *magnum opus, On the Holy Spirit* (375).

BIBLICAL EXEGESIS IN *ON THE HOLY SPIRIT*

The Pneumatomachi were maintaining that it was proper only to give glory to the Father through the Son in the Holy Spirit. A specific question had come to Basil from a close friend whom he had mentored, Amphilochius of Iconium, asking whether or not it was also proper in corporate worship to glorify the Father with the Son together with the Holy Spirit.[58] The aversion of the Pneumatomachi to the conglorification of the Spirit with the Father and the Son thus became the

---

57 Haykin, *Spirit of God*, 37–38.
58 Basil, *On the Holy Spirit* 1.1, 3.

occasion Basil needed to make a detailed reply to the views of Eustathius and the Pneumatomachi.

The core of Basil's *On the Holy Spirit* was essentially a detailed exposition of much of the biblical testimony about the Spirit's person.[59] A number of key themes informed Basil's argument. From the presence of the Spirit in the baptismal formula of Matthew 28, he argued that the mention of "Father, Son, and Spirit" in this formula "testifies to their union and fellowship." Thus he went on to state, "The Lord has delivered to us a necessary and saving dogma: the Holy Spirit is to be ranked with the Father."[60] Then, from a variety of biblical texts that speak of the Spirit's activities Basil showed how the Spirit "is indivisibly and inseparably joined to the Father and the Son" since he does what only God can do. The Spirit sanctifies the angels, for example, and enables them to remain steadfast in their allegiance to God, something he could not do unless he were divine. The holiness of the angels is not inherent, but results from their communion with One who is innately holy, namely the Spirit.

> How can the Seraphim sing, "Holy, holy, holy," without the Spirit teaching them to constantly raise their voices in praise? If all God's angels praise him, and all his host, they do so by cooperating with the Spirit. Do a thousand thousands of angels serve him? Do ten thousand times ten thousand stand before him? They accomplish their proper work by the Spirit's power.[61]

Basil also pointed to the titles given by Scripture to the Spirit to argue for his deity. For instance, the ascription of the term "Lord" to the Spirit in 2 Corinthians 3:16–18 was indisputable proof of the "excellence of the Spirit's glory."[62] It is noteworthy that Basil did not explicitly call the Spirit "God" nor did he speak of the Spirit as "one in being" (*homoousios*) with the Father and the Son. While his argument clearly

---

59 Basil, *On the Holy Spirit* 10–28.
60 Basil, *On the Holy Spirit* 10.24, 25, trans. David Anderson, *St Basil the Great: On the Holy Spirit* (Crestwood: St. Vladimir's Seminary Press, 1980), 45, 46.
61 Basil, *On the Holy Spirit* 16.37, 38, trans. Anderson, *On the Holy Spirit*, 60, 64.
62 Basil, *On the Holy Spirit* 21.52, trans. Anderson, *On the Holy Spirit*, 81.

indicates his belief in the full deity of the Spirit, his refusal to use the term *homoousios* seems to indicate an ongoing concern about the modalistic danger of this term. Nicene Trinitarian orthodoxy had to be affirmed over against Arian subordinationism but without any hint of modalism.[63]

Then, the Spirit is the One who gives saving knowledge of God, but only God can reveal God. In Basil's words:

> When, by means of the illuminating power, we fix our eyes on the beauty of the invisible image and through that image are led up to the supremely beautiful spectacle of the Archetype, the Spirit of knowledge is inseparably present there [with the Father and the Son]. To those who love the vision of the truth the Spirit supplies in himself the power to behold the image. He does not give the revelation from without, but in himself leads to the knowledge [of the image]. For just as "no one knows the Father except the Son" [Matthew 11:27], so "no one can say Jesus is Lord except in the Holy Spirit" [1 Corinthians 12:3]. For it does not say "through the Spirit" but "in the Spirit." ...And, as it is written, "in your light we shall see light" [Psalm 36:9], that is, in the illumination of the Spirit [we shall see] "the true light that enlightens every man that comes into the world" [John 1:9]. Thus, in himself he makes known the glory of the Only-Begotten, and in himself provides the knowledge of God to the true worshippers. Therefore, the way of the knowledge of God is from the one Spirit through the one Son to the one Father.[64]

Here Basil is building on such passages as Hebrews 1:3 and Colossians 1:15 in which the Son is described as the image of the Father, whom Basil calls the "Archetype." During the course of the Arian controversy, it had become commonplace to argue that the Son's being the image of the Father meant that there was a community of nature between the Son and the Father. But knowledge of the image and, by extension,

---

63 Barnes, "Fourth Century as Trinitarian Canon," 62.
64 Basil, *On the Holy Spirit* 18.47, trans. Michael A.G. Haykin. See also *On the Holy Spirit* 26.64 for similar argumentation.

its archetype is impossible without the Spirit who reveals the Son—here Basil is drawing upon 1 Corinthians 12:3. Moreover, this knowledge is given by the Spirit "in himself." Knowledge of God does not come through an intermediary like an angel, but is given by God by/in himself, namely in the Spirit, who must therefore be divine. This text then tells us why the Spirit is inextricably joined to the Father and the Son. His epistemic relationship to the Father and the Son speaks of an ontological union.[65] As Basil noted in one of his letters: "Therefore we never divorce the Paraclete from his unity with the Father and the Son; for our mind, when it is lit by the Spirit, looks up to the Son and in him as in an image beholds the Father."[66]

Now, if the Spirit is God, how does his relationship to the Father differ from that of the Son to the Father? This was a vital question for fourth-century Greek theologians, since, as has been noted, they ever feared the spectre of Sabellianism that denied the hypostatic differences between the persons within the Godhead. Basil turned to such Scripture texts as John 15:26, 1 Corinthians 2:12 and Psalm 33:6 to argue that the Spirit "proceeds from the mouth of the Father, and is not begotten like the Son."[67] Basil quickly qualified this image. The terms "breath" and "mouth" must be understood in a manner befitting God. The comparison of the Spirit with breath does not mean that he is the same as human breath, which quickly dissipates upon exhalation, for the Spirit is a living being with the power to sanctify others. This image well reflects the nature of our knowledge about God. On the one hand, it indicates the intimate relationship of the Father and the Spirit so the Spirit has to be glorified with the Father and the Son. On the other hand, the image reminds us that the Spirit's mode of existence is ineffable, even as the being of the Godhead is beyond human comprehension.[68]

Basil died at the beginning of 379 and never saw the triumph of his theological position, which took place two years later through the work of his younger brother Gregory of Nyssa.

---

65 Hildebrand, *Trinitarian Theology of Basil of Caesarea*, 187, 190–191.
66 Basil, *Letter* 226.3, trans. Michael A.G. Haykin.
67 Basil, *On the Holy Spirit* 18.46, trans. Anderson, *On the Holy Spirit*, 73. See also *On the Holy Spirit* 16.38.
68 Haykin, *Spirit of God*, 143–147.

THE COUNCIL OF CONSTANTINOPLE (381) AND ITS CREED

With the death of the emperor Valens (328–378), patron and protector of the Arians, in the disastrous rout at Hadrianople in Thrace in 378, the purple passed to a Spaniard, Theodosius I (347–395), who, in his theological convictions, was committed to Nicene trinitarianism. Determined to establish the church on the bedrock of the Nicene Creed, Theodosius travelled to Constantinople, entering the city on November 24, 380, and called for a council to meet in Constantinople the following May.

Theodosius desired the theologians at the council to see if they could persuade the Pneumatomachi to abandon their deficient view of the Spirit. In the words of the historian Socrates, Theodosius and "the bishops who shared the same faith spared no efforts" to bring the Pneumatomachi "into unity with them."[69] However, the gulf which lay between the orthodox and the Pneumatomachi, thirty-six bishops under the leadership of Eleusius of Cyzicus—Eustathius appears to have died by then—was so wide, that it could not have been bridged without one side sacrificing all they held dear. Thus, the Pneumatomachi, after rejecting the proposed union, left the council. After their departure, the council approved a confessional statement that may well have been crafted in the discussions with the Pneumatomachi. Moreover, it is quite probable that one of the leading figures behind the composition of this creedal statement was Basil's younger brother, Gregory. He had drunk deeply from the well of both Scripture and his brother's doctrine of the Spirit. Like Basil, he was overwhelmingly convinced that the Spirit is a full member of the Godhead. Yet, also like his brother, he was hesitant to employ the term "God" with regard to the Spirit.

Without a doubt, the Niceno-Constantinopolitan Creed is one of the most significant texts from the early church. The third article, which deals with the Spirit, runs thus:

> We believe in the Holy Spirit, the Lord, the giver of life, who proceeds from the Father; with the Father and the Son he is worshipped and glorified; he has spoken through the Prophets.

---

69 Socrates, *Church History* 5.10.

The biblical grounding of this article is patent upon inspection. The use of the term "Lord" for the Spirit, as in 2 Corinthians 3:16–18, for example, had been a key part of Basil's argument for the deity of the Spirit. Then, to call the Spirit "the giver of life" is to ascribe to him a work that only God can do. This term may reflect the pneumatology of Genesis 1:2, but more likely it is a reference to the Spirit's role in giving new life in Christ, as found in a passage like John 3:3–8. The clause "who proceeds from the Father" is taken from John 15:26. One significant change, though, has been made: in place of the preposition "from the side of" (*para*) in John 15:26 there is the preposition "from within" (*ek*), a change based on 1 Corinthians 2:12. This clause serves to differentiate the person of the Spirit from the person of the Son. Whereas the Son is begotten of the Father, the Spirit proceeds from the Father. It is also noteworthy that the verb "proceeds" is in the present tense, which is "tantamount to saying that like the Father he [i.e. the Spirit] had no beginning."[70]

The "all-important clause," as J.N.D Kelly puts it, is the affirmation that the Holy Spirit "with the Father and the Son is worshipped and glorified."[71] If the Spirit's conglorification and co-adoration with the Father and the Son is affirmed, it must be because he is fully God. As it stands, it would have been impossible for the Pneumatomachi to have subscribed to this statement.[72] One of Basil's closest friends, Gregory of Nazianzus, was the president of the council at this point, and he was critical of the creedal statement because it did not say explicitly that the Spirit is God or declare the *homoousion* of the Spirit.[73] Why the omission of such terms? Adolf-Martin Ritter has argued plausibly that it was this creed that was employed to seek reconciliation with the Pneumatomachi.[74] Nevertheless, behind the reserved

---

70 Harold O.J. Brown, *Heresies* (Garden City: Doubleday & Co., 1984), 142–143.
71 Kelly, *Early Christian Creeds*, 342.
72 Adolf-Martin Ritter, *Das Konzil von Konstantinopel und sein Symbol. Studien zur Geschichte und Theologie des II. Ökumenischen Konzils* (Göttingen: Vandenhoeck & Ruprecht, 1965), 301.
73 John A. McGuckin, *St Gregory of Nazianzus: An Intellectual Biography* (Crestwood: St Vladimir's Seminary Press, 2001), 367–368.
74 Ritter, *Das Konzil von Konstantinopel*, passim.

language was a very clear stance on the deity of the Spirit.[75] The final clause, "who spoke through the prophets," is based on verses like 2 Peter 1:20–21 and Ephesians 3:5. While it may have primary reference to the Old Testament prophets, it is important to note that Basil could describe the inspiration of the whole Bible as prophetic. Undoubtedly he considered the prophetism of the Scriptures a proof of the divinity of the Spirit who inspired them.[76]

While the Niceno-Constantinopolitan Creed must be viewed as a *norma normata* ("a rule that is ruled"), it is a rule that faithfully reflects the biblical view of God and, as such, it stands as one of the great landmarks of Christian theology.

A CODA

Just before the council convened in Constantinople, Gregory of Nazianzus was installed as the bishop of the city, and Gregory of Nyssa, who had come to Constantinople for the impending council, was asked to preach at the induction. Also present at the installation of Nazianzen were some monks from Mesopotamia, including, according to Reinhart Staats, quite possibly the author known as Macarius (300–c.391).[77] Gregory of Nyssa had a deep admiration for these brothers, for they were men

> full of the Spirit, namely, [these] men from Mesopotamia. There, the charismata are still a living reality; there the preached Word is confirmed by the Spirit.... [Similarly, with] the apostles, the

---

75 Behr, *The Nicene Faith*, 2:378–379.

76 A. de Halleux, "La profession de l'Esprit-Saint dans le symbole de Constantinople," *Revue Théologique de Louvain* 10 (1979): 30–31; Hildebrand, *Trinitarian Theology of Basil of Caesarea*, 109–114.

77 Reinhart Staats, "Die Basilianische Verherrlichung des Heiligen Geistes auf dem Konzil zu Konstantinopel 381. Ein Beitrag zum Ursprung der Formel 'Kerygma und Dogma,'" *Kerygma und Dogma* 25 (1979): 232–253. For major studies of Macarius' life and theology, see Hermann Dörries, *Die Theologie des Makarios-Symeon* (Göttingen: Vandenhoeck & Ruprecht, 1978); Columba Stewart, *'Working the Earth of the Heart': The Messalian Controversy in History, Texts, and Language to AD 431* (Oxford: Clarendon Press, 1991); Marcus Plested, *The Macarian Legacy: The Place of Macarius-Symeon in the Eastern Christian Tradition* (Oxford: Oxford University Press, 2004).

miracles assisted and the Word was considered to be credible because of the charismata. I...mean that mighty deeds possess much persuasive power.... But what must be thought of the present situation? Do you not see similar works of faith? I consider the great deeds of our fellow servants as such wonders. ...According to their outward appearance they are old men, venerable persons to see, with shiny white hair and their mouths shut in silence. They do not struggle with words, they do not study rhetoric; but they have such great power over the spirits that, with one command, they expel demons not by the art of rhetoric, but through the power of faith.[78]

This passage well reveals Nyssen's deep admiration for Spirit-filled men like Macarius whose hearts' desire was to live in such a way as to give glory to the One whom Macarius joyfully confessed as the "consubstantial Trinity."[79] Those who fought for the doctrine of the Trinity in the fourth-century—men like Gregory of Nyssa, his brother Basil and their hero Athanasius—were not so enamoured with philosophical reflection that they neglected the Scriptural admonition to be full of the Spirit and to walk in the Spirit (Ephesians 5:18; Galatians 5:16).

---

78 Trans. Johannes van Oort, "The Holy Spirit and the Early Church: The Experience of the Spirit," *HTS Teologiese Studies/Theological Studies* 68, no.1 (2012): 5–6, altered (http://www.hts.org.za/index.php/HTS/article/view/1154/2238; accessed November 8, 2016).

79 Macarius, *Homily* 17.15. For Macarius' thought and life, see the following chapter.

9

"Rivers of dragons and mouths of lions and dark forces"

The Holy Spirit and the holiness of the Christian in Macarius[1]

> [It is] impossible to separate the soul from sin unless God should calm and turn back this evil wind, inhabiting both the soul and body. —MACARIUS[2]

In one of John Wesley's most frequently preached sermons, *The Scripture-Way of Salvation*, the Methodist leader sought to sum up the

---

[1] This chapter originated as a paper delivered on September 17, 2010, to the Society for Christian Psychology.

[2] Macarius, *Homily* 2.3.

Wesleyan vision of the *ordo salutis* and correct certain misunderstandings of that rich vision. At one point Wesley was concerned to stress that in the overwhelming experience of conversion it was natural for those who go through

> such a change [to] imagine that all sin is gone! That it is utterly rooted out of their heart, and has no more any place therein! How easily do they draw that inference, 'I *feel* no sin; therefore I *have* none.' ...But it is seldom long before they are undeceived, finding sin was only suspended, not destroyed. Temptations return and sin revives, showing that it was but stunned before, not dead. They now feel two principles in themselves, plainly contrary to each other: 'the flesh lusting against the spirit,' nature opposing the grace of God.[3]

Wesley then turned to a somewhat obscure fourth-century monastic author whom he called Macarius—known to modern scholars as either Pseudo-Macarius or Macarius-Symeon but whom this chapter will give the name by which he has gone for centuries, namely, Macarius—to make the same point:

> How exactly did Macarius, fourteen hundred years ago, describe the present experience of the children of God! "The unskilful (or unexperienced), when grace operates, presently imagine they have no more sin. Whereas they that have discretion cannot deny that even we who have the grace of God may be molested again."[4]

Wesley had been introduced to a German Pietist translation of Macarius' homilies in the colony of Georgia, at the close of July 1736, by some Moravian friends.[5] Wesley so appreciated these homilies that he would

---

3 John Wesley, *Sermons II, 34–70*, ed. Albert C. Outler (*The Works of John Wesley*, vol. 2; Nashville: Abingdon Press, 1985), 158–59.

4 Wesley, *Sermons II, 34–70*, ed. Outler, 159.

5 John Wesley, *Journals and Diaries I (1735–38)*, ed. W. Reginald Ward and Richard P. Heitzenrater (*The Works of John Wesley*, vol. 18; Nashville: Abingdon Press, 1988), 405–406.

later edit and reprint some of them in the first volume of his *A Christian Library*, a collection of Christian literature designed for lay preachers.[6] The major themes of the Macarian texts available to Wesley did indeed nicely dovetail with the Methodist leader's interests, for in them Macarius especially set forth the biblical dimensions and theological implications of the salvific work of the Holy Spirit and explored the experience of the believer, who, though indwelt by the Spirit, nevertheless battles indwelling sin. In what follows, these major themes of Macarian theology and spirituality are explored as they are found primarily in one collection of Macarian texts, Collection II, the *Fifty Spiritual Homilies*, which have exercised a significant influence upon both Eastern and Western Christianity.

WHO WAS MACARIUS?

While there is much that is unclear about Macarius, the author of these works, he appears to have been especially active between the 380s and the first decade of the fifth century.[7] He had strong ties to Syrian Christianity, although his mother tongue was most likely Greek. He would thus have been very comfortable with the theological

---

6 For reflection on Wesley's reading and use of Macarius, see Howard A. Snyder, "John Wesley and Macarius the Egyptian," *The Asbury Theological Journal* 45, no.2 (Fall 1990): 55–60, and especially Mark T. Kurowski, "The First Step toward Grace: John Wesley's Use of the Spiritual Homilies of Macarius the Great," *Methodist History* 36, no.2 (January 1998): 113–124. For a general study of Wesley's reading of patristic literature, see Richard P. Heitzenrater, "John Wesley's Reading of and References to the Early Church Fathers" in S.T. Kimbrough, Jr., *Orthodox and Wesleyan Spirituality* (Crestwood: St Vladimir's Seminary Press, 2002), 25–32.

7 For major studies of Macarius' life and theology, see Hermann Dörries, *Die Theologie des Makarios-Symeon* (Göttingen: Vandenhoeck & Ruprecht, 1978); Columba Stewart, *'Working the Earth of the Heart': The Messalian Controversy in History, Texts, and Language to AD 431* (Oxford: Clarendon Press, 1991); Marcus Plested, *The Macarian Legacy: The Place of Macarius-Symeon in the Eastern Christian Tradition* (Oxford: Oxford University Press, 2004). See also the helpful studies by George A. Maloney, "Introduction" to his trans., *Pseudo-Macarius: The Fifty Spiritual Homilies and the Great Letter*, The Classics of Western Spirituality (New York: Paulist Press, 1992), 1–33, and Alexander Golitzin, "A Testimony to Christianity as Transfiguration: The Macarian Homilies and Orthodox Spirituality" in Kimbrough, ed., *Orthodox and Wesleyan Spirituality*, 129–156.

ambience of Greek Christian life and piety.[8] His ministry seems to have been situated on the frontier of the Roman empire in upper Syria and in southern Asia Minor, where he was the spiritual mentor of a number of monastic communities.[9]

Four collections of his homilies are extant.[10] In their *Rezeptionsgeschichte*, they have been historically linked to Messalianism, an ascetic movement that was condemned at various councils, including the ecumenical Council of Ephesus in 431 as well as the earlier Synod of Side in Pamphylia (c.395), which was presided over by Amphilochius of Iconium, the protégé and close friend of Basil of Caesarea, the famous Cappadocian theologian, whose life and thought we have already looked at in previous chapters. According to those who condemned them, the Messalians argued that there was an indwelling demonic power in each human soul, and that only intense and ceaseless prayer could break the power that this demonic power held over the soul. Consequently, they were said to refuse to work so that they could devote their entire time to prayer. They were also said to affirm physical experiences of the Spirit, and made light of the sacraments of the church as well as the ministry of those in official positions of power.[11] In the words of Robert Murray, the Messalians "laid too much

---

8 Plested, *Macarian Legacy*, 14–15.

9 Plested, *Macarian Legacy*, 15–16.

10 For discussion of the four collections, see Stuart K. Burns, "Pseudo-Macarius and the Messalians: The Use of Time for the Common Good" in R.N. Swanson, ed., *The Use and Abuse of Time in Christian History* (Woodbridge: The Boydell Press for The Ecclesiastical History Society, 2002), 3 n.7; Plested, *Macarian Legacy*, 9–12.

11 Stewart, 'Working the Earth of the Heart,' 52–69, *passim*; Maloney, "Introduction," 8–9; David Roach, "Macarius the Augustinian: Grace and Salvation in the Spiritual Homilies of Macarius-Symeon," *Eusebeia* 8 (Fall 2007): 77–78.

On the question of the relationship of Macarius to the Messalians, see, in addition to the monographs cited in note 6, John Meyendorff, "Messalianism or Anti-Messalianism? A Fresh Look at the «Macarian» Problem" in Patrick Granfield and Josef A. Jungmann, ed., *Kyriakon: Festschrift Johannes Quasten* (Münster: Verlag Aschendorff, 1970), II, 585–590; Reinhart Staats, "Messalianism and AntiMessalianism in Gregory of Nyssa's *De Virignitate*," *The Patristic and Byzantine Review* 2 (1983): 27–44; Stuart K. Burns, "Charisma and spirituality in the early Church: A study of Messalianism and Pseudo-Macarius" (Ph.D. thesis, University of Leeds, 1990); and Alexander Golitzin, "Temple and Throne of the Divine Glory: 'Pseudo-Macarius' and Purity of Heart,

stress on experience of the Spirit for the liking of ecclesiastics in the institutional Church."[12]

Although there are a number of clear points of contact between the Messalians and Macarius, especially with regard to Macarius' deep interest in the Spirit, the burden of current scholarly opinion is that Macarius cannot be regarded as a Messalian.[13] Confirmation of this perspective of recent Macarian scholarship is found in Macarius' strong connections to the Cappadocians, in particular, Basil and his brother Gregory of Nyssa, which was noted in the previous chapter.[14] The deep admiration for Macarius on the part of Nyssen is further evident in the fact that the Cappadocian father copied significant portions of Macarius' *Great Letter*, and used it as the basis for his own *De instituto christiano*. It was this connection with the Cappadocians that undoubtedly helped preserve the Macarian corpus.

Another key factor for the preservation of Macarius' writings was the fact that he shared with the Cappadocians a profound concern to defend the deity of the Spirit.[15] In general, "the Macarian writings are profoundly Trinitarian,"[16] with a particular focus on the deity of the Holy Spirit, which would situate them in the 370s–390s during the Pneumatomachian controversy and its wake. For Macarius, the Spirit is "uncreated" and fully divine for he is the One who brings us into union with God.[17]

Together with Some Remarks on the Limitations and Usefulness of Scholarship" in Harriet A. Luckman and Linda Kulzer, eds., *Purity of Heart in Early Ascetic and Monastic Literature. Essays in Honor of Juana Raasch, O.S.B.* (Collegeville: Liturgical Press, 1999), 107–17.

12 Robert Murray, *Symbols of Church and Kingdom: A Study in Early Syriac Tradition* (Cambridge: Cambridge University Press, 1975), 35.

13 See, for example, Stewart, 'Working the Earth of the Heart' and Burns, "Pseudo-Macarius and the Messalians," 1–12.

14 See also Plested, *Macarian Legacy*, 46–58, passim.

15 Plested, *Macarian Legacy*, 57–8.

16 Plested, *Macarian Legacy*, 42.

17 Plested, *Macarian Legacy*, 50.

THE TRAGEDY OF THE FALL[18]

The awful devastation caused by the Fall of Adam and the experiential reality of the tyranny of sin that ensued for his progeny as a result of his disobedience regularly impressed themselves upon the mind of Macarius.[19] Prior to the Fall, Adam was clothed with the glory of the Holy Spirit,[20] and thus knew the Spirit's personal instruction as well as that of the Word of God—the "Word was everything to him."[21] He lived in total purity, was pleasing to God in all areas of his life and he had sovereign control over his thoughts and actions.[22] When he disobeyed God's Word of his own free will, though, his disobedience became the doorway through which all kinds of evil were sowed in the world, as well as being the vehicle for the entrance of "tumult, confusion, and battle" into the inner being of men and women.[23] After the Fall, Adam and his descendants lost both God and their God-given beauty. God, ever "the Lover of mankind," wept over his fallen creation,[24] for they were now marred by corruption, spiritual ugliness, and "a great stench" that emanated from their souls.[25] Fallen men and

---

18 I have used Maloney's translation in what follows since it is most readily available. The other major English translation of Collection II is A.J. Mason, *Fifty Spiritual Homilies of St. Macarius the Egyptian* (London: Society for Promoting Christian Knowledge, 1921). When reference is made to the Greek in the text, then the relevant column and section in J.-P. Migne, ed., *Patrologiae cursus completus...series Graeca* (Paris, 1860), 34:449–822, henceforth abbreviated as PG34, is given in brackets after the citation of the primary source.

I have also made very occasional use of the seven untranslated homilies published by G.L. Marriott: *Macarii Anecdota: Seven Unpublished Homilies of Macarius*, Harvard Theological Studies, Vol.5 (Cambridge: Harvard University Press, 1918). Following the numbering of Plested (*Macarian Legacy*, 10 n.5), these are Homilies 51–57. Where they are used I have designated the reference by the name of Marriott with the appropriate page in brackets.

19 See Plested, *Macarian Legacy*, 35–36 and Roach, "Macarius the Augustinian," 78–79 for an overview of Macarius' thinking about the impact of the fall.

20 Macarius, Homily 5.11, 12; 12.6–8; 20.1.

21 Macarius, Homily 12.6–8 (Maloney, *Fifty Spiritual Homilies*, 99–100).

22 Macarius, Homily 12.7–8; 15.25.

23 Macarius, Homily 15.49. See also Homily 1.7.

24 Macarius, Homily 4.16; 30.7; 46.3.

25 Macarius, Homily 30.7–8. See also Homily 24.4.

women were now, in one of Macarius' most trenchant descriptions, like "houses of prostitution and ill-fame in which all sorts of immoral debaucheries go on."[26] Dominating their lives was a love of this age and its passions and concerns.[27] Instead of their Maker being their Lord, Satan himself became their prince and ruler, and filled their hearts with spiritual darkness.[28]

Ever true to his nature as a wicked tyrant, Satan did not spare any area of human existence from his deadly touch and control. The "evil prince corrupted" the human frame "completely, not sparing any of its members from its slavery, not its thoughts, neither the mind nor the body."[29] When men and women act under the impulse of these evils, they think that they are doing so on the basis of their "own determination." But the reality is they are controlled by the power of sin.[30] From Macarius' vantage-point, every fallen human being is so under sin's dominion that he or she can "no longer see freely but sees evilly, hears evilly, and has swift feet to perpetrate evil acts."[31]

Although this extremely realistic view of the Fall and its impact would appear to commit Macarius to a strongly determinist perspective with regard to the human condition, in line with the voluntarism of Greek patristic tradition, Macarius vehemently maintained that men and women ultimately commit evil of their own free will. As he asserted on one occasion: "Our nature...is capable of both good and evil, either of divine grace or of the opposing power, but never through compulsion."[32] However, this ability to choose appears to extend solely to individual sinful acts.[33] What human beings cannot do is remove the deeply-rooted interiority of sin itself. Its dominion within the

---

26 Macarius, *Homily* 12.2.
27 Macarius, *Homily* 21.2; 24.2.
28 Macarius, *Homily* 5.2; 21.2.
29 Macarius, *Homily* 2.1 (Maloney, *Fifty Spiritual Homilies*, 44). See also *Homily* 16.6.
30 Macarius, *Homily* 15.49.
31 Macarius, *Homily* 2.2 (Maloney, *Fifty Spiritual Homilies*, 45).
32 Macarius, *Homily* 15.25 (PG34.592D), trans. Michael A.G. Haykin.
33 Mariette Canévet, "Macaire" in A. Rayez, A. Derville and A. Solignac, *Dictionnaire de spiritualité* (Paris: Beauchesne, 1980), X, 31–32; Golitzin, "A Testimony to Christianity as Transfiguration," 132.

human heart is far too strong to be defeated by human energy alone.[34] It is "impossible," Macarius stated on one occasion, "to separate the soul from sin unless God should calm and turn back this evil wind, inhabiting both the soul and body."[35] Again, as he put it elsewhere: "without the Lord Jesus and the working of divine power," that is, the Holy Spirit, "no one can…be a Christian."[36]

"THE SWEETNESS OF THE SPIRIT"[37]

This situation can only be changed for the better, in Macarius' thinking, through a person persistently crying out to God for help to transform him or her from "bitterness to sweetness."[38] So it is that Macarius can argue that "even the man confirmed in evil, or the one completely immersed in sin and making himself a vessel of the devil…still has freedom to become a chosen vessel."[39] Given Macarius' views about the devastation that has resulted from the Fall, some of which has been detailed above, this statement must be taken to mean that Macarius believes human beings have enough freedom to cry out to God for salvation.[40]

Without God's aid through the gift of the Spirit, no one will ever "return to their senses from their intoxication with the material realm."[41] Without the life-giving power of the Spirit, one is dead "as far as the kingdom goes, being unable to do any of the things of God," for "the Spirit is the life of the soul."[42] And so great is the plague of sin in the human heart, healing is only found through the medicine of the Holy

---

34 Macarius, *Homily* 3.4; 27.22; Stewart, 'Working the Earth of the Heart,' 74; Golitzin, "Temple and Throne of the Divine Glory," 124–125.

35 Macarius, *Homily* 2.3 (Maloney, *Fifty Spiritual Homilies*, 45). See also *Homily* 3.4.

36 Macarius, *Homily* 17.10 (Maloney, *Fifty Spiritual Homilies*, 139).

37 Macarius, *Homily* 47.15 (Maloney, *Fifty Spiritual Homilies*, 238, altered).

38 Macarius, *Homily* 2.3; 4.4, 8; 18.2; 20.1; 31.1; 44.9; 47.7, 10. The quote is from *Homily* 31.1 (PG 34.728D; Maloney, *Fifty Spiritual Homilies*, 194, altered). See also Golitzin, "A Testimony to Christianity as Transfiguration," 132.

39 Macarius, *Homily* 15.40 (PG34.604A; Maloney, *Fifty Spiritual Homilies*, 123, altered).

40 Macarius, *Homily* 46.3.

41 Macarius, *Homily* 24.5 (PG 34.665B–C), trans. Michael A.G. Haykin.

42 Macarius, *Homily* 30.3, 6 (Maloney, *Fifty Spiritual Homilies*, 191, 192).

Spirit.[43] Macarius also likens the conversion of a person to the taming of a horse. Prior to being tamed, an unconverted person is like a "wild and indomitable" horse. But once "he hears the Word of God and believes, he is bridled by the Spirit. He puts away his wild habits and carnal thoughts, being now guided by Christ, his rider."[44]

The apostle Paul was, for Macarius, a prime example of such conversion. He had been living under the "tyrannical spirit of sin," and as a persecutor of the church he can be rightly described as being "steeped in evil and turned back to a wild state." But Christ arrested his progress in sin, and "flooding him with ineffable light," liberated him from sin's domination. Here, Macarius stated, we see Christ's "goodness…and his power to change."[45] From another angle, the Spirit comes into the entirety of a person's being to put it in order and beautify it, just as "a house that has its master at home shows forth an abundance of orderliness, and beauty and harmony."[46]

This gift of the Spirit in conversion, though, is only the beginning of what formed a major aspect of Macarius' theological reflections, namely, the remarkable nature of life in the Spirit. Sometimes the believer's life is flooded with the joy of the Spirit and he is like "a spouse who enjoys conjugal union with her bridegroom."[47] On other occasions, he finds himself overwhelmed by grief as he prays in accordance with the "love of the Spirit towards mankind."[48] Other times there is "a burning of the Spirit" which enflames the heart with regard to the things of God.[49] Then, just as "deep, conjugal love" between a man and a woman lead them to marry and leave father and mother and all other earthly loves, so "true fellowship with the Holy Spirit, the heavenly and loving Spirit" ultimately brings freedom from the loves of this age.[50]

---

43 Macarius, *Homily* 20.7 (PG34.653A), trans. Michael A.G. Haykin.
44 Macarius, *Homily* 23.2 (Maloney, *Fifty Spiritual Homilies*, 156).
45 Macarius, *Homily* 44.8 (Maloney, *Fifty Spiritual Homilies*, 225–26).
46 Macarius, *Homily* 11.3; 33.3 (Maloney, *Fifty Spiritual Homilies*, 202). See also *Homily* 5.9; 27.19.
47 Macarius, *Homily* 18.7.
48 Macarius, *Homily* 18.8 (Maloney, *Fifty Spiritual Homilies*, 144).
49 Macarius, *Homily* 25.9 (Maloney, *Fifty Spiritual Homilies*, 163).
50 Macarius, *Homily* 4.15 (Maloney, *Fifty Spiritual Homilies*, 56–7, altered).

It bears noting that the gift of the Spirit is dependent on the crosswork of Christ. Likening the cross to the work of a gardener, Macarius argued that through the cross, Christ, "the heavenly and true gardener," removed from the barren soul "the thorns and thistles of evil spirits," as well as uprooting and burning with fire "the weeds of sin." With the removal of these, he can now plant in the soul "the most beautiful paradise of the Spirit."[51] The gift of the Spirit is a fruit of the death of Christ.

Macarius thinks about the cross in primarily two ways.[52] On the one hand, the cross is a place of healing and Christ is "the true physician" who has come to heal "everyone afflicted by the incurable wound of sin."[53] Then, the cross is conceived of as a place of ransom, where Christ's life is given in payment for those of sinners. Thus, Macarius argued that Christ's blood was poured out on the cross so that there would be "life and deliverance for humanity."[54] Again, he could state that Christ came to earth to "suffer on behalf of all and to buy them back with his blood."[55]

"RIVERS OF DRAGONS AND MOUTHS OF LIONS AND DARK FORCES"[56]

The gift of the indwelling Spirit, though, does not mean that the one whom he indwells is now exempt from spiritual warfare, for, "where the Holy Spirit is, there follows...persecution and struggle."[57] As Marcus Plested has noted, Macarius argued for "a profoundly militant

---

51 Macarius, *Homily* 28.4 (Maloney, *Fifty Spiritual Homilies*, 185, altered).

52 For Macarius' thinking about the cross, see especially Christine Mengus, "Le «cœur» dans les «Cinquante Homélies spirituelles» du Pseudo-Macaire (III)," *Collectanea Cisterciensia* 59 (1997): 124–126; Roach, "Macarius the Augustinian," 80–81.

53 Macarius, *Homily* 20.4–8. The quotes are from *Homily* 20.6 (PG 34.653A) and 20.4 respectively.

54 Macarius, *Homily* 47.8 (Maloney, *Fifty Spiritual Homilies*, 235).

55 Macarius, *Homily* 24.3 (Maloney, *Fifty Spiritual Homilies*, 158). See especially *Homily* 11.9–15 for Macarius' most detailed development of the cross as a place of ransom.

56 Macarius, *Homily* 16.13 (Maloney, *Fifty Spiritual Homilies*, 134). For this expression, see also *Homily* 15.50; 43.3.

57 Macarius, *Homily* 15.12 (Maloney, *Fifty Spiritual Homilies*, 112).

Christianity."[58] There is persecution of the church by the powers of this age.[59] The faithful believer is "nailed to the cross of Christ" and knows what it is to experience "the stigmata and wounds of the Lord."[60] And there is struggle within the heart of the Christian, such that even the most mature Christian can fall back into a life of sin.[61] In part, Macarius argued, this is because of the malice of Satan, who is "without mercy and hates humans," and thus never hesitates to attack Christians.[62] In part, though, it is because Christians, even "those who are intoxicated with God" and "bound by the Holy Spirit," are not under constraint to do that which pleases God, for they still have their free will.[63] Thus Macarius read Ephesians 4:30 to mean that it was up to Christians' "will and freedom of choice to honour the Holy Spirit and not to grieve him" through sin.[64]

Macarius personally knew men who seemed to be making great progress in the Christian life and then, through yielding to sin, lost everything. One man, who was a Roman aristocrat, seeking to follow Christ, sold his possessions and freed all of his slaves. He soon gained a reputation for being a holy man. Pride entered in and eventually he "fell completely into debaucheries and a thousand evils."[65] Yet another suffered as a confessor in what was probably the last great imperial Roman persecution of the church, namely, that of Diocletian. He was horribly tortured. While in prison, a Christian woman sought to minister to him, but tempted by sexual lust, they "fell into fornication."[66]

---

58 Plested, *Macarian Legacy*, 37. For discussion of this theme, see Plested, *Macarian Legacy*, 36–38; Christine Mengus, "Le «cœur» dans les «Cinquante Homélies spirituelles» du Pseudo-Macaire (II)," *Collectanea Cisterciensia* 59 (1997): 36–38; Golitzin, "Temple and Throne of the Divine Glory," 125.

59 Macarius, *Homily* 15.12. See also *Homily* 9.2–7.

60 Macarius, *Homily* 10.1 (PG34.541A); 53.17 (Marriott, 36; trans. Michael A.G. Haykin). See also *Homily* 12.5.

61 Macarius, *Homily* 8.5; 15.4, 14, 16, 36; 26.17.

62 Macarius, *Homily* 15.18 (Maloney, *Fifty Spiritual Homilies*, 114).

63 Macarius, *Homily* 15.40 (PG34.604B), trans. Michael A.G. Haykin. The phrase "bound by the Spirit" is taken from Paul's statement in Acts 20:22. See also *Homily* 15.36; 27.10–11.

64 Macarius, *Homily* 27.9 (Maloney, *Fifty Spiritual Homilies*, 178).

65 Macarius, *Homily* 27.14 (Maloney, *Fifty Spiritual Homilies*, 180).

66 Macarius, *Homily* 7.15 (Maloney, *Fifty Spiritual Homilies*, 180).

The Christian experience of life in the Spirit in this world was thus one of great struggle against evil powers, whom, in a memorable turn of phrase, Macarius likened to "rivers of dragons and mouths of lions and dark forces."[67]

Ultimately, though, it is not the human will that is the determinant factor in perseverance. It is "the power of the divine Spirit" that is the critical necessity for a person to attain to eternal life. True to the pneumatological focus in much of his thought, Macarius thus concluded: "if [a person] thinks he can effect a perfect work by himself without the help of the Spirit, he is totally in error. Such an attitude is unbecoming one who strives for heavenly places, for the kingdom."[68]

A CONCLUDING WORD

Macarius' vision of the Christian life then is one of victorious liberation from the tyranny of sin by the power of the Spirit of Christ.[69] It begins with a heart dominated by evil, due to Adam's disobedience. Conversion brings liberty from this dreadful state of affairs, but plunges the believer into a warfare with indwelling sin and external spiritual enemies. Although the human will is now truly free to follow Christ or go back into a life of sin, ultimately it is the grace of the Spirit that spells victory in this war.

In many ways, Macarius' homilies are not marked by the deep theological sophistication of his contemporary, Gregory of Nyssa, whom he influenced and who, like Macarius, was deeply interested in the twin themes of theological anthropology and pneumatology. Nevertheless, Macarius' deeply realistic approach to the human condition, his emphasis on the vital necessity of the Holy Spirit to effect eternal transformation, and his desire to take seriously human responsibility reveal him to be a thinker worthy of attention in our day that is also marked by a fascination with spirituality and a passionate interest in what it means to be truly human.

---

67 Macarius, *Homily* 16.13 (Maloney, *Fifty Spiritual Homilies*, 134).
68 Macarius, *Homily* 24.3,5 (Maloney, *Fifty Spiritual Homilies*, 158).
69 Plested, *Macarian Legacy*, 78–79.

10

"The most glorious City of God"
Augustine of Hippo and *The City of God*[1]

> ...the earthly city glories in itself, the Heavenly City glories in the Lord.—AUGUSTINE[2]

THE FALL OF THE WESTERN ROMAN EMPIRE

Scholars have long reflected on and debated the reasons behind the so-called fall of the western Roman empire. A multitude of suggestions,

---

1 Augustine, *City of God* 1.1, trans. Michael A.G. Haykin. Unless otherwise indicated the translation followed in this paper is that of Henry Bettenson, *St Augustine, Concerning the City of God against the Pagans* (London: Penguin, 2003). This chapter has appeared as "'The Most Glorious City of God': Augustine of Hippo and *The City of God*" in *The Power of God in the Life of Man. Papers read at the 2005 Westminster Conference* (London: The Westminster Conference, 2005), 37–57. Used by permission of The Westminster Conference.

2 Augustine, *City of God* 14.28.

ranging from the ridiculous to the extremely plausible—things like climactic change, lead poisoning of the aristocracy, excessive government bureaucracy and the demise of the urban middle class—have been made.[3] One classical approach, that of the eighteenth-century historian Edward Gibbon (1737–1794), maintained that the fall was intimately tied to the growth of Christianity.[4] There is no doubt that many of the most brilliant thinkers of late antiquity—men like Hilary of Poitiers (c.315–c.367), Basil of Caesarea, John Chrysostom and the main subject of this chapter, Augustine of Hippo—devoted their energies to the life of the church and not to that of the state, possibly draining valuable resources from the political sphere. But Gibbon's explanation is probably shaped as much by his bitter dislike of the Christian faith as it is by historical evidence. Another perspective worth noting is that of Arther Ferrill, who has presented a convincing argument for a military explanation for the collapse of Roman hegemony in Western Europe.[5] It is vital to note, however, that none of these various theories can be regarded as cogent if they do not account for why the West was submerged beneath a tidal wave of Germanic tribes while the eastern half of the empire continued in transmogrified form as the Byzantine empire.[6]

Increasingly, however, historians of this period are reticent to talk of a *fall* of Roman imperial power. They much prefer to speak in terms of a *transformation*, a transition from the empire of late antiquity to the various quasi-Romanized Germanic kingdoms of the early

---

3 See Donald Kagan, Steven Ozment and Frank M. Turner, *The Western Heritage*, 6th ed. (Upper Saddle River: Prentice Hall, 1998), 192–193. See the list of 210 suggestions—in German—for the fall of Rome in Bryan Ward-Perkins, *The Fall of Rome and the End of Civilization* (Oxford: Oxford University Press, 2005), 32.

4 Edward Gibbon, *History of the Decline and Fall of the Roman Empire*, 3 vol. (London: W. Strahan and T. Cadell, 1776–1781).

5 Arther Ferrill, *The Fall of the Roman Empire: The Military Explanation* (London: Thames and Hudson, 1986). For an excellent overview of Roman military strategy and the military weaknesses that led to the collapse of Roman might, see Michael F. Pavkovic, "Grand Strategy of the Roman Empire," *Military Chronicles* 1, no.1 (May/June 2005): 14–30.

6 Barry Baldwin, "Roman Empire" in Everett Ferguson, ed., *Encyclopedia of Early Christianity*, 2nd ed. (New York: Garland Publishers, 1997), 2:993.

mediæval era.⁷ This perspective has a long pedigree, dating back at least to the time of Gibbon when the Italian Abbé Galliani (1728–1787), the Neapolitan ambassador to France, wrote, "The fall of empires? What can that mean? Empires being neither up or down they do not fall. They change their appearance."⁸ In recent days, its leading advocate has been Peter Brown, who has also written the definitive biography of Augustine.⁹ In a 1997 reflective essay, "The World of Late Antiquity Revisited," Brown wrote that in his 1971 book, which had argued for this new view of the closing days of the Roman world, he was able to discuss the history of this period without invoking "the widespread notion of decay."¹⁰

Nevertheless, as Bryan Ward-Perkins has argued in a study defending the traditional notion of a fall of Rome, if we look at the textual and material evidence from the period in question, one cannot escape the fact that "the coming of the Germanic peoples was very unpleasant for the Roman population, and…the long-term effects of the dissolution of the empire were dramatic."¹¹ And when one reads the various contemporary witnesses to this great historical event, it is invariably the notions of "collapse," "demise" and "end" that predominate. For instance, after the cataclysmic defeat of the Romans at the Battle of Adrianople in 378, when the emperor Valens, many of his senior officers and close to two-thirds of the imperial army in the eastern Roman empire were slain by a combined army of Germanic Goths and the Huns, Ambrose, bishop of Milan and Augustine's early mentor, was certain that "the end of the world is coming [*mundi finis*]" and that he and his contemporaries were in "the wane of the age [*occasu saeculi*]."¹²

---

7 John P. McKay, Bennett D. Hill and John Buckler, *A History of Western Society*, 7th ed. (Boston: Houghton Miflin Co., 2003), 184–185; Ward-Perkins, *Fall of Rome*, 3–5.

8 Cited McKay, Hill and Buckler, *History of Western Society*, 184.

9 Peter R.L. Brown, *Augustine of Hippo: A Biography*, rev. ed. (Berkeley: University of California Press, 2000).

10 Peter R.L. Brown, "The World of Late Antiquity Revisited," *Symbolae Osloenses* 72 (1997): 14–15.

11 Ward-Perkins, *Fall of Rome*, 10.

12 Ambrose, *Exposition of the Gospel according to Luke* 10.10. For a brief account of the events leading up to the battle and the battle itself, see F. Homes Dudden, *The Life and Times of St. Ambrose* (Oxford: Clarendon Press, 1935), I, 166–172.

Seventeen years later, the Bible scholar and translator Jerome, writing from the relative tranquility of a monastery in Bethlehem, was convinced after hearing of Hunnic invasions of the eastern empire that "the Roman world was falling" apart, and this had to mean the end of history.[13]

What some have identified as the "true moment of collapse, the moment of irreversible disaster"[14] for imperial power in the West was the crossing by huge numbers of barbarian warriors—Vandals, Suevi and the (non-Germanic) Alans—over the frozen surface of the Rhine, Rome's natural frontier in that part of the empire, during the winter of 406/407.[15] They poured into the western provinces of the empire, wresting forever those areas of the *imperium* from Roman rule. But the event truly emblematic of the passing of Roman might was the three-day sack of Rome in August 410. Alaric, more of a profiteer than determined enemy of Rome, and his Visigoths, who were largely Arian by theological conviction, entered the city on August 24. Over the course of the next three days, the symbolic heart of the empire went through what Augustine would later describe as "devastation, butchery, [and] plundering."[16] A number of leading senators were slain, women were raped, even some who had devoted themselves to celibacy for Christ's sake, and others taken hostage.[17] Among the latter was an important Roman aristocrat, Galla Placidia (c.388/390–450), the half-sister of Honorius (r.395–423), the emperor in the West. Her capture by Alaric has led some scholars to think that Alaric had dreams of replacing Honorius. Galla Placidia ended up marrying Alaric's brother-in-law Athaulf, who ruled over the Visigoths for five years after Alaric's death in 410.[18]

---

13 Jerome, *Letter* 60.16.
14 R.P.C. Hanson, "The Reaction of the Church to the Collapse of the Western Roman Empire in the Fifth Century," *Vigiliae Christianae* 26 (1972): 273.
15 Henry Chadwick, *The Church in Ancient Society: From Galilee to Gregory the Great* (Oxford: Oxford University Press, 2001), 510–511.
16 Augustine, *City of God* 1.7, trans. Bettenson, *City of God*, 12.
17 Chadwick, *Church in Ancient Society*, 511; Augustine, *City of God* 1.16.
18 Chadwick, *Church in Ancient Society*, 511–512.

CHRISTIAN REACTIONS TO THE SACK OF ROME (410)[19]

Rome had long ceased to be the real political heart of the empire. That role had been assumed in the west by Ravenna in northern Italy and in the east by Constantinople. Her status in the early fifth century was largely iconic, the symbol of an entire way of life; her sack by a foreign invader—the first since the Celts had taken the city in 390 B.C.—spoke volumes, however, to a world accustomed to finding meaning below the surface of a text through allegorization. Pagans, Augustine tells us, were sure that the disaster was attributable to the abandonment of the worship of the old gods.[20] Augustine quoted them as saying to believers, "Look at all the terrible things happening in Christian times [*tempora Christiana*], the world is being laid waste...and Rome destroyed."[21] This pagan conviction is rooted in the long-held belief that it was Roman *pietas*—namely, Rome's submission to the gods and her fulfillment of her duty toward them—that had guaranteed her earthly triumphs and stability. It is telling that two pagan authors, Zosimus (*fl.*491–518) and Rutilius Namatianus (*fl.* fifth century), though writing after the sack of the city, say little about this momentous event. Their grief was probably too great for words.[22]

Many Christians were equally stunned and shocked by the horrors that had overtaken the city of Rome. Jerome, for instance, was absolutely overwhelmed by the reports he heard and for a while could do little else but weep.[23] When he did write down his thoughts, he did so through the medium of apocalyptic language. "The whole world is

---

19 See the helpful summary of these responses in Hanson, "Reaction of the Church to the Collapse of the Western Roman Empire," 272–287.
20 Augustine, *City of God* 1.1; *Retractions* 2.69.
21 Augustine, *Sermon* 81.7, 9, trans. Edmund Hill, *Sermons III (51–94) on the New Testament* in *The Works of Saint Augustine: A translation for the 21st Century*, III/3 (Brooklyn: New City Press, 1991), 364, 365. This sermon was preached in either 410 or 411 and represents one of Augustine's earliest responses to the sack of Rome.
22 It was Rutilius, writing around 417, who could call Rome "queen of the world and brightest jewel in the vault of Heaven" and that the "stars...have never seen a more beautiful Empire" [cited David F. Wright, "Rome, August 24, 410, and New York, September 11, 2001: Augustine and the End of the World," *Scottish Bulletin of Evangelical Theology* 21, no.1 (Spring 2003): 59].
23 Jerome, *Letters* 126.2; 127.12.

sinking into ruin," he told one correspondent.[24] To another, he stated that 2 Thessalonians 2:7,[25] that intriguing verse long understood by Patristic exegetes to be a reference to Roman rule, had been fulfilled and that the coming of "Antichrist is at hand."[26] After detailing the various parts of the empire that had been impacted by the invaders, Jerome used a line from the first-century poet Lucan to help him describe his feelings. In one of his poems, Lucan had asked, "If Rome be weak, where shall we look for strength?"[27] Jerome suggested that the then-current circumstances demanded modifying his words to say, "If Rome perishes, how shall we look for help?"[28] Jerome, like so many other Christians of his day, seems to have been utterly unable to conceive of a Romeless world.[29]

An excellent window into Jerome's thinking around this time is found in one of his letters in which he cited Psalm 79:1–3 as extremely relevant to what had happened in Rome:

> Oh God, the nations have come into your inheritance; they have defiled your holy temple; they have made Jerusalem an orchard. They have given the dead bodies of your servants to be meat unto the birds of the sky, the flesh of your saints to the beasts of the earth. They have shed their blood like water around Jerusalem and there was none to bury them.[30]

---

24 Jerome, *Letter* 128.5. For the Latin, see I. Hilberg, ed., *Sancti Eusebii Hieronymii Epistulae III: Epistulae CXXI–CLIV* (*Corpus Scriptorum Ecclesiasticorum Latinorum*, vol. 56/1; 2nd ed.; Vienna: Österreichischen Akademie der Wissenschaften, 1996), 161.

25 For Augustine's reading of this verse, see *City of God* 20.19. He regarded the words of the apostle as "obscure."

26 Jerome, *Letter* 123.15 (Hilberg, ed., *Sancti Eusebii Hieronymii Epistulae III*, 91).

27 Lucan, *Pharsalia* 5.274.

28 Jerome, *Letter* 123.16 (Hilberg, ed., *Sancti Eusebii Hieronymii Epistulae III*, 94).

29 Here Jerome was also echoing a long-standing Christian conviction that the collapse of the Roman empire automatically meant the end of the world had come. See Tertullian, *To Scapula* 2; Lactantius, *The Divine Institutes* 7.25. This conviction existed side by side with various anti-imperial sentiments as noted below. See also R. A. Markus, "The Roman Empire in Early Christian Historiography" in his *From Augustine to Gregory the Great: History and Christianity in Late Antiquity* (London: Variorum Reprints, 1983), no.IV, 343–344.

30 Jerome, *Letter* 127.12, trans. W.H. Freemantle, *The Principal Works of St. Jerome,*

In its original context, the psalmist is, of course, referring to Jerusalem, the centre of worship under the old covenant. Jerome does not appear to sense any incongruity, however, in applying the text also to the Rome of his day. This is an amazing shift from earlier pre-Constantinian, Latin Christian attitudes to Rome. The latter are well seen in two early texts. The first is a description of the Roman empire by the North African theologian Tertullian. Unlike Jerome, when Tertullian looks for a biblical city that best typifies Rome it was not Jerusalem. Rather, referring to the use of the term Babylon in Revelation, he states that this ancient Near Eastern imperial capital is the best "metaphor of the Roman city," for, "like Babylon, [Rome] is great, and proud of empire, and at war against the saints of God."[31] An official record in Latin of the trial of some believers from Scillium, a town in the Roman province of Numidia in North Africa, around 180, contains a similar view of Rome. Speratus, one of a number who was martyred for the faith on that occasion, is recorded as telling the proconsul of Africa: "I do not recognize the empire of this world; but rather I serve that God whom no man sees nor can see with these eyes."[32]

EUSEBEIAN IMPERIAL THEOLOGY

The acclamation of Constantine as emperor at York in 306 and his subsequent reign of thirty-one years necessitated a fundamental change in perspective about the empire, for Constantine not only secured legal toleration for Christianity but his actions also bespoke a conviction that he had been called by God to be the church's patron. As we saw in chapter 6, the legislation enacted by Constantine and those texts that we have from his hand reveal a man who was sincerely

---

Nicene and Post–Nicene Fathers, Second Series, Vol. 6 (reprint; Grand Rapids: Eerdmans, 1978), 257, altered.

31 Tertullian, *Against Marcion* 3.13, trans. Ernest Evans, *Tertullian: Adversus Marcionem* (Oxford: Clarendon Press, 1972), 211.

32 *The Acts of the Scillitan Martyrs*, trans. Herbert Musurillo, *The Acts of the Christian Martyrs* (Oxford: Clarendon Press, 1972), 87. It is noteworthy that Greek-speaking theologians like Origen in the eastern Roman empire had a more positive evaluation of the empire. See W.H.C. Frend, "The Roman Empire in Eastern and Western Historiography" in his *Religion Popular and Unpopular in the Early Christian Centuries* (London: Variorum Reprints, 1976), no.IX, 26–27.

convinced that he had been given a divine mission to inculcate virtue in his subjects and persuade them to worship the true God proclaimed in the Christian faith. This conviction was wedded to an intense ambition for personal power, but that does not diminish its sincerity.[33]

Fourth-century Christian leaders thus found themselves having to re-evaluate their understanding of the role of the Roman empire in history.[34] For much of that century it was the re-evaluation espoused by Eusebius of Caesarea, sometimes called the father of church history, that seems to have prevailed in many circles.[35] Drawing upon an earlier strain of thinking in Greek-speaking circles that had viewed aspects of the empire in a more positive light than the Latin-speaking witnesses cited above, Eusebius argued that the establishment of the *pax Romana* under the imperial rule of Augustus Caesar (r.27 B.C.– A.D.14) was a direct fulfillment of Scripture texts like Psalm 72:7–8, Isaiah 2:4 and Micah 5:4–5, which predicted political peace at the time of the coming of the Messiah.[36] Constantine's similar political achievement, coupled with an overt commitment to the advance of the Christian faith, marked out his reign as another high point in God's providential purposes in history. Eusebius thus concluded his famous narrative of the history of the church on a note of optimism, for Constantine had "combined the Roman Empire into a single whole, as in former days"— a reference to the Augustan achievement—and brought it all under his "peaceful rule, from the rising of the sun to the farthest dark."[37]

---

33 Vital in orienting my perspective on Constantine has been Timothy D. Barnes, *Constantine and Eusebius* (Cambridge: Harvard University Press, 1981).

34 For studies of this re-orientation, see Frend, "Roman Empire in Eastern and Western Historiography"; Markus, "Roman Empire in Early Christian Historiography."

35 For helpful summaries of Eusebius' view, see Frend, "Roman Empire in Eastern and Western Historiography," 27–28; Markus, "Roman Empire in Early Christian Historiography," 343–344; Glenn F. Chesnut, Jr., "'The Patterns of the Past: Augustine's debate with Eusebius and Sallust" in John Deschner, Leroy T. Howe and Klaus Penzel, ed., *Our Common History as Christians: Essays in Honor of Albert C. Outler* (New York: Oxford University Press, 1975), 69–95, *passim*; Avihu Zakai and Anya Mali, "Time, History and Eschatology: Ecclesiastical History from Eusebius to Augustine," *The Journal of Religious History* 17 (1993): 393–402.

36 Eusebius, *The Preparation for the Gospel* 1.4; Eusebius, *The Proof of the Gospel* 7.2.

37 Eusebius, *Church History* 10.9, trans. Paul L. Maier, *Eusebius: The Church History* (Grand Rapids: Kregel, 1999), 370.

Laws were now passed that "reflected liberality and true piety," so that, in Eusebius' glowing prose,

> all tyranny was eradicated, and the kingdom that was theirs was preserved, secure and undisputed, for Constantine and his sons alone. They, having first cleansed the world of hatred to God and knowing all the good He had conferred on them, showed their love of virtue and of God, their devotion and gratitude to the Almighty, by their actions for all to see.[38]

Implicit in these historical reflections is the view that God's providential guidance of history had reached its zenith in the Christian Roman empire.[39] And when it had run its course, history would end.

One other element of Eusebeian imperial theology that needs to be noted is evident in a sermon given on July 25, 336, the year before Constantine's death. Eusebius had been asked to preach at the celebration of the thirtieth anniversary of Constantine's accession to power. The main theme of his sermon is that the empire of Constantine is a visible image of the heavenly kingdom, a manifestation on earth of the ideal monarchy that exists in heaven. Eusebius went on to affirm that Constantine governs it in accordance with the divine archetype, ever keeping his eyes on heaven to find the pattern for his government. In other words, in Eusebius' mind the Roman state has become a sacred realm.[40]

Over the course of the fourth century, this Eusebeian theology of empire became integral to popular Christian thought. It surely informs the way Jerome responded to the fall of Rome. At the other end of the empire, it can be found in the poetry of the Spaniard Prudentius (c.348–c.405), who borrowing words that the first-century poet Virgil put in Jupiter's mouth about Rome—"I set no limits to their fortune and/No time; I give them empire without end"[41]—applied them directly, and then said:

---

38 Eusebius, *Church History* 10.9, trans. Maier, *Eusebius: The Church History*, 371.
39 Zakai and Mali, "Time, History and Eschatology," 399–401.
40 Eusebius, *Oration in Praise of Constantine* 3.5. See also Barnes, *Constantine and Eusebius*, 254.
41 Virgil, *Aeneid* 1.278–279.

> Do we still doubt that Rome to You, O Christ,
> Has given herself and yielded to your laws,
> And that with all her people and great men
> She now extends her realm beyond the stars?[42]

Little wonder then that the taking of Rome by the Visigoths was such a shock, and how readily understandable that Christians, imbued with the Eusebius' imperial theology, were prepared to think that the end of the world was imminent. And how strange must Augustine's *The City of God*, with its vast and deeply Scriptural critique of the optimism of this imperial theology, have seemed to many of his contemporaries.

AUGUSTINE—A SKETCH OF HIS LIFE

Augustine is a seminal thinker in the history of the church and Western civilization. It can be said of Augustine with regard to the realm of theology what Cassius says of Julius Caesar, in William Shakespeare's *Julius Caesar*: "he doth bestride the narrow world like a colossus, and we petty men walk under his huge legs."[43] Apart from the Scriptural authors, no other figure had a greater impact on Christian thought through the Middle Ages than Augustine.[44] And when we come to the Reformation, those two leading figures, Martin Luther (1483–1546) and John Calvin (1509–1564), quote Augustine "more often than any other theologian and see themselves as recapturing his emphases and his spirit for the condition of the church at their time."[45] As Benjamin B. Warfield rightly notes: "When the great revival of religion which

---

42 Prudentius, *Against Symmachus* 1.587–590, trans. M. Clement Eagan, *The Poems of Prudentius*, Vol.2 (Washington: The Catholic University of America Press, 1965), 134, altered.

43 William Shakespeare, *Julius Caesar*, Act I, Scene 2, lines 135–137.

44 For this impact of Augustine, see the collection of essays in Irene Backus, ed., *The Reception of the Church Fathers in the West: From the Carolingians to the Maurists* (Leiden: E.J. Brill, 1997), vol. 1.

45 John E. Hare, "Augustine, Kant, and the Moral Gap" in Gareth B. Matthews, ed., *The Augustinian Tradition* (Berkeley: University of California Press, 1999), 252. See also Manfred Schulze, "Martin Luther and the Church Fathers," trans. James C.G. Greig and Johannes van Ort, "John Calvin and the Church Fathers" in Backus, ed., *The Reception of the Church Fathers in the West*, 2:573–626 and 2:661–700, respectively.

we call the Reformation came...it was, on its theological side, a revival of 'Augustinianism.'"[46] And, as Gerald Bonner has written, Augustine "continues to attract large numbers of students, who are fascinated by his personality and his ideas...and many of these, while recognizing the flaws in Augustine's teachings, would admit to having received illumination and inspiration from his thought."[47]

The facts of Augustine's early life are well-known, because he recorded them in his justly famous *Confessions* (397–401).[48] Born on November 13, 354, in what was then the Roman province of Numidia, he was the son of a poor minor official, Patricius (died c.371) and his Christian wife Monica (331–387).[49] Of the two, it was his mother who had a much greater influence on his life. Shortly after his conversion, Augustine would note that his mother's prayers had been instrumental in bringing him to a living faith in Christ.[50] One of the leading patrologists of our day, Jaroslav Pelikan, well sums up Augustine's years before his conversion. He says of the North African that he "moved from one preoccupation to another, from preoccupation with self to a dozen years as a member of the murky Manichean sect, to various kinds of neo-Platonism, to orthodox Christianity."[51]

---

46 Benjamin B. Warfield, "Augustine" in his *Calvin and Augustine*, ed. Samuel G. Craig (Philadelphia: The Presbyterian and Reformed Publ. Co., 1956), 319, 320, 322–323.

47 Gerald Bonner, "They Speak to Us across the Centuries: 7. Augustine," *The Expository Times* 109, no.10 (July 1998): 293.

48 The standard biography of Augustine is that of Peter Brown—see n.9 in this chapter. Two other helpful biographical studies are those of Henry Chadwick, *Augustine: A Very Short Introduction* (Oxford: Oxford University Press, 2001) and Gary Wills, *Saint Augustine* (New York: Viking, 1999). See also the overview by Robert A. Markus, "Life, Culture, and Controversies of Augustine" in Allan D. Fitzgerald, ed., *Augustine through the Ages: An Encyclopedia* (Grand Rapids: Eerdmans, 1999), 498–504 and the interesting little study by Karla Pollmann, *St Augustine the Algerian* (Göttingen: Duehrkohp & Radicke, 2003).

49 On his parents, see Allan D. Fitzgerald, "Patricius" and Angelo di Berardino, "Monnica" in Fitzgerald, ed., *Augustine through the Ages*, 621 and 570–571 respectively. Monica's name can also be spelt as "Monnica."

50 Augustine, *The Happy Life* 6.

51 Jaroslav Pelikan, "Writing as a Means of Grace" in his et al., *Spiritual Quests: The Art and Craft of Religious Writing* (Boston: Houghton Miflin Co., 1988), 88.

Conversion to Christ came in the late summer of 386, in a garden in Milan where Augustine was working as an imperial rhetor.[52] The critical moment came through the reading of a Pauline text, Romans 13:13–14, of which, Augustine later wrote, "the light of confidence flooded into my heart and all the darkness of doubt was dispelled."[53] In his *Confessions*, Book 9, Augustine described more fully how he later understood God's saving work in his life:

> During all those years [of rebellion], where was my free will? What was the hidden, secret place from which it was summoned in a moment, so that I might bend my neck to your easy yoke and take your light burden on my shoulders, Christ Jesus, my Helper and my Redeemer? How sweet all at once it was for me to be rid of those fruitless joys which I had once feared to lose and was now glad to reject! You drove them from me, you who are the true, the sovereign joy. You drove them from me and took their place, you who are sweeter than all pleasure, though not to flesh and blood, you who outshine all light, yet are hidden deeper than any secret in our hearts, you who surpass all honor, though not in the eyes of men who see all honor in themselves.[54]

In the spring of 387, at the Saturday evening Easter vigil service, Augustine was baptized by the bishop of Milan, Ambrose. The following year, he moved back to his hometown in North Africa. By 391, he had decided to move to the coastal town of Hippo Regius, some 150 miles from Thagaste, in order to found a monastery where he and others might devote themselves to the reading of the Scriptures. But things did not turn out as he intended. As Augustine later recalled in a sermon that he preached in the mid-420s:

> A slave may not contradict his Lord. I came to this city to see a friend, whom I thought I might gain for God, that he might live

---

52 rhetor: a teacher of rhetoric.
53 Augustine, *Confessions* 8.12, trans. R.S. Pine-Coffin, *Saint Augustine: Confessions* (Harmondsworth: Penguin, 1961), 178.
54 Augustine, *Confessions* 9.1, trans. Pine-Coffin, *Confessions*, 181.

with us in the monastery. I felt secure, for the place already had a bishop. I was grabbed. I was made an elder (*presbyter factus sum*)...and from there, I became your bishop.[55]

Such a procedure was apparently not unusual in the North African church of late antiquity.[56] Some who were "ordained" in this way undoubtedly took the first opportunity to escape the responsibilities imposed upon them. But not so Augustine, who saw in this unlooked-for experience God's unexpected call to a vocation as a preacher of the gospel. As he said, "a slave may not contradict his Lord."

Within a couple of years of his becoming bishop of Hippo, which happened in 395, Augustine had an experience that Bonner deems to be the most decisive of his life after his conversion. A request had come from an old friend from Milan, Simplicianus (died c.400), who would succeed Ambrose as the bishop of the congregation in that city, for some insight into the meaning of the Pauline text of Romans 9:10–29, which deals with God's electing love of Jacob and his rejection of Esau.[57] Augustine plunged into the study of Romans and Paul's other letters and was led to see that any attempt to uphold "the freedom of choice of the human will" was fundamentally misguided from a biblical standpoint. As he studied the Pauline corpus, "the grace of God had the upper hand," as he put it. In particular, it was his meditation on 1 Corinthians 4:7 ("What do you have that you have not received?") that brought about the realization that divine "grace alone is all-sufficient" to move sinners toward Christ. Everything the believer has, even faith itself, must be seen as sheer gift.[58] This revolution in

---

55 Augustine, *Sermon* 355.2, cited Brown, *Augustine of Hippo*, 131.

56 Chadwick, *Church in Ancient Society*, 475.

57 For Augustine's interaction with Romans throughout his life, see especially Pamela Bright, "Augustine" in Jeffrey P. Greenman and Timothy Larsen, ed., *Reading Romans through the Centuries: From the Early Church to Karl Barth* (Grand Rapids: Brazos Press, 2005), 59–80. See also J.P. Burns, "The Interpretation of Romans in the Pelagian Controversy," *Augustinian Studies* 10 (1979): 43–54; W.S. Babcock, "Augustine's Interpretation of Romans (AD 394–396)," *Augustinian Studies* 10 (1979): 55–74; idem, "Augustine and Paul: The Case of Romans IX," *Studia Patristica* 16 (1985): 473–479; C.P. Bammel, "Augustine, Origen and the Exegesis of St. Paul," *Augustinianum* 32 (1992): 341–367.

58 Bright, "Augustine" in Greenman and Larsen, ed., *Reading Romans*, 70–71.

Augustine's thinking bore fruit in his classic account of the sovereignty of God's grace at work in his own life, the *Confessions*, and also equipped him spiritually for his later struggle with the theological errors of Pelagianism.

This submission to Scripture points to another key element of Augustine's life, namely his vocation as a preacher of the gospel. Numerous accounts of his life sketch Augustine's career chiefly in terms of the controversies in which he took part. But there is something very inadequate about this approach. Augustine's primary task through the decades of his ministry was the care of souls entrusted to him. And a central expression of that care were the sermons that he regularly preached. He preached on Saturdays as well as Sundays, and daily during Lent and the week following Easter. *Notarii*, that is stenographers, would take the sermon down in shorthand and then transcribe it into longhand. Of the estimated 8,000 sermons that Augustine preached, 559 are extant.[59] This constant interaction with the Scriptures nourished his thought as no other words could.[60] And when he died in Hippo on August 28, 430, he did so reading four of the penitential psalms of David that he had had copied out and pasted to the walls of his bedroom.

THE CITY OF GOD (412–427)—AN INTRODUCTION [61]

It is thus typically Augustinian that it was the Scriptures that gave him the central theme for *The City of God*. In Book 11.1, Augustine explicitly

---

59 Stanley P. Rosenberg, "Interpreting Atonement in Augustine's Preaching" in Charles E. Hill and Frank A. James III, ed., *The Glory of the Atonement: Biblical, Historical & Practical Perspectives. Essays in Honor of Roger Nicole* (Downers Grove: InterVarsity Press, 2004), 227; Hubertus R. Drobner, "Studying Augustine: An Overview of Recent Research" in Robert Dodaro and George Lawless, eds., *Augustine and His Critics: Essays in Honour of Gerald Bonner* (London: Routledge, 2000), 22–23. See Éric Rebillard, "Sermones" in Fitzgerald, ed., *Augustine through the Ages*, 774–789 for a listing of most of Augustine's extant sermons.

60 Bright, "Augustine" in Greenman and Larsen, eds., *Reading Romans*, 80.

61 Studies of *The City of God* are legion. The following have been especially helpful in the writing of this chapter: Robert Austin Markus, *Saeculum: History and Society in the Theology of St. Augustine* (1970, reprint, Cambridge: Cambridge University Press, 2000); Gerard J.P. O'Daly, "*Ciuitate dei*" in Cornelius Mayer, ed., *Augustinus-Lexikon* (Basel: Schwabe & Co. AG, 1986–1994), 1:970–1010; J. van Oort, *Jerusalem and Babylon: Study into Augustine's "City of God" and the Sources of His Doctrine of the Two Cities*

notes a number of passages in the Psalms that use the phrase "city of God"—Psalm 87:3; 48:1–2,8; 46:4. It was especially the first of these verses—"Glorious things are spoken of you, O city of God"—that gave Augustine the theme for his book. As he describes this community at the very beginning of the book, she is "the most glorious City of God (*gloriosissimam civitatem Dei*)."[62] In the New Testament, this term is also found in Hebrews—explicitly in 12:22 and by implication in 11:10 and 16—and Revelation—explicitly in 3:12 and implicitly in 21:2 and 10. The Scriptures also develop the idea of a divine city under the type of the heavenly Jerusalem (see Galatians 4:24–26 and Hebrews 12:22) and of an earthly city by means of the symbol of Babylon (particularly in Revelation).[63] Given these biblical roots of the basic idea of the two cities, it is not surprising to find authors before Augustine using this typology. A number of Latin-speaking writers, including Tertullian, Ambrose and the Donatist exegete Tyconius (died c.400), use the typology of two cities, though none of them does so as a way of explaining the course of history.[64] The latter appears to be completely original to Augustine.[65]

By Augustine's own admission, *The City of God* was "a long and arduous" task, a "huge work" as he says at its close.[66] The Latin text runs to

---

(Leiden: E.J. Brill, 1991); Gerard O'Daly, *Augustine's City of God: A Reader's Guide* (Oxford: Clarendon Press, 1999); Carol Harrison, *Augustine: Christian Truth and Fractured Humanity* (Oxford: Oxford University Press, 2000), 194–222. See also the essays in Dorothy F. Donnelly, ed., *The City of God. A Collection of Critical Essays* (New York: Peter Lang, 1995) and Mark Vessey, Karla Pollmann and Allan D. Fitzgerald, ed., *History, Apocalypse, and the Secular Imagination: New Essays on Augustine's City of God* (Bowling Green: Philosophy Documentation Center, 1999).

62 Augustine, *City of God* 1. Preface, trans. Michael A.G. Haykin.

63 O'Daly, *Augustine's City of God*, 53–54; Van Oort, *Jerusalem and Babylon*, 312–318; Charles Kannengiesser, *Handbook of Patristic Exegesis: The Bible in Ancient Christianity* (Leiden: E.J. Brill, 2004), II, 1180.

64 Van Oort, *Jerusalem and Babylon*, 274–312; O'Daly, *Augustine's City of God*, 54–58. On especially Tyconius' influence on Augustine, see Paula Fredriksen, "Tyconius" in Fitzgerald, ed., *Augustine through the Ages*, 853–855; Van Oort, *Jerusalem and Babylon*, 254–274; and some of the papers in Pamela Bright, ed. and trans., *Augustine and the Bible* (Notre Dame: University of Notre Dame Press, 1986), "Part II: A Conflict of African Hermeneutics: Augustine and Tyconius."

65 Van Oort, *Jerusalem and Babylon*, 318; O'Daly, *Augustine's City of God*, 62.

66 Augustine, *City of God* 1. Preface; 22.30.

about a quarter of million words. Not surprisingly, at times it is repetitious and rambling, replete with diversions and sidebars. Some of the latter—dealing with subjects like the relationship of true philosophy to skepticism, the meaning of the miraculous, and the incarnation as an expression of divine humility—are extremely interesting windows into Augustine's thinking.[67] All of this means that it is not easy to produce a comprehensive summary of the book.[68] But at the work's heart was Augustine's mature reflection on God's purposes in the realm of history, a reflection that sought to be rigorously biblical and that represented a well thought out rejection of the Eusebian vision of history.

Although the taking of Rome by the Visigoths provided the immediate reason for beginning the work, there is every indication that even if this event had not happened, Augustine would have written this massive tome. Book 1, as we shall see, contains a significant response to this unnerving event, but the other twenty-one books hardly mention it. As Johannes van Oort puts it: "*The City of God* is not an occasional pamphlet that developed into a comprehensive work, but one of Augustine's principal works, written after a long process of maturation."[69] So it was that the actual process of writing began when Augustine was in middle age, a man in his late fifties. When he had finished it, he was seventy-three, an old man by Roman standards.

The work falls into two distinct parts, each of which has sub-sections. The first part of the book consists of Books 1–10. There Augustine first deals directly with questions of theodicy raised by Christians with regard to the fall of Rome and pagan attacks on Christianity in light of that event (Books 1–5). In the second sub-section, Books 6–10, Augustine attacks the pagan idea that worship of gods is necessary in order to secure eternal life. The second part of the book has three sub-sections, each consisting of four books. In Books 11–14, Augustine deals with the origin of the two cities, the City of God and the City of Man. The next sub-section, Books 15–18, focus on the course of these two cities

---

67 Trevor Rowe, *St Augustine: Pastoral Theologian* (London: Epworth Press, 1974), 104.
68 Van Oort, *Jerusalem and Babylon*, 63.
69 Van Oort, *Jerusalem and Babylon*, 87.

Augustine of Hippo
(354–430)

through history, while the last sub-section, Books 19–22, deals with the final, and radically differing, destinations for these cities.[70]

THE CITY OF GOD 1–10

The first five books of *The City of God*, which were probably begun in 412 and were definitely completed by late 415,[71] are essentially a theodicy. They are Augustine's reply to the numerous acute human problems with which he had to deal after the sack of Rome. Christians, fleeing from the sack of the imperial city, had flooded across to North Africa, and were deeply distressed by experiences that they had undergone and events they had witnessed. Christians had been tortured and others entirely deprived of their worldly goods.[72] Many believers had been slain and their bodies left to rot in the open air,[73] while numerous others had been taken into captivity.[74] Most distressing to some was the fact that Christian women and girls had been violated and some had even taken their own lives rather than submit to rape.[75]

To the questions raised by all of this human suffering, Augustine sought—especially in Book 1—to give reasoned biblical answers.[76] For instance, he insisted that while a believer may lose his possessions, he can never lose the inner riches produced by saving faith.[77] Then, Augustine emphasized, death is common to all men, but what makes it an evil is when the soul goes to a hellish destination after death.[78] Moreover, as Augustine points out, funerals, while a good thing, are for the living rather than the dead.[79] Augustine takes considerable space in dealing with the question of whether or not it was sin for Christian women to commit suicide in order to avoid being raped.[80]

---

70 Van Oort, *Jerusalem and Babylon*, 75–76.
71 O'Daly, "Ciuitate dei" in Mayer, ed., *Augustinus-Lexikon*, 1:974.
72 Augustine, *City of God* 1.10–11.
73 Augustine, *City of God* 1.12–13.
74 Augustine, *City of God* 1.14–15.
75 Augustine, *City of God* 1.16–18.
76 See also the discussion by Wright, "Augustine and the End of the World," 63–68.
77 Augustine, *City of God* 1.10.
78 Augustine, *City of God* 1.11.
79 Augustine, *City of God* 1.11–12.
80 Augustine, *City of God* 1.16–28.

Augustine of Hippo and *The City of God*   153

The North African theologian first of all makes it clear that to be a victim of rape in no way pollutes the person raped since "purity is a virtue of the mind."[81] Augustine is conscious that there may be "a sense of shame (*pudorem*)" that fills the victim, but in the eyes of God there has been no sin committed by that person. Then, although Augustine does not wish to countenance suicide—as he says, "in the sacred canonical books" there is no "injunction or permission" given "to commit suicide...to avoid or escape any evil"[82]—he is prepared to consider the possibility that these women had actually been commanded by God to sacrifice themselves, much like Samson's self-sacrifice or the command given to Abraham to slay Isaac.[83] The reason for this is a pastoral one: Augustine was extremely reluctant to condemn these women when some of his Christian contemporaries viewed them as martyrs.[84]

These first five books are also a response to those pagans who were blaming Christianity for the ills that had befallen the Roman state and who felt that the sack of Rome had shown the impotency of the God of the Christians.[85] Essentially, Augustine argues from a selective survey of Roman history that it is the pagan religion of Rome that is unable to protect its adherents from calamities. Long before Roman rulers ever embraced Christianity, Rome had suffered horrible wars and various disasters.[86] In fact, the growth of the Roman state really had nothing to do with the favour of the pagan gods—it was entirely owing to the one true God whom Christians worship. It is this God, "the author and giver of felicity, who...gives earthly dominion both to good men and evil."[87]

What Augustine is doing in this first quarter of *The City of God* is showing that God never intended the Christian religion to necessarily entail all manner of earthly happiness for its adherents—such happiness is for the life to come! Citing Matthew 5:45, Augustine emphasizes

---

81 Augustine, *City of God* 1.16–18.
82 Augustine, *City of God* 1.20, trans. Bettenson, *City of God*, 31.
83 Augustine, *City of God* 1.26.
84 Augustine, *City of God* 1.26.
85 Augustine, *City of God* 1.29–30.
86 Augustine, *City of God* 2–4.
87 Augustine, *City of God* 4.33, trans. Bettenson, *City of God*, 176. See also *City of God* 5.21–22.

that in this world God causes sunshine and rain to come upon both the righteous and the unrighteous.[88] For the righteous, the experience of the good things of this world is so tempered by the challenges of life that they yearn for the complete peace and joy of the kingdom to come. Hardships in their lives are a way that God sanctifies them. What is critical, Augustine points out, is to realize that while both the good and the wicked go through earthly trials, these trials have very different effects upon the two types of people. As he puts it:

> Though the sufferings are the same, the sufferers remain different. Virtue and vice are not the same, even if they undergo the same torment. The fire which makes gold shine makes chaff smoke.... Stir a cesspit, and a foul stench arises; stir a perfume, and a delightful fragrance ascends. But the movement is identical.[89]

For Christians to make sense of their lives, they must view them eschatologically—in the light of eternity. Undergirding these pastoral reflections is Augustine's other-worldly perspective that rightly sees "the imperfection and impermanence of all human life" in this world, even that of the saints.[90]

Books 6–10, written between 415 and 417, extend Augustine's critique of Roman religion. Not only are the pagan gods—and the demonic powers that lie behind them—incapable of giving earthly happiness, they are also utterly impotent when it comes to future blessing and life in the world to come.[91] A large part of this section also contains

---

88 Augustine, *City of God* 1.8.

89 Augustine, *City of God* 1.8, trans. Bettenson, *City of God*, 14. Augustine had made similar remarks in a sermon that he preached within months, possibly even weeks, of the sack of Rome. "Adversity comes as a fire. Does it find you as gold? If so, it rids you of impurity. Does it find you as chaff? If so, it reduces you to ash" (Augustine, *Sermon* 81.7).

90 Wright, "Augustine and the End of the World," 68. See also Hans von Campenhausen, "Augustine and the Fall of Rome" in his *Tradition and Life in the Church: Essays and Lectures in Church History*, trans. A.V. Littledale (Philadelphia: Fortress Press, 1960), 206–207.

91 This is Augustine's own characterization of Books 6–10. See Augustine, *City of God* 10.32.

Augustine's rebuttal of a philosophical position that had once been quite attractive to the North African, namely Platonism.

THE CITY OF GOD 11–22

In the second half of *The City of God*, Augustine charts the course of the City of God and the earthly city in history. In doing so, he is engaging in a fundamental critique of the Eusebeian imperial theology of history. Unlike those who upheld this ideology, Augustine sees no central role for the Roman empire in the history of salvation.

Books 11–14, which were written by 418, deal with the origins of the two cities, but Augustine devotes much of these books to various discussions that deal with such things as how to understand Genesis 1[92] and why sexual intercourse even within marriage is for the sole purpose of procreation—which Augustine believes is the central purpose of sex—bears about it a sense of shame.[93] Augustine traces the origins of the two cities back to the early days of the universe when God made the angels, whom, he says, "form the greater part" of "the Holy City."[94] Correspondingly, the earthly city takes its rise with the fall of some of these angels into sin. While the one company who stood fast in glory burns "with holy love of God; the other smoulders with the foul desire for its own exaltation."[95] And when Adam was created, there was within him, as it were, the potential for adding citizens to both of these two cities. "For from that man were to come all men," Augustine observes, "some of them to join the company of the evil angels in their punishment, others to be admitted to the company of the good angels in their reward."[96]

Then, at the close of this sub-section, in *City of God* 14.28, Augustine provides one of his most succinct descriptions of the two cities:

> We see then that the two cities were created by two kinds of love: the earthly city was created by self-love reaching the point of

---

92 Augustine, *City of God* 11.19–34.
93 Augustine, *City of God* 14.16–26.
94 Augustine, *City of God* 11.9. See also *City of God* 11.28: the City of God is "eternally immortal in heaven, consisting of the holy angels who cleave to God", trans. Bettenson, *City of God*, 463.
95 Augustine, *City of God* 11.34, trans. Bettenson, *City of God*, 468.
96 Augustine, *City of God* 12.28, trans. Bettenson, *City of God*, 508.

contempt for God, the Heavenly City by the love of God carried as far as contempt of self. In fact, the earthly city glories in itself, the Heavenly City glories in the Lord. The former looks for glory from men, the latter finds its highest glory in God.... In the former, the lust for domination lords it over its princes as over the nations it subjugates; in the other, both those put in authority and those subject to them serve one another in love, the rulers by their counsel, the subjects by obedience. The one city loves its own strength shown in its powerful leaders; the other says to its God, "I will love you, my Lord, my strength."[97]

Here Augustine contrasts the two communities by means of their deepest passions, for Augustine was rightly convinced that the core of a society is found in what it loves and cherishes most highly.[98] As he says elsewhere: love—love for God and love for our neighbour—is the central thing that God commands, the implication being that it is the most important thing in human existence.[99] Also noteworthy about this text is that Augustine depicts the contrast between these two cities in political terms. In the City of God, there is a loving relationship between ruler and ruled, in which leaders lead in such a way as to benefit those being led, for the leaders are seeking to "serve...in love (*serviunt...in caritate*)." It is quite otherwise in the earthly city, where "a lust for domination" (*dominandi libido*) prevails that creates the desire to conquer other nations and acquire empire.[100] Earlier in the book, Augustine made a similar remark when he bluntly described many of the great empires of the ancient world as "gangs of criminals on a large scale."[101] In Augustine's words:

> ...to attack one's neighbours, to pass on to crush and subdue more remote peoples without provocation and solely from the thirst

---

97 Augustine, *City of God* 14.28, trans. Bettenson, *City of God*, 593.
98 Frederick Van Fleteren, "*De Civitate Dei*: Miscellaneous Observations" in Donnelly, ed., *The City of God*, 418–419.
99 Augustine, *City of God* 19.14.
100 O'Daly, *Augustine's City of God*, 159.
101 Augustine, *City of God* 4.4, trans. Bettenson, *City of God*, 139.

for dominion—what is one to call this but brigandage on the grand scale?[102]

The description of the earthly city in such stark terms would immediately call to mind for Augustine's readers the Roman *imperium*, and it would indicate Augustine's implicit criticism of any identification of the City of God with this earthly realm.

This text, coming immediately before the next sub-section that traces the course of the two cities in history, namely Books 15–18, also serves as an introduction to this narrative.[103] As Augustine traces the historical path of these two cities, he does so by first elaborating in Books 15–16 on the way in which these two cities appear in the biblical account in Genesis. Typical of his emphasis in this elaboration is his statement at the outset of Book 15 that the City of God is a pilgrim city that is not at home in this world:

> Scripture tells us that Cain founded a city, whereas Abel, as a pilgrim, did not found one. For the City of the saints is up above, although it produces citizens here below, and in their persons the City is on pilgrimage until the time of its kingdom comes.[104]

Given the repetitive way in which Augustine describes the City of God in these terms,[105] there is little doubt that the state of being a pilgrim in this world is an essential aspect of the City of God. The City of God has no home here in this world, but is on its way to its true home in

---

102 Augustine, *City of God* 4.6, trans. Bettenson, *City of God*, 142. Cf. *City of God* 2.17.

103 Unlike the first 14 books of the *City of God* that can be dated with some certainty, there are divergent opinions about when the rest of the books were composed. See O'Daly, "*Ciuitate dei*" in Mayer, ed., *Augustinus-Lexikon*, 1:973–974; O'Daly, *Augustine's City of God*, 34–35; James J. O'Donnell, "Augustine, City of God" (http://faculty.georgetown.edu/jod/augustine/civ.html; accessed February 14, 2017).

104 Augustine, *City of God* 15.1, trans. Bettenson, *City of God*, 596.

105 For the numerous references to the City of God as a community of pilgrims and the discussion of this characterization, see Van Oort, *Jerusalem and Babylon*, 131–142.

the world to come.[106]

Then, in Book 17, he looks at the pathway of the City of God in other historical narratives from the Old Testament. Finally, in roughly half of the last book of this sub-section, Book 18, he traces in a rather impressionistic fashion the course of the earthly city.[107] For information for this book, he is heavily dependent upon Eusebius of Caesarea's *Chronological Canons*, which synchronizes in tabular form the important dates of the various civilizations of the ancient world from the time of Abraham down to 325/326.[108] Augustine selects one great eastern power—the Assyrian empire, which he confuses with imperial Babylon—and one western power, Rome, to show the way the earthly city is dominated by the striving for power.[109] In the second half of Book 18, Augustine deals with the Old Testament prophecies that foretold the coming of Christ, pursues an excursus on the authority of the Septuagint, mentions the birth of Christ and ends the chapter with a discussion of persecution of the church.[110]

The final sub-section of the book, Books 19–22, focus on the eschatological ends of the two cities. The earthly city—which he describes with such terms as "the city of the Devil"[111] and an "irreligious city"[112]—will find its end in the everlasting punishment of hell.[113] The City of God, on the other hand, will find its true home in the unending glory of God's presence and the felicity of the beatific vision.[114] It is here that Augustine unfolds his mature understanding of the millennial period as the present reign of Christ in the church,[115] has a huge discussion

---

106 Van Oort, *Jerusalem and Babylon*, 138–139.
107 Augustine, *City of God* 18.1–26.
108 Andrew Carriker, "Eusebius of Caesarea" in Fitzgerald, ed., *Augustine through the Ages*, 339.
109 Augustine, *City of God* 18.2.
110 Augustine, *City of God* 18.27–54.
111 Augustine, *City of God* 20.11. See also *City of God* 21.1.
112 Augustine, *City of God* 18.51, trans. Bettenson, *City of God*, 834. For other descriptions of this city, see Van Oort, *Jerusalem and Babylon*, 130.
113 Especially see Augustine, *City of God* 19.28; 21.
114 Augustine, *City of God* 20.17; 22.30.
115 Augustine, *City of God* 20.7–13. On Augustine's thinking about the millennium, see Zakai and Mali, "Time, History and Eschatology," 411–416.

on the possibility of present-day miracles[116] and a lengthy exploration of the nature of the resurrection body.[117]

THE AUGUSTINIAN THEOLOGY OF HISTORY

What has Augustine achieved in this massive work? First of all, he has shown that the Christian life is a life of pilgrimage. The eternal world to come is the believer's true home. Those who are journeying toward this goal are part of a holy community that lives by faith, hope and self-denying love,[118] and that is thus marked by humility and obedience to God.[119] Nor can this community be fully identified with any earthly kingdom, for none of these kingdoms are eternal. Augustine thus refused to see the so-called Christian Roman empire as the eschatological goal of history, as Eusebius seems to have done. The fulfillment of God's purposes, therefore "does not stand or fall with the fate of Rome, or indeed with any earthly society."[120] It is not the future of the Roman empire, even if it is ruled by Christians, that defines the meaning of history. Rather, it is the future of the pilgrim City of God that reveals the true nature of the historical realm.[121]

In this age, though, the City of God often goes through tribulation and hardship. Augustine refuses to countenance the fundamentally pagan idea that religious commitment automatically issues in health, wealth and prosperity. Christians do go through suffering. But, Augustine skillfully argues, suffering is never simply that and nothing else.

---

116 Augustine, *City of God* 22.7–10.
117 Augustine, *City of God* 22.11–21, 25–28. It is noteworthy that in *City of God* 22.17, against those who would disparage women, Augustine affirms that women will indeed retain their gender in the resurrection.
118 Augustine, *City of God* 15.18, 21; 19.12, 20–23.
119 Augustine, *City of God* 19.23.
120 Markus, "Roman Empire in Early Christian Historiography," 347.
121 G.W. Trompf, *Early Christian Historiography: Narratives of Retributive Justice* (London: Continuum, 2000), 273. As Augustine views it, the greatness of the Christian Roman emperors has little to do with their political and military achievements, but everything to do with their piety. Theodosius I is offered as an example, when Augustine says of him, that he "was more glad to be a member" of the church "than to be ruler of the world" (Augustine, *City of God* 5.26, trans. Bettenson, *City of God*, 223). Also see the comments of Wright, "Augustine and the End of the World," 68.

Rather, it is how suffering is borne. It can be "either a curse or a blessing, since it hardens and degrades the godless, but purifies the devout and frees them" to seek God and find in him their true wealth and joy.¹²²

Thus, there is an ambiguity about history when it is viewed solely in the light of this age. Both good and bad befall those in the pilgrim City of God and those inhabitants of the earthly city. No clear distinction can be made between the two communities if one simply looks at the circumstances affecting them.¹²³ This obviously demands that we view history from its eschatological end-point. But this also means that Christians cannot stand aloof from the needs of their fellow-citizens, for afflictions come and they affect all in an earthly community. Christians therefore can and should be good citizens and involved in the life of the earthly communities surrounding them.¹²⁴ As Augustine said in a sermon preached at the time of the sack of Rome:

> I beg you, I beseech you, I exhort you all to be meek, to show compassion on those who are suffering, to take care of the weak; and at this time of many refugees from abroad, to be generous in your hospitality, generous in your good works. Let Christians do what Christ commands, and the blasphemies of the pagans can hurt none but themselves.¹²⁵

A CONCLUDING WORD FROM AUGUSTINE

A key place in Augustine's *City of God* is occupied by Book 19.¹²⁶ Here the North African theologian develops the argument that human existence at its best is ultimately social in nature and orientation.¹²⁷

---

122 Von Campenhausen, "Augustine and the Fall of Rome," 206.

123 Rowe, *St Augustine*, 116–117.

124 Augustine, *City of God* 19.26. Also see Harrison, *Augustine: Christian Truth and Fractured Humanity*, 212; Åke Bergvall, *Augustinian Perspectives in the Renaissance* (Uppsala: Uppsala University, 2001), 173–177.

125 Augustine, *Sermon* 81.9, trans. Hill, *Sermons*, III, 366.

126 For an excellent overview and analysis of Book 19, see Oliver O'Donovan, "Augustine's *City of God* XIX and Western Political Thought" in Donnelly, ed., *The City of God*, 135–149.

127 Harrison, *Augustine: Christian Truth and Fractured Humanity*, 206–207.

This social dimension of the City of God is readily seen in a comment that he made in a sermon on Psalm 85:

> When therefore death shall be swallowed up in victory, these things shall no longer be: there will be full and eternal peace. We shall be in a City, of which, brethren, when I speak I find it hard to leave off, especially when offences wax common. Who would not long for that City from which no friend goes out, into which no enemy enters, where is no tempter, no seditious person, no one dividing God's people, no one wearying the Church in the service of the devil; since the prince himself of all such is cast into eternal fire, and with him those who consent unto him, and who have no will to retire from him? There shall be peace made pure in the sons of God, all loving one another, seeing one another full of God, since God shall be all in all. We shall have God as our common object of vision, God as our common possession, God as our common peace. For whatever there is which he now gives unto us, he himself shall be unto us instead of his gifts; this will be full and perfect peace. This he speaks unto his people: this it was which he would hearken unto who said, "I will hearken what the Lord God will say unto me: for he shall speak peace unto his people, and to his saints, and unto those who turn their hearts unto him." Look, my brothers and sisters, do you wish that unto you should belong that peace which God utters? Turn your heart unto him: not unto me, or unto that one, or unto any man. For whatever man would turn unto himself the hearts of men, he falls with them. ...Our joy, our peace, our rest, the end of all troubles, is none but God: blessed are they that turn their hearts unto him.[128]

---

128 Augustine, *On the Psalms* 85.7

11

"The words of the Lord are always sweet"
Preaching God's Word in the ancient church[1]

> If I am weighed down by one great sorrow, it is sorrow over Christians, over my brothers, who enter the church in their bodies but leave their hearts outside. —AUGUSTINE[2]

Early Christianity was a "bookish" religion, which made it quite exceptional in its Græco-Roman context. Except for Judaism, in no other religion in the Roman empire, the main geographical context for the development of the Christian faith, were books so central.[3] At the

---

1 This chapter was given as a talk, "Scripture in the Early Church," on January 16, 2017, at the 2017 Winter Conference at Reformation Bible College, Sanford, Florida.
2 Augustine, *Sermon* 62.12.18.
3 Larry W. Hurtado, *Destroyer of the Gods: Early Christian Distinctiveness in the Roman World* (Waco: Baylor University Press, 2016), 105–141.

heart of the Christian faith were the Holy Scriptures, what we call the Old and New Testaments, which were faithfully copied and disseminated, read and preached. In addition, numerous other texts—letters and defenses of the Christian faith, hymns and theological treatises, exegetical commentaries and sermons—were also produced in such prodigious numbers that Larry Hurtado has rightly commented, "among the many other Roman-era religious groups, there is simply no analogy for this variety, vigor and volume in Christian literary output."[4]

Obviously, one key reason for this overall "bookishness" is the role that the Bible played in the expansion of the ancient church. In his classic study of early Christian evangelism, Michael Green has noted that from the days of Pentecost down to the third century—and we might add, well into the fourth century—

> we find the same story repeated time and again. Discussion with Christians, arguments with them, annoyance at them, could lead enquirers to read these "barbaric writings" [i.e. the Scriptures] for themselves. And once they began to read, the Scriptures exercised their own fascination and power. Many an interested enquirer...came to Christian belief through finding, as he read, that "the Word of God is living and active and sharper than any two-edged sword," and that "the sacred Scriptures are able to instruct you for salvation through faith in Jesus Christ."[5]

Through personal conversation, private reading and public proclamation, the Holy Scriptures played a key role in the witness of the ancient church in drawing sinful men and women to Christ. This chapter seeks to outline the specific role that public proclamation or preaching actually played in this advance of the church. In doing so, some of the details of the social context in which this preaching took place are first noted. The leading preacher of the pre-Constantinian period, Origen, is then briefly discussed. Finally, a number of examples from the golden age of patristic preaching, namely, the fourth century, are

---

4 Hurtado, *Destroyer of the Gods*, 119.

5 Michael Green, *Evangelism in the Early Church*, rev. ed. (Grand Rapids: Eerdmans, 2003), 352.

examined to help contemporary readers appreciate the value of the sermons from this period.

THE SOCIAL CONTEXT OF EARLY CHRISTIAN PREACHING

It is important to note that for the first 250 years of Christianity's existence, the main geographical context of the church, namely, the Roman empire, was one in which it was illegal to be a Christian. This meant that the church could not meet for worship, and preaching in public venues that were especially constructed for such a purpose was not permitted. Rather, Christians met in what we call house-churches, that is, the homes of middle-class or well-to-do believers, who provided space for congregational worship and proclamation. One sees the beginning of such house-churches in the New Testament. In Corinth, for instance, Paul did some of his teaching and preaching in the home of Titius Justus (Acts 18:7), though a brother named Gaius also had a church meeting at his house (Romans 16:23). At Laodicea, a sister named Nympha opened her home for the Laodicean church's worship and preaching (Colossians 4:15), while Philemon hosted the church in Colossae (Philemon 1–2). And in Rome, some believers regularly met in the home of Paul's co-workers Prisca and Aquila (Romans 16:3).[6]

The house church was actually vital to the early Christian mission, for most Christian teaching and preaching seems to have taken place in houses from the first century to the beginning of the fourth century.[7] Incidentally, the use of the home in this way was not atypical of intel-

---

6 For other examples, see Acts 16:14–15, 40 (the house of Lydia), Acts 20:6–12 (the apartment in Troas) and Romans 16:1–2, where the mention of Phoebe being a patron may imply a house church at Cenchreae. It is not without significance that the second-century apocryphal work, *The Acts of Paul and Thecla*, consistently depicts Paul teaching in someone's home. See, for instance, *The Acts of Paul and Thecla* 2:1–3 and 10.6, where Paul is said to have preached in the house of Onesiphorus.

7 Reidar Hvalvik, "In Word and Deed: The Expansion of the Church in the pre-Constantinian Era" in Jostein Ådna and Hans Kvalbein, ed., *The Mission of the Early Church to Jews and Gentiles* (Tübingen: Mohr Siebeck, 2000), 270. For more detail regarding the first century, see Roger W. Gehring, *House Church and Mission: The Importance of Household Structures in Early Christianity* (Peabody: Hendrickson Publishers, 2004), especially 119–228.

lectual life in Græco-Roman culture. As Stanley Kent Stowers has noted, "The private home was a centre of intellectual activity" and "seems to have been the most popular place for philosophers and sophists to hold their classes."[8]

All of this changed in the fourth century, with the toleration extended to Christianity by Constantine's Edict of Milan (February 313). Christians could now meet for worship in public, and thus began to build basilicas as the architectural context of their worship and preaching. Instead of congregations of 100–150 believers gathering for worship as in the pre-Constantinian era, some of these basilicas could accommodate up to 4,000 worshippers. There is little doubt that this shift would have entailed some substantial differences in the experience of preaching. For one, preachers now needed to have strong voices capable of projection in these large buildings. Augustine, for example, wrestled with making himself heard. On one occasion, for example, while preaching in Carthage, he urged his hearers, "as you can hear, my voice is weak; help me by not making any noise."[9]

Moreover, it bears remembering that while the extent of literacy in the ancient world is not easy to determine, it would not have been much higher than 10–12 per cent among Greek and Roman males. In the Jewish community, it would have been somewhat higher, but among women in both Gentile and Jewish circles, it would have been much lower, maybe as low as 2 per cent.[10] In part, among the Greeks and Romans, this had to do with a fact already noted: "Greco-Roman religions were not centered around a sacred text; there was no holy writ to be studied, copied, memorized, and transmitted."[11] With regard

---

8 Stanley Kent Stowers, "Social Status, Public Speaking and Private Teaching: The Circumstances of Paul's Preaching Activity," *Novum Testamentum* 26, no. 1 (January, 1984): 65–66.

9 Cited Daniel E. Doyle, "Introduction to Augustine's Preaching" in *Essential Sermons*, trans. Edmund Hill and ed. Boniface Ramsey (Hyde Park: New City Press, 2007), 20.

10 Hurtado, *Destroyer of the Gods*, 108; E. Randolph Richards, "Will the Real Author Please Stand Up? The Author in Greco-Roman Letter Writing" in Paul Copan and William Lane Craig, ed., *Come Let Us Reason: New Essays in Christian Apologetics* (Nashville: B&H, 2012), 123. For an excellent study of this subject, see especially W.V. Harris, *Ancient Literacy* (Cambridge: Harvard University Press, 1989).

11 Moyer V. Hubbard, *Christianity in the Greco-Roman World* (Grand Rapids: Baker, 2010), 69.

to corporate worship, this meant that believers would not be bringing their Bibles to church, as is common among contemporary Western evangelicals, since most early Christians were simply illiterate and would not have owned copies of the Scriptures. On the other hand, since Christianity is, above all things, a belief system in which books or sacred writings are utterly central, it was vital for Christian adherents to know the Scriptures. Though they could not read them and since it was essential for them to be known, memorization and the use of mnemonic techniques were widespread.

THE EARLIEST CHRISTIAN SERMONS

The earliest extant sermons outside of the New Testament are the texts known as *2 Clement* and *On the Passover* by Melito of Sardis (died c.190). The first of these sermons may well have been preached in Corinth in the mid-second century, though Rome and also Alexandria have been suggested as possible places where it was delivered.[12] It is largely a series of ethical admonitions to avoid hypocrisy. In *2 Clement*, the preacher urges his hearers:

> …let us not seek to be men-pleasers, nor let us desire to please only ourselves by our righteousness, but also those who are without, so that the Name may not be blasphemed on our account. For the Lord says, "My name is continually blasphemed among all the nations," and again, "Woe to him on whose account my name is blasphemed."[13] Why is it blasphemed? Because you do not do what I desire. For when the Gentiles (*ta ethnē*) hear from our mouths the oracles of God, they marvel at their beauty and greatness. But when they discover that our actions are not worthy of the words we speak, they turn from wonder to blasphemy, saying it is a myth and a delusion.[14]

---

12 Paul Parvis, "*2 Clement* and the Meaning of Christian Homily," *The Expository Times* 117 (2006): 268; Alan Kreider, *The Patient Ferment of the Early Church: The Improbable Rise of Christianity in the Roman Empire* (Grand Rapids: Baker Academic, 2016), 198 n.67.

13 The first quote is from Isaiah 52:5; the second quote is from an unknown source.

14 *2 Clement* 13.1–3, trans. Michael W. Holmes in his ed. and trans., *The Apostolic Fathers*, 3rd ed. (Grand Rapids: Baker Academic, 2007), 155, altered. For an excellent

Melito of Sardis, the author of the other homily, was remembered for his remarkable spirituality. We know of sixteen books by him, but his homily on the Passover and the way that it typifies the work of Christ on the cross is the only complete work to come down to us.[15]

Out of the thousands of sermons that must have been preached during the second century, these are the only two that are extant. Most of these sermons would have been extemporaneous, given to small house-churches, and unless someone took notes as they were being preached, they would not be remembered beyond the lives of their hearers.[16]

THE PREACHING OF ORIGEN

In the middle of the second century, though, there is suddenly a cornucopia of sermonic material, much of it from the hand of one man, Origen, nicknamed by some as Adamantius, "man of steel."[17] He was born into a wealthy Egyptian Christian home in Alexandria. His father, Leonidas, who was martyred in 202, recognized the talent of his eldest child and gave him a superb education in Greek literature as well as supervising his learning to recite the Bible by heart.[18] However, since the property of condemned Christians was confiscated by the imperial treasury, Origen and his family were now destitute. It was only through the generosity of a rich Christian widow that Origen was able to continue his studies. In 206, another bout of persecution led to all of the teachers in Alexandria going into hiding. Origen took their

---

overview of the homily, see Parvis, "*2 Clement* and the Meaning of Christian Homily," 265–270.

15 For this sermon, see *The Homily on the Passion by Melito Bishop of Sardis, and Some Fragments of the Apocryphal Ezekiel*, ed. Campbell Bonner (Philadelphia: University of Philadelphia Press, 1940); *Melito of Sardis: On Pascha and Fragments*, trans. Stuart G. Hall (Oxford: Clarendon Press, 1979).

16 Kreider, *Patient Ferment*, 200; Hildegund Müller, "Preacher: Augustine and His Congregation" in Mark Vessey with Shelley Reid, ed., *A Companion to Augustine* (Oxford: Wiley Blackwell, 2012), 299.

17 Jerome, *On Illustrious Men* 54, in *Saint Jerome: On Illustrious Men*, trans. Thomas P. Halton (Washington: The Catholic University of America Press, 1999), 77.

18 Timothy D. Barnes, *Constantine and Eusebius* (Cambridge: Harvard University Press, 1982), 82.

place, we are told, giving instruction to new converts and other Christians until neighbours denounced him and he was nearly arrested at his home. Origen escaped and continued to teach in house churches. At least seven of his pupils died as martyrs.[19]

After the cessation of this persecution, and though Origen was but a young man, he was appointed the head of a catechetichal school in Alexandria. Soon his fame as a Bible scholar and preacher of the Word began to spread throughout Egypt and the eastern Mediterranean. A Christian by the name Ambrose, who had been converted from the heresy of Gnosticism through the preaching and teaching of Origen, became Origen's patron and benefactor. Ambrose paid for a veritable team of shorthand writers and copyists—around twenty or so![20]—to take down Origen's dictation and reproduce his tracts, sermons, and commentaries in multiple copies.[21]

Origen appears to have had prodigious energy, doing work in every major field of Christian thought, including writing expository sermons on nearly all of the books of the Bible, though we only possess around 400 of his sermons.[22] There are 16 on Genesis, 13 on Exodus, 16 on Leviticus, 28 on Numbers, 13 on Deuteronomy, 26 on Joshua, 9 on Judges, 4 on 1 Kings, 32 on Isaiah, 45 on Jeremiah, 14 on Ezekiel, 120 on the Psalms, 22 on Job, 7 on Proverbs, 8 on Ecclesiastes and 2 on the Song of Songs. In the New Testament, the only sermons extant are 39 that he preached on the Gospel of Luke.[23] The fifth-century church historian Socrates noted that Origen normally preached on Wednesdays and Fridays, though we know that he preached his sermons on Luke on Sundays.[24] Given that his sermons would have been delivered

---

19 Barnes, *Constantine and Eusebius*, 83.

20 Hermann J. Vogt, "Origen of Alexandria (185–253)" in Charles Kannengiesser, *Handbook of Patristic Exegesis: The Bible in Ancient Christianity* (Leiden: Brill, 2004), I, 539.

21 Barnes, *Constantine and Eusebius*, 83–84.

22 R.P. Lawson, "Introduction" to his trans. and annotated, *Origen: The Song of Songs: Commentary and Homilies*, Ancient Christian Writers, No.26 (New York: Newman Press, 1956), 16.

23 Joseph T. Lienhard, "Origen and the Crisis of the Old Testament in the Early Church," *Pro Ecclesia* 9, no.3 (2000): 362–363.

24 Socrates, *Church History* 5.22; Lawson, "Introduction," 16.

in house-churches, it is not surprising that his sermons have a conversational tone about them. They have little rhetorical adornment and generally have a fairly simple structure: after an introduction, a passage of Scripture is exegeted, application is made followed by a final exhortation.[25]

His sermonic corpus on the Old Testament is of great significance, for in the third century the church was still battling the Gnostics, who denied the inspiration of the Old Testament. As Joseph T. Lienhard has argued, Origen's Old Testasment sermons and commentaries helped ensure that the Old Testament would be a key part of the Christian Bible.[26] Origen's preaching is also important as he stands at the fountainhead of that exegetical tradition that views the Song of Songs as entailing more than a depiction of human love and romance, a tradition that stretches from Origen down to the Victorian preacher C.H. Spurgeon (1834–1892). Thus, in the first of his two extant sermons on this portion of the wisdom books, which Origen would have preached probably in the early 240s,[27] the Alexandrian preacher tells his hearers that by "the Bridegroom understand Christ, and by the Bride the Church without spot or wrinkle."[28] We will see the patristic flowering of this way of reading the Song of Songs in the preaching of Gregory of Nyssa.

One final point before we leave Origen. We have an eyewitness account of the impact of his preaching from Gregory Thaumaturgus. Gregory had come to Beirut from his native Pontus around 231, intending to become a lawyer. But he met Origen in Caesarea and became one of his students there—Origen having moved to that city in Palestine the previous year in 230. He studied with Origen for seven years, at the close of which he gave a speech of appreciation of his teacher. In the speech, he articulated why Origen's preaching had such an impact on him:

---

25 Thomas K. Carroll, *Preaching the Word*, Message of the Fathers of the Church, Vol. 11 (Wilmington: Michael Glazier, 1984), 61.
26 Lienhard, "Origen and the Crisis of the Old Testament," 355ff.
27 Lawson, "Introduction," 17.
28 *Homily 1 on the Song of Songs*.1, trans. Lawson, *Origen: The Song of Songs*, 267.

Of all men now living, I have never known or heard of one who had meditated as he had on the pure and luminous words [of the Bible] and had become so expert at fathoming their meaning and teaching them to others. I do not think he could have done that unless he had had the Spirit of God in him, for the same grace is needed for understanding the prophecies as for making them. No one can understand the prophets unless the Spirit who inspired the prophets himself give him understanding of his word.[29]

AUGUSTINE THE PREACHER

The fourth-century church found herself in a very different social setting. Christianity was now a legal religion, and spacious church buildings were now erected to house Christian congregations. There is no way justice can be done to this entire era of preaching in the rest of this chapter, therefore focus is placed on two traditions of preaching—that of Latin North Africa, represented by Augustine, and that of Greek Cappadocia, represented by three men, Asterius of Amasea (c.350–c.410), Basil of Caesarea and Basil's younger brother, Gregory of Nyssa.

I have sketched out Augustine's life in chapter 10, so I will not repeat that here. As you will remember, Augustine's primary vocation was pastor of the church in Hippo. Of the estimated 8,000 sermons Augustine preached, some 559 are extant,[30] and thirty of these were only recently discovered in 1990.

In 1990, the city library in Mainz published a catalogue of its manuscripts. One codex in particular, which contained sermons by Augustine, caught the eye of the French patristic scholar François Dolbeau.

---

29 Gregory Thaumaturgus, *Panegyric Addressed to Origen* 15 (PG10.1093), trans. Carroll, *Preaching the Word*, 62.

30 Stanley P. Rosenberg, "Interpreting Atonement in Augustine's Preaching" in Charles E. Hill and Frank A. James III, ed., *The Glory of the Atonement: Biblical, Historical & Practical Perspectives: Essays in Honor of Roger Nicole* (Downers Grove: InterVarsity Press, 2004), 227; Hubertus R. Drobner, "Studying Augustine: An overview of recent research" in Robert Dodaro and George Lawless, ed., *Augustine and His Critics: Essays in Honour of Gerald Bonner* (London: Routledge, 2000), 22–23; Doyle, "Introduction to Augustine's Preaching," 13. See Éric Rebillard, "Sermones" in Fitzgerald, ed., *Augustine through the Ages*, 774–789 for a listing of most of the extant sermons.

Upon investigation, Dolbeau found that the codex was a late fifteenth-century manuscript that contained 62 homilies. Of this number, 9 turned out to be fuller versions of homilies previously known, while 21 were completely unknown, or if known, known only through fragments cited by early mediæval commentators.[31] They do not contain, as Henry Chadwick noted in an article on the sermons, the sort of information that revolutionizes aspects of our understanding of Augustine's life. But they contain two *emphases* that dominated Augustine's thinking: first, "true religion is inward and a matter of the heart—outward acts are secondary and a means to a spiritual end"; and second, "true faith will issue in a reformed moral life."[32]

Both of these emphases can be found in sermons where Augustine dealt with the fact that there were far too many in the church who were really pagan at heart. Over the course of the fourth century, things developed to the point that, by the 380s, Christianity was the only legal religion in the Roman empire. One of the results of this was that the church became flooded with men and women whose Christianity was all too frequently mixed up with pagan practices. Augustine stood against this, powerfully declaring that the Christian faith issued in a life in harmony with that faith.

On one occasion in 399, for instance, some Christians in Carthage had participated in a civil celebration in honour of "the genius of Carthage." Asked to preach by the church there, Augustine was forthright in his condemnation of mixing Christianity and Roman paganism:

> If I am weighed down by one great sorrow, it is sorrow over Christians, over my brothers, who enter the church in their bodies but leave their hearts outside....All must come within the church, body and soul; why should the body, which is seen by men, be within, while that which is seen by God is left outside? ...We certainly do preach against idols: it is from the heart we want to uproot them.[33]

---

31 Henry Chadwick, "New Sermons of St Augustine," *Journal of Theological Studies* 47 (1996): 69–71.

32 Chadwick, "New Sermons of St Augustine," 80–81.

33 Augustine, *Sermon* 62.12.18, trans. R.A. Markus, *The End of Ancient Christianity* (Cambridge: Cambridge University Press, 1990), 113.

Here is a call for total devotion, body and soul, and an attack on the centre of idolatry, the human heart. Some of the professing Christians appeared to have argued that the festival was harmless, that the genius of Carthage was no god and therefore the banquet was not idolatry. But, Augustine pleaded with them:

> [You say] "we know he is no god—would that they [i.e. the pagans] knew it too; but for the sake of the infirm who do not know this, you must not trouble their consciences"....How do you think you can avoid people being taken in by idols whom they assume to have been honoured by Christians? You may say "God knows my heart;" alright, but your brother does not know it. If you are infirm, beware of falling into more serious illness; if you are healthy, beware of causing your brother to fall ill.

Participation would not only offend weak Christian consciences, but also prevent pagans being confronted with Christian truth.

> We want to bring in the remaining pagans; you are rocks in their path. They will say in their heart: why should we leave the gods whom Christians worship along with us.

What did Augustine see himself doing in his sermons? Well, first, as in the sermon just examined, Augustine believed that an important function of his preaching was to inform his hearers of the Christian worldview and doctrine, and how it was to be lived. As David Dunn-Wilson notes: "To survey the doctrine set out in the sermons would be, in effect, to examine Augustinian theology in its entirety."[34] Augustine preached a good number of sermons against various heretical positions, an indicator that he saw the sermon as a vehicle for substantial doctrinal teaching.[35] In fact, in one of his letters he likened churches to "sacred lecture halls for the people."[36]

---

[34] David Dunn-Wilson, *A Mirror for the Church: Preaching in the First Five Centuries* (Grand Rapids: Eerdmans, 2005), 95.

[35] Rosenberg, "Interpreting Atonement in Augustine's Preaching" in Hill and James III, ed., *Glory of the Atonement*, 229.

[36] Augustine, *Letter* 91.3, cited Rosenberg, "Interpreting Atonement in Augustine's

Second, Augustine was well aware that a preacher must not only teach (*docere*) but also delight (*delectare*), for he knew by personal experience that the engagement of the affections was central to true faith.[37] Augustine was well fitted for such a role because of his superb literary training. His preaching appealed to intellectuals because of his vast knowledge of Roman history and classical literature.[38] But it is noteworthy that he also crafted his sermons for those who were not learned. He used words that they could understand and asked them sometimes in the middle of the sermon if he had "expounded the text too hastily."[39]

A quick perusal of his sermons reveals Augustine to be a master of similes: "hope" is like an egg, the Scriptures are "the hem of Christ's garment," human life is likened to a leaky ship, and human beings are "frailer than glass." Augustine drew his imagery from diverse sources: the law-courts, farms, doctor's surgeries, orchards and athletic contests.[40] In one of the newly-discovered sermons, preached in 397 on loving God, Augustine drew upon chariot-racing to illustrate what love of God should be like:

> You have a favorite charioteer; you urge all the people you love to watch him with you, to love him with you, to cheer him on with you, to go crazy about him with you. If they don't love him, you revile them, you call them idiots.... The doting fans of a charioteer are totally absorbed in the spectacle; they don't exist except in the fellow they are gazing at. Such a fan is utterly unaware of himself, has no idea where he is. Accordingly, someone less interested in that sport who is standing next to him and sees him so excited will say, "He's miles away." You too, if possible, be miles away from yourself when you are in God.[41]

Preaching" in Hill and James III, ed., *Glory of the Atonement*, 232.
37 Dunn-Wilson, *A Mirror for the Church*, 93.
38 Dunn-Wilson, *A Mirror for the Church*, 93.
39 Dunn-Wilson, *A Mirror for the Church*, 93.
40 Dunn-Wilson, *A Mirror for the Church*, 94.
41 Augustine, *Sermons* 90A.8, 9, trans. Edmund Hill, *The Works of Saint Augustine: A Translation for the 21st Century*, Part III, Vol. 11: Newly Discovered Sermons (Hyde Park: New City Press, 1997), 81, 82.

Augustine was also transparent in his preaching, apologizing when he felt he had not done justice to a text and promising to return to it later. And unlike classical speakers who rarely regarded brevity as a virtue, Augustine never forgot that the congregation had to stand during the preaching, and so he would apologize if his sermon was too long.[42]

At the heart of Augustine's preaching was the interpretation of Scripture, a task that he loved, for "the words of the Lord," he said, "are always sweet."[43] There is little doubt that his constant interaction with the Scriptures nourished his thought as no other words did.[44] This love for Scripture was rooted in the conviction that in the Bible God speaks to his people. As he said on one occasion, "Let us treat scripture like scripture, like God speaking."[45] And on another: "The divine scriptures cannot lie, the mouth of Truth cannot utter a lie."[46] He knew much of the Scriptures by heart, and quoted them from memory when he was preaching. In fact, the African bishop was not only concerned that people come to hear the Word proclaimed but, if they could, that they also read it privately. As he stated in one of his sermons: "Copies of the Lord's gospels are on sale all the time....Buy one for yourself, and just you read it when you've got the time; or rather, make sure you get the time."[47] As Chadwick comments, this concern "to encourage private Bible study" clearly "presupposes a degree of literacy in his congregation."[48]

THREE CAPPADOCIAN PREACHERS

Thomas Carroll has noted that the Greek-speaking church in the fourth century reached its apex in preaching in the province of Cappadocia (now central Turkey). This is quite remarkable, in view of the fact that

---

42 Dunn-Wilson, *A Mirror for the Church*, 93–94; Müller, "Preacher: Augustine and His Congregation," 302.
43 Augustine, *Sermon* 75.1, on 1 John 5:2, cited Dunn-Wilson, *A Mirror for the Church*, 94.
44 Bright, "Augustine" in Greenman and Larsen, ed., *Reading Romans*, 80.
45 Augustine, *Sermon* 162C.15, trans. Hill, *Works of Saint Augustine*, III/11: 176.
46 Augustine, *Sermon* 110A.3, trans. Hill, *Works of Saint Augustine*, III/11: 96.
47 Augustine, *Sermon* 114B.14, trans. Hill, *Works of Saint Augustine*, III/11: 113. See also *Sermon* 198.20.
48 Chadwick, "New Sermons of St Augustine," 82.

Cappadocia was renowned for its boorishness. According to one epigram, the average Cappadocian was as little likely to speak Greek well as a tortoise might be taught to fly.[49] There were three great Cappadocian preachers and theologians—Basil of Ceasarea, his close friend Gregory of Nazianzus and Basil's younger brother Gregory of Nyssa. We will consider the preaching of Basil and his brother Gregory. But first, let us look at a sermon of another Cappadocian, Asterius of Amasea.

Born in Cappadocia around the same time as Augustine, the 350s, Asterius became bishop of Amasea, the provincial capital of Pontus on the shore of the Black Sea, toward the end of the fourth century. At a certain point in his education, Asterius had carefully studied the speeches of Demosthenes (384–322 B.C.), one of the great orators of classical Greece. This helped Asterius develop as a powerful preacher in his own right. The twenty or so sermons that have come down to us "show rare rhetorical skill, a vivid and disciplined imagination, great power of expression, and, above all, intense moral conviction."[50] One of them is a very fine expository sermon on the question asked our Lord by the Pharisees in Matthew 19:3: "Is it lawful for a man to divorce his wife on any grounds?" (CSB).

Asterius begins by noting that in this Scripture text, "the Spirit lays before us" a thing of beauty, for implicitly it speaks of the marriage bond that God established in the beginning:

> In marriage...both soul and body are united, so that character is mingled with character, and flesh with flesh. How, then, are you going to sever the bond of marriage without suffering? How can you withdraw from this union easily and without pain, after taking your sister and wife not as a servant of a few days, but as a partner for life, a sister by reason of her formation and creation, for you were both made of the same element of earth and of the same substance, and wife because of the conjugal union, because

---

49 Anthony Meredith, *Gregory of Nyssa* (London: Routledge, 1999), 11.

50 Galusha Anderson and Edgar Johnson Goodspeed, "Introduction" to their trans. of Asterius, *Ancient Sermons for Modern Times* (New York: The Pilgrim Press, 1904), 7. Quotations from Asterius' sermon on divorce are taken from this edition.

of the law of marriage? ...I refer back to the utterance of Adam: "This is flesh of my flesh and bone of my bones, This shall be called my wife."[51] Not without reason is this utterance preserved in writing; for, uttered by the first man, it is the common covenant of men, made with the whole class of women, who are joined by law to their husbands.[52]

Asterius then describes what marriage is from the vantage-point of the wife:

[S]he is a companion [to her husband], a helper, a partner with whom to pass your life, and to bring children into the world, an aid in sickness, a comfort in distress, the guardian of the hearth, the custodian of the household goods, having the same sorrows, the same joys, sharing with you your wealth, if wealth be yours, or mitigating hard poverty, resourcefully and sturdily bearing up against its grievous consequences, and because of her marriage with you, enduring the toilsome rearing of children. And if perchance a change of affairs overtakes the husband, and he being overwhelmed sinks into obscurity, and those who have been considered friends, measuring their friendship by the duration of his prosperity, desert him in his adversity, while the servants run away from both master and misfortunes. Only the wife is left, a partner of his distress, serving her husband amid manifold evils. She wipes away his tears, and heals his stripes if he be smitten. She follows him when he is led to prison; and if permitted to enter with him, she cheerfully shares his confinement.[53]

Having set forth something of the beauty of marriage, Asterius then looks at the general reasons given by men for divorce:

---

51 See Genesis 2:23.
52 Asterius, *On Divorce* in Asterius, *Ancient Sermons for Modern Times*, trans. Anderson and Goodspeed, 134, 139–140, altered.
53 Asterius, *On Divorce* in Asterius, *Ancient Sermons for Modern Times*, trans. Anderson and Goodspeed, 141–142, altered.

> Now what can the man seeking divorce say to this? And what sort of specious defense of his own fickleness can he offer? "My wife's disposition," he says, "is mean and hateful, and her tongue is violent, and her tastes are not domestic, and her house is ill-managed." So be it. Granted. I am so far persuaded, and accept it, like the judges who are not very critical in hearing, but are readily carried away by the invectives of advocates. But tell me, when you first married her, did you not know that you were being joined to a human being? And does anybody fail to see that to a human being sin attaches? For perfection is of God alone. And do you yourself, then, never sin? Do you not cause your wife pain by your conduct? Are you free from all fault?[54]

Are there no just reasons for divorce? Asterius does admit that adultery is the only one. Thus, if the man can prove that his wife has committed adultery, or vice versa, Asterius says:

> I will at once become the advocate of the injured man, and directing my discourse against the adulteress, will take my stand beside the husband, no longer his foe, but his valiant ally, commending him who flees the treacherous woman, and severs the tie which bound him to an asp and a viper. For the Creator of all is the first to absolve this man as justly indignant, and right in driving the plague from his house and hearth. For marriage exists for these two things, love and offspring, neither of which is compatible with adultery. For there is no love when affection turns toward another; and honor in bringing children into the world is destroyed, when their parentage is made doubtful.[55]

But Asterius seeks to conclude on a positive note and thus exhorts his hearers:

---

54 Asterius, *On Divorce* in Asterius, *Ancient Sermons for Modern Times*, trans. Anderson and Goodspeed, 145–146.

55 Asterius, *On Divorce* in Asterius, *Ancient Sermons for Modern Times*, trans. Anderson and Goodspeed, 153–154.

But pray let both parties to the marriage contract practise self-control—the unbroken bond of wedlock. For where the honor of marriage is maintained, there is, of necessity, affection and peace, with no vulgar and unlawful desire to excite the soul, and expel legitimate and righteous love.[56]

Turning to Basil of Caesarea, we find that a good number of his sermons are also focused on issues relating to Christian virtue and moral formation.[57] (I sketched out Basil's life in chapter 7.) In one of his sermons, known as *Homily 20*, preached early in his ministry—possibly around the year 364—he went through what may be considered a classic study of the grace of humility. Basil begins by explaining just how necessary it is for men and women to strive to be humble:

> Would that man had abided in the glory which he possessed with God—he would have genuine instead of fictitious dignity. For he would be ennobled by the power of God, illumined with divine wisdom, and made joyful in the possession of eternal life and its blessings. But, because he ceased to desire divine glory in expectation of a better prize, and strove for the unattainable, he lost the good which it was in his power to possess. The surest salvation for him, the remedy of his ills, and the means of restoration to his original state is in practicing humility and not pretending that he may lay claim to any glory through his own efforts but seeking it from God.[58]

The way of salvation, Basil assures his hearers then and his readers now, is a path of humility. Lest one think that Basil is here asserting some kind of works-righteousness, look at the final sentence. There Basil emphasizes that possessing the hope of eternal glory is the gift of God, given only to those who humble themselves to accept it. It cannot be achieved by human effort.

---

56 Asterius, *On Divorce* in Asterius, *Ancient Sermons for Modern Times*, trans. Anderson and Goodspeed, 153–154.

57 For the life of Basil, see especially Philip Rousseau, *Basil of Caesarea* (Berkeley: University of California Press, 1994).

58 Basil, *Homily 20*, trans. Wagner, *Ascetical Works*, 475.

Having outlined the necessity of humility, the question immediately arises as to the nature of this virtue. What does it look like? Basil's answer to this question is not contained in one single passage of this homily, but is scattered throughout the sermon. First of all, foundational to humility is the recognition by men and women that they are entirely destitute of all true righteousness and holiness. To obtain these, one must cast oneself upon God's mercy and so confess that one is made right with God—i.e. justified—by Christ alone.[59] In other words, becoming a Christian is intrinsically a humbling experience. What makes human beings truly great—what brings them glory, something that the ancients passionately sought—is to look away from themselves to God. In Basil's words:

> But what is true glory and what makes a man great? "In this," says the Prophet, "let him that glories, glory that he understands and knows that I am the Lord."[60] This constitutes the highest dignity of man, this is his glory and greatness: truly to know what is great and to cleave to it, and to seek after glory from the Lord of glory. The Apostle tells us: "He that glories may glory in the Lord," saying: "Christ was made for us wisdom of God, righteousness and sanctification and redemption; that, as it is written: he that glories may glory in the Lord."[61] Now, this is the perfect and consummate glory in God: not to exult in one's own righteousness, but, recognizing oneself as lacking true righteousness, to be justified by faith in Christ alone.[62]

This passage clearly reveals Basil's fundamental opposition to any idea that we can save ourselves by our own good works, something enunciated within thirty years of Basil's death by Pelagius (fl.400–420).[63] Thus, it is not surprising that humility leads the believer to recognize

---

59 David Amand, *L'Ascèse monastique de saint Basile* (Maredsous: Editions Maredsous, 1948), 313.
60 Jeremiah 9:24.
61 1 Corinthians 1:30–31.
62 Basil, *Homily 20*, trans. Wagner, *Ascetical Works*, 478–479, altered.
63 Amand, *L'Ascèse monastique*, 313 n.230.

that he or she has nothing at all about which to boast. Our knowledge of God, our good deeds and our possessions are all entirely rooted in the grace, goodness and mercy of God.

> Why...do you glory in your goods as if they were your own instead of giving thanks to the Giver for His gifts? "For what do you have that you have not received? And if you received it, why do you glory as if you had not received it?" [1 Corinthians 4:7]. You have not known God by reason of your righteousness, but God has known you by reason of his goodness. "After that you have known God," says the Apostle, "or rather are known by God." You did not apprehend Christ because of your virtue, but Christ apprehended you by his coming.[64]

Basil can therefore urge all of his hearers, both past and present, to "strive for glory with God, for his is a glorious recompense." This striving for glory with God is, in Basil's perspective, the most important practical demonstration of humility.

Finally, let's consider one text from Gregory of Nyssa, who was regarded in his day as one of the most eminent preachers in the Greek-speaking churches. Gregory's preaching at the Council of Constantinople, for instance, led to a friendship with the Roman emperor Theodosius I, who had called the council to resolve the Arian controversy, in particular the debate about the deity of the Holy Spirit.[65] There is every indication that Gregory of Nyssa played a significant role in drafting the third article of the Niceno-Constantinopolitan Creed that affirmed the Spirit's deity, for, after the council, Theodosius declared him to be one of the guarantors of Trinitarian orthodoxy. Communion, for Gregory, was essential to being regarded as orthodox.[66] And when the emperor's wife, Aelia Flavia Flaccilla (356–386) and their daughter Aelia Pulcheria (385–386) both died in 386, Gregory was asked to preach their funeral sermons.

---

64 Basil, *Homily* 20, trans. Wagner, *Ascetical Works*, 480, altered.
65 Gregory of Nyssa was asked to preach the funeral sermon for Meletius of Antioch, the first president of the council, who died during its proceedings. See also the end of chapter 8, for more on Gregory of Nyssa.
66 *Theodosian Code* 16.1.3.

About five or six years later, a young wealthy Christian widow of the imperial court by the name of Olympias (c.360/365–408) asked Gregory for an interpretation of the Song of Songs. He sent her a series of sermons he had preached to his congregation at Nyssa during a Lenten period in the early 390s.[67] They followed Origen's basic interpretative stance that this portion of Scripture was primarily about the love of Christ for his people, and vice versa. Or as Gregory puts it: "the Song of Songs...lies before us, for our guidance in all matters having to do with philosophy and the knowledge of God."[68]

Take, for example, Gregory of Nyssa's explanation of the statement of the bride in Song of Songs 1:5, "I am dark and beautiful." His investigation of this phrase convinced him that it speaks of "the Bridegroom's measureless love of humanity—the Bridegroom who, in his love, clothes his Beloved with beauty." Gregory continues to explain what the Bride is essentially saying in her statement:

> Do not marvel that Righteousness has loved me. Marvel rather that when I was dark with sin and at home in the dark because of my deeds, he by his love made me beautiful, exchanging his own beauty for my ugliness. For having transferred to himself the filth of my sins, he shared his own purity with me and made me a participant in his own beauty—he who first made something totally desirable out of one who had been repulsive.[69]

Our theological and cultural climate tends to be dismissive of this interpretative approach to the Song of Songs, but, in doing so, are we not the poorer? And have we not lost some of this homiletical tradition's riches, such as this tremendous statement of what my Calvinistic Baptist forebears would call justification by the imputed righteousness of Christ?

---

67 Richard A. Norris, "Introduction: Gregory of Nyssa and his Fifteen Homilies on the Song of Songs" in his translation of Gregory of Nyssa, *Homilies on the Song of Songs*, Writings from the Greco-Roman World, No.13 (Atlanta: Society of Biblical Literature, 2012), xx–xxiii.
68 Gregory of Nyssa, *Homily 2*, trans. Norris, *Homilies on the Song of Songs*, 47, 49.
69 Gregory of Nyssa, *Homily 2*, trans. Norris, *Homilies on the Song of Songs*, 51.

12

"O blessed gatekeeper of heaven"[1]
Petrine texts, bishops and the papacy[2]

> The saying is trustworthy: If anyone aspires to the office of overseer, he desires a noble task.
> —1 TIMOTHY 3:1

Among the texts at the very fountainhead of theological reflection regarding the governance of the church is the apostle Paul's (died c.67) maxim that "whoever aspires to the office of an overseer/bishop (ἐπίσκοπον), desires a beneficial task."[3] When the monastic leader

---

1 The quote is taken from Hilary of Poitiers, *Commentary on Matthew* 16.7 (*Patrologia Latina* 9.1010A).

2 This chapter originally appeared in Benjamin L. Merkle and Thomas R. Schreiner, ed., *Shepherding God's Flock: Biblical Leadership in the New Testament and Beyond* (Grand Rapids: Kregel, 2014), 119–139. Used with permission.

3 1 Timothy 3:1.

John Cassian (c.360–c.435) reflected on the nature of the Christian life three-and-a-half centuries later, however, his opinion about bishops could not have been more different than Paul's: "a monk"—that is, one striving to live a holy life for the benefit of other believers—"must by all means flee from women and bishops"![4] A substantial monograph would be needed to detail the way the church moved from Paul's positive endorsement of the desire to be an overseer to the negative perspective of Cassian about episcopal leadership—such leaders are a danger to the monk's soul, and presumably their office endangers their own souls as well. This chapter has a much more modest goal: it seeks to elucidate the development of ecclesial oversight in the western church, particularly as it relates to the papacy, a development that, for some, more than justifies Cassian's pessimism. First, though, we look at the emergence of monepiscopacy—necessary soil for the papal plant.

"MONARCHY IS SUPERIOR": THE RISE OF MONEPISCOPACY

According to the witness of the New Testament, along with the authority of the apostolic band, there are two distinct groups of residential ministers in the churches of that time: the bishops or overseers (*episkopoi*), who are described elsewhere in the New Testament as elders (*presbyteroi*), and the deacons (*diakonoi*).[5] While this two-tier model of ministry remained a live option throughout the second century, a shift toward three offices—a bishop, elders and deacons—appeared immediately after the New Testament era in the church at Antioch-on-the-Orontes (Syrian Antioch). In his correspondence, Ignatius, bishop of the congregation in what was then the third largest city in the Roman world, seems to have assumed a three-tier model to be

---

4   John Cassian, *The Institutes* 11.18, trans. Boniface Ramsey, *John Cassian: The Institutes*, Ancient Christian Writers, No.58 (New York: Newman Press, 2000), 247.

5   See Philippians 1:1; 1 Timothy 3:1–13. For the identification of the *episkopos* and *presbyteros*, see Acts 20:17 and 28, as well as Titus 1:5–9. See also *Didache* 15 that seems to equate bishops and elders since it mentions only "bishops and deacons." As Philip Schaff noted: the "undeniable identity of presbyters and bishops in the New Testament" is a fact "conceded even by the best interpreters among the church fathers, by Jerome, Chrysostom, and Theodoret" [Philip Schaff, *History of the Christian Church* (New York: Charles Scribner's Sons, 1889), II, 139].

normative,[6] though it is noteworthy that in his letter to the church at Rome, he makes no mention of a bishop.[7] Ignatius' view of the ministry turned out to be the wave of the future, for by the close of the second century it had been all but universally embraced by the church within the Roman *imperium*. It also bears noting, as Philip Schaff once wisely observed, "this primitive catholic Episcopal system must by no means be confounded with the later hierarchy" of bishops in the Middle Ages.[8]

Recognizing that any explanation for the development of the episcopate during the second and third centuries must needs be complex,[9]

---

6   See, for example, Ignatius, *Letter to Polycarp* 6.1 and Ignatius, *Letter to the Smyrnaeans* 8.1.

7   John Knox, "The Ministry in the Primitive Church" in H. Richard Niebuhr and Daniel D. Williams, ed., *The Ministry in Historical Perspectives* (New York: Harper & Brothers, 1956), 23.

8   Schaff, *History of the Christian Church*, I, 144. See also Kenneth A. Strand, "The Rise of the Monarchical Episcopate," *Andrews University Seminary Studies* 4 (1966): 70–71.

9   For a listing of these various factors, see Schaff, *History of the Christian Church*, I, 132–154; Adolf von Harnack, *The Mission and Expansion of Christianity in the First Three Centuries*, trans. and ed. James Moffatt, 1908 ed. (reprint, New York: Harper & Brothers, 1962), 439–486; John Knox, "Ministry in the Primitive Church," 24–25; Strand, "Rise of the Monarchical Episcopate"; Henry Chadwick, *The Early Church*, rev. ed. (London: Penguin Books, 1993), 49.

Seeking to understand this development is fraught not only with issues that relate to the history of the ancient church, but that also have to do with the interpretative horizon of the one seeking to trace this historical phenomenon. Roman Catholic, Eastern Orthodox and Anglo-Catholic authors have generally argued that the single-bishop model arose because it was put in place by the apostles. Protestant scholars, on the other hand, have usually maintained that the episcopacy emerged out of an original Presbyterian or even Congregational model. And in more recent days—roughly paralleling the rise of the Pentecostal and Charismatic movements in the late nineteenth and twentieth centuries—there have been those who have argued for an earlier charismatic and more "fluid" situation with regard to ministry that gave way to more formal structures as the initial fervor of the apostolic era waned. See Strand, "Rise of the Monarchical Episcopate," 67–68. To cite one example of authorial convictions shaping an argument's direction, see Everett Ferguson on the congregationalism of the apostolic era: "The 'Congregationalism' of the Early Church" in D.H. Williams, ed., *The Free Church and the Early Church: Bridging the Historical and Theological Divide* (Grand Rapids: Eerdmans, 2002), 129–140.

at least six key factors should be identified. First, in the midst of their life-and-death struggles with the heresy of Gnosticism and persecution from the Roman state, churches learned that it was profoundly helpful to have one main preaching elder, the bishop, as the focal point of church unity.[10] Then, by the time of Cyprian, correspondence between one church and another was being handled by the bishop in his own name, which was a shift from the previous century when such correspondence was directly between churches, with the bishop, if involved, acting as a secretary.[11] Furthermore, when an individual was ordained, it was not often possible for every presbyter from neighbouring churches to attend. It came to be considered sufficient if simply the bishops from the other churches were present. There is also evidence that the presidency of the Lord's Supper facilitated the acceptance of the pre-eminence of one elder, namely, the one who came to be called the bishop.[12] The complexity of organization in some of the urban churches—for example, at Rome, Alexandria and Antioch—also pushed these churches in the direction of monepiscopacy. For instance, Cornelius mentions in a letter during his episcopate at Rome—he was bishop from 251–253—that the church in the imperial capital had "46 presbyters, 7 deacons, 7 sub-deacons, 42 acolytes, [and] 52 exorcists, readers and door-keepers."[13] Finally, there was the ideological ambience of a larger culture that made anything but hierarchical structures appear less than credible. As Eusebius of Caesarea commented in the sermon he gave at the celebration of Constantine's thirtieth anniversary as emperor:

---

10 Henry Chadwick, "The Role of the Christian Bishop in Ancient Society" in his *Heresy and Orthodoxy in the Early Church* (Aldershot: Variorum, 1991), no. III: 3.

11 Ferguson, "'Congregationalism' of the Early Church," 132–134. See, for example, *The Shepherd of Hermas*, Vision 2.4.3, where an individual named Clement (Is this Clement of Rome?) seems to serve the churches in Rome as a secretary. See also Allen Brent, "Was Hippolytus a Schismatic?" *Vigiliae Christianae* 49 (1995): 218–219.

12 George H. Williams, "The Ministry of the Ante-Nicene Church (c.125–325)" in Niebuhr and Williams, ed., *Ministry in Historical Perspectives*, 27–28.

13 Cited Eusebius, *Ecclesiastical History* 6.43.11, trans. Hugh Jackson Lawlor and John Ernest Leonard Oulton, *Eusebius: The Ecclesiastical History and the Martyrs of Palestine* (London: SPCK, 1954), I, 211–212. See the comments of Walter Ullmann, *A Short History of the Papacy in the Middle Ages*, 2nd ed. (London: Routledge, 2003), 5.

Monarchy is superior to every other constitution and form of government. For polyarchy, where everyone competes on equal terms, is really anarchy and discord. This is why there is one God, not two, three, or even more.[14]

Eusebius is, of course, defending Constantine's monarchical rule and his elimination of imperial colleagues, but the same reasoning was used to defend monepiscopacy.[15]

"THE CHAIR OF PETER": TWO EARLY CLAIMS FOR THE PRIMACY OF ROME

Claims for the primacy of the bishop of Rome over fellow bishops go back to Victor I, who was bishop from 189 to 198. Drawing upon archaeology and a variety of literary sources, Peter Lampe has persuasively argued that prior to Victor's episcopate, the governance of the various house-churches in Rome was through a collegial presbyterate with each house-church having its own presiding elder. Victor sought to change this, however, and impose himself as a monarchical bishop.[16] Victor's convictions regarding his authority were on full display during the Quartodeciman controversy in the early 190s. Victor threatened the churches in Asia Minor with excommunication if they did not give up their adherence to the Jewish calendar in their celebration of Christ's resurrection, for these churches were not confining their celebration of this central Christian festival to the Lord's day, as was done at Rome and in numerous other centres.[17] Victor's desire to impose

---

14 Eusebius, *Oration in Honour of Constantine on the Thirtieth Anniversary of his Reign* 3, trans. Maurice Wiles and Mark Santer, ed., *Documents in Early Christian Thought* (Cambridge: Cambridge University Press, 1975), 234.
15 Chadwick, "Role of the Christian Bishop in Ancient Society," 3.
16 Peter Lampe, *From Paul to Valentinus: Christians at Rome in the First Two Centuries* (Minneapolis: Fortress Press, 2003), especially 397–408.
17 Eusebius of Caesarea, *Ecclesiastical History* 5.23–25. Allen Brent and John M. Rist interpret Victor's threat of excommunication as being "aimed at those Asian Christians in the city of Rome itself who followed their native practice." See Brent, "Was Hippolytus a Schismatic?" 220, and John M. Rist, *What Is Truth? From the Academy to the Vatican* (Cambridge: Cambridge University Press, 2008), 227. In other words, this is not a claim by the bishop of Rome to a wider primacy.

the custom of celebrating the resurrection solely on the Lord's day, however, provoked a storm of protest from a number of bishops, including Irenaeus of Lyons, who together appear to have persuaded Victor to desist from an imprudent use of authority.

In the century that followed, Cyprian, who fully embraced the idea that there can be only one legitimate bishop within a given geographical area, found himself embroiled in a bitter controversy with Stephen, bishop of Rome (254–257), over whether heretics and schismatics who returned to the church were to be baptized or not.[18] This controversy is usually described as a controversy about rebaptism, though, in many ways, the real issue at stake had to do not so much with baptism as with the Holy Spirit.[19] Was the Spirit present within heretical or schismatic assemblies? If not, then, as Cyprian argued, the only valid baptism that the Spirit would honour as a true baptism is that given within the church that he indwelt; thus heretics and schismatics were to be baptized.[20] Stephen disagreed, and argued that the laying on of hands would suffice as the rite of reception into the church if the person had already undergone baptism into the Triune name. It is noteworthy that he appealed at one point to his "occupancy of the chair of Peter (*cathedram Petri*)"[21] to support his argument. This is a clear reference to Matthew 16:16–18, and it appears to have been the first occasion that a bishop of Rome used what would become a standard argument in the fourth and fifth centuries.[22]

---

18 The bitterness of this controversy can be seen, for example, in Stephen's last word about Cyprian, cited by Firmilian of Caesarea (died c.269), that the African bishop was "a bogus Christ, a bogus apostle, and a crooked dealer" [Cyprian, *Letter* 75.25.4, trans. G.W. Clarke, *The Letters of St. Cyprian of Carthage*, Ancient Christian Writers, No.47 (New York: Newman Press, 1989), IV, 94].

19 Michel Réveillaud, "Note pour une Pneumatologie Cyprienne" in F.L. Cross, ed., *Studia Patristica*, Texte und Untersuchungen, Vol. 81 (Berlin: Akademie-Verlag, 1962), 6:181–82.

20 Allen Brent, "Introduction" to his trans., *St Cyprian of Carthage, On the Church: Select Treatises*, Popular Patristics Series, No. 32 (Crestwood: St Vladimir's Seminary Press, 2006), 32–33.

21 Cyprian, *Letter* 75.17.2, trans. Clarke, *Letters of St. Cyprian of Carthage*, IV, 89.

22 Walter Ullmann, "Leo I and the Theme of Papal Primacy," *Journal of Theological Studies*, n.s. 11 (1960): 29–30; J.N.D. Kelly, *The Oxford Dictionary of Popes* (Oxford: Oxford University Press, 1986), 21; Hanns Christof Brennecke, "Papacy" in Hans

By the time of the Council of Nicæa in 325, monepiscopacy had largely triumphed throughout the church in the Roman world, as is clearly seen in the focus of some of the canons of this first ecumenical council upon the proper working of the episcopate.[23] Canon 6 specifically recognized the authority of the bishops of Alexandria, Rome and Antioch—and by implication the bishops of other important cities like Carthage—over the bishops of churches in smaller towns located near these major urban centres, evidence of a further level of hierarchy within the governance of the church. The Nicene canons distinguished the bishops of these significant cities by the term "metropolitan" (μητροπολίτη), though it is striking that there is no privileging of the bishop of Rome over his fellow metropolitan bishops.[24]

"MAKE ME BISHOP OF ROME...": THE EPISCOPATE OF DAMASUS I

Critical for what R.A. Markus has called "the creation of the papacy with jurisdictional rights acknowledged" by most other bishops in the West were the Roman episcopates between Damasus I (366–384) and Leo I (440–461).[25] Relatively little is known about Damasus' early years until his appointment as a deacon in the church at Rome during the episcopate of Liberius (352–366) in the early 350s.[26] Liberius had been a firm opponent of Arianism and supporter of the principled stand of Athanasius of Alexandria for Nicene Trinitarianism. And he

---

Dieter Betz, et al., ed., *Religion Past & Present: Encyclopedia of Theology and Religion* (Leiden: Brill, 2011), IX, 490.

23 See especially Canons 2–8, 15. For the text of the canons, see "Canons of the Council of Nicaea," Fourth-Century Christianity (http://www.fourthcentury.com/index.php/nicaea-325-canons; accessed December 8, 2013).

24 For an overview of the fourth-and fifth-century conciliar canons dealing with the episcopate, see George H. Williams, "The Ministry in the Later Patristic Period (314–451)" in Niebuhr and Williams, ed., *Ministry in Historical Perspectives*, 60–66.

25 R.A. Markus, "Papacy and Hierarchy" in his *From Augustine to Gregory the Great: History and Christianity in Late Antiquity* (London: Variorum Reprints, 1983), No.XVII:17.

26 For a positive evaluation of the life and career of Damasus, see Stanley Morison, "An Unacknowledged Hero of the Fourth Century, Damasus I 366-384" in Charles Henderson, Jr., ed., *Classical, Mediaeval, and Renaissance Studies in Honor of Berthold Louis Ullman* (Rome: Edizioni di storia e letteratura, 1964), 241–263. Also see the overview by Kelly, *Oxford Dictionary of Popes*, 32–34.

had undergone exile in Thrace for these convictions from 355 to 358.[27] During Liberius' exile, the clergy in Rome had elected Felix II (355–365), who had distinct sympathies for Arianism, as their bishop. In 358, the Arian emperor Constantius II, at whose behest Liberius had been exiled, brought significant pressure to bear upon the exiled bishop to renounce his previous allegiances. Liberius eventually agreed to give up his support of Athanasius and sign a creedal statement in which he confessed the Son to be merely "like (ὅμοιος)" the Father, a clear rejection of the Nicene Creed's affirmation of the oneness of being of the Father and the Son. Satisfied that Liberius now shared his Arianism, Constantius allowed him to return to Rome, where he expected him to work with Felix as his co-bishop.

The congregations in Rome, however, rejected this arrangement and compelled Felix to relocate to the suburbs of the city, where he had a church built for his ministry. Constantius died in 361, whereupon Liberius felt the freedom once again to declare his support for the Nicene Creed. At Liberius' death in 366, a group of his closest supporters elected a deacon by the name of Ursinus (died c.385) to succeed him, but Felix's followers—Felix having died the previous year—contested the election and nominated Damasus as bishop. The rivalry between these two groups was so intense that it led eventually to sanguinary conflict on three distinct occasions, one of which, according to the pagan historian Ammianus Marcellinus (325/330–c.391–400), left 137 dead in the Christian basilica of Santa Maria Maggiore. It is noteworthy that Marcellinus traced this violence back to the "superhuman desire" each man had to "seize the bishopric" (*supra humanum modum ad rapiendam episcopi sedem ardentes*) of Rome.[28]

---

27 For what follows regarding Liberius' episcopate, I am indebted to the masterly summary by Kelly, *Oxford Dictionary of Popes*, 30–31. For more extensive studies, see James Barmby, "Liberius (4)" in William Smith and Henry Wace, ed., *A Dictionary of Christian Biography* (London: John Murray, 1882), III, 717–724; and J. Zeiller, "La question du pape Libère," *Bulletin d'ancienne littérature et d'archéologie chrétienne* 3 (1913), 20–51.

28 Marcellinus, *History* 27.3.12–13, trans. John C. Rolfe, *Ammianus Marcellinus*, Loeb Classical Library, rev. ed. (Cambridge: Harvard University Press, 1952), III, 19, altered. For help obtaining this text I am indebted to Mr. Kevin Hall of Louisville, KY.

Damasus emerged the victor from this shameful conflict, but at a frightful cost to his credibility. In the early 370s, a charge of homicide was also leveled against Damasus, though it was never proven.[29] Christian critics were scandalized by the opulent lifestyle he adopted—possibly to reach the Roman aristocracy, one of the last bastions of paganism—and the impact of his sermons upon upper-class Roman women in particular led to his being called derisively "the ladies' ear-tickler"![30] No wonder the prominent pagan aristocrat Vettius Agorius Praetextatus (c.315–384), mocking the whole idea of Christian conversion, is said to have told Damasus: "Make me bishop of Rome and I will become a Christian immediately."[31]

Help in understanding Damasus' thought about the Roman episcopate is actually found in a letter written to him in 375 by one of his protégés, namely Jerome, who had been baptized as a believer in Rome in the mid-360s and had subsequently served as Damasus' secretary in the 380s. Jerome is reflecting on the havoc that Arianism had wrought in the churches of the east:

> Since the East…is tearing piecemeal the undivided tunic of Christ, woven from the top throughout, and foxes are destroying the vineyard of Christ, so that among the broken cisterns that have no water it is difficult to locate the fountain sealed and the garden enclosed, I have considered that I ought to consult the chair of Peter (*cathedram Petri*), and the faith praised by the mouth of the Apostle. I now ask for food for my soul, from the place whence I received the garment of Christ.
>
> Neither the vast expanse of ocean, nor all the breadth of land which separates us could keep me from seeking the pearl of great

---

29 Henry Chadwick, *The Church in Ancient Society: From Galilee to Gregory the Great* (Oxford: Oxford University Press, 2001), 316–318.

30 Chadwick, *Early Church*, 160–162; Chadwick, *Church in Ancient Society*, 317; Bernard Green, *The Soteriology of Leo the Great* (Oxford: Oxford University Press, 2008), 10–11.

31 Cited Jerome, *Against John of Jerusalem* 8 (Patrologia Latina 23.377C-D). For a discussion of this remark of Praetextatus, see Burton L. Visotzky, "Hillel, Hieronymus and Praetextatus," *Journal of the Ancient Near Eastern Society* 16–17 (1984–1985), 217–224.

price. "Wherever the body is, there will the eagles be gathered together." Now that evil children have squandered their patrimony, you alone keep your heritage intact. There the fertile earth gives back a hundredfold the pure seed of the Lord. Here the corn, cast into the furrows, degenerates into darnel or wild oats. It is now in the West that the sun of righteousness arises; whilst in the East Lucifer, who had fallen, has set his throne above the stars. "You are the light of the world." "You are the salt of the earth." You are vessels of gold and silver. Here the vessels of clay or wood await the iron rod and eternal fire.

...I am speaking with the successor of the fisherman, with the disciple of the cross. Following none in the first place but Christ, I am in communion with your holiness, that is with the chair of Peter (*cathedrae Petri*). I know that upon this rock the Church is built. Whoever shall eat the Lamb outside this house is profane. If any be not with Noah in the ark, he shall perish in the flood.[32]

Here Jerome uses a variety of biblical images to describe the church. There is, for example, "the sealed fountain and the enclosed garden" from Song of Songs 4:12—a verse that had been interpreted ecclesiologically since at least the time of Cyprian[33]—as well as Noah's ark. Interwoven among these images are at least two allusions to Matthew 16:16–18: Damasus sits on the "chair of Peter," which is the rock on which the church is built, and therefore, by implication, has a primacy over other episcopal sees. This emphasis on the apostle Peter as the source of Damasus' authority is what Walter Ullmann has called "the basic petrinological theme," which turns out to have been a key feature of Damasus' thinking.[34]

---

32 Jerome, *Letter* 15 (Patrologia Latina 22.355B–D), trans. E. Giles, ed. *Documents Illustrating Papal Authority, A.D. 96–454* (London: SPCK, 1952), 148–149, modernized and slightly altered.

33 See Cyprian, *Letter* 69.2.1; 74.11.2. In the first of these texts Cyprian also uses Noah's ark as a type of the church. For Cyprian's exegesis of Song of Songs 4:12, see especially Giuseppe Nicotra, "Interpretazione di Cipriano al Cap. IV, Vers. 12, della Cantica," *La Scuola Cattolica* 68 (1940): 380–387.

34 Ullmann, *Short History of the Papacy*, 11.

In 380, the emperor Theodosius I issued the Edict of Thessalonica, which declared the "religion which the divine Peter the Apostle is said to have given to the Romans, and which it is evident that the Pontiff (*pontificem*) Damasus and Peter, Bishop of Alexandria, a man of apostolic holiness, follow,"[35] to be the only legal religion of the empire. Damasus must have been deeply gratified by this public recognition of the authority of the Roman bishop and the link to the apostle Peter. The following year, after the Niceno-Constantinopolitan Creed, which effectively closed the debate on the nature of the Godhead in the Arian controversy, had been drawn up at the Council of Constantinople, Theodosius issued an edict on July 30, 381, to confirm the council's doctrinal conclusions. Eleven bishops were explicitly named as the guarantors of the orthodox faith contained in the creedal statement.[36] Damasus was not among them. By way of response, a synod in Rome in 382 issued a formal statement that explicitly grounded the primacy of the bishop of Rome on Jesus' words to Peter in Matthew 16:17:

> ...though all the catholic churches diffused throughout the world are but one bridal chamber of Christ, yet the holy Roman church has been set before the rest by no conciliar decrees, but has obtained the primacy by the voice of our Lord and Saviour in the gospel: "you are Peter, and on this rock I will build my church..." There is added also the society of the most blessed apostle Paul... who was crowned on one and the same day, suffering a glorious death, with Peter in the city of Rome, under Caesar Nero; and they alike consecrated the above-named Roman church to Christ the Lord, and set it above all others in the whole world by their presence and venerable triumph.[37]

---

35 *Codex Theodosianus* 16.1.2, trans. The Library of Original Sources, ed. Oliver J. Thatcher (New York: University Research Extension, [1907]), 70, altered.

36 *Codex Theodosianus* 16.1.3.

37 Damasus, *Post has omnes* (Patrologia Latina 13.374B–C) in Giles, ed. *Documents Illustrating Papal Authority*, 131. For a discussion of this text, see Ullmann, *Short History of the Papacy*, 10–11; Chadwick, *Church in Ancient Society*, 321–322.

Since Peter, along with Paul, had planted the church in Rome, whatever privileges and responsibilities were accorded to Peter were the Roman bishop's by inheritance.[38]

It was probably to further buttress his authority and influence that Damasus penned an epigram around the time of this Synod of Rome that recalled an old belief that originally Peter and Paul had been buried together on the Via Appia after their martyrdoms:

> Whoever you may be that seek the names of Peter and Paul should know that the saints dwelt here once. The East sent the disciples; that we readily admit. But on the account of the merit of their blood (they have followed Christ through the stars and attained to the ethereal bosom and the realms of the holy ones) Rome has gained a superior right to claim them as her citizens. Damasus would thus tell of your praises as new stars.[39]

Here, Damasus claimed that although Peter and Paul had journeyed from the orient, their dwelling at and especially their dying in Rome gave the church there "a superior right" to claim them as their very own. Damasus could thus refer to Rome as an "apostolic see (*sedes apostolica*)."[40] In other words, Damasus was asserting that apostolic authority had been transferred from the east to the west, from early Christian centres like Jerusalem and Antioch, where Peter and Paul had been active, to Rome, where they had died together.

---

38 The belief that Peter and Paul founded the church in Rome goes back to Irenaeus; see his *Against Heresies* 3.3.1–2.

39 Cited Chadwick, *Church in Ancient Society*, 324. For a discussion of this epigram, see Henry Chadwick, "St. Peter and St. Paul in Rome: The Problem of the *Memoria Apostolorum ad Catacumbas*," *Journal of Theological Studies*, n.s., 8 (1957), 34–35; "Pope Damasus and the Peculiar Claim of Rome to St. Peter and St. Paul" in Henry Chadwick, *History and Thought of the Early Church* (London: Variorum Reprints, 1982), no.III; and Chadwick, *Church in Ancient Society*, 324–325. For the dating of this epigram, see Chadwick, *Church in Ancient Society*, 325.

40 Ullmann notes that the term "apostolic see" is first consistently used by Damasus: "Leo I and the Theme of Papal Primacy," 43 n.2, and Ullmann, *Short History of the Papacy*, 10.

"SO GREAT IS OUR AUTHORITY": FROM SIRICIUS TO ZOSIMUS

A letter of Damasus' successor, Siricius (384–399), to Himerius of Tarragona, written in the year after Siricius became bishop of Rome, continued this vein of interpretation.[41] He informed Himerius that as the bishop of Rome he had a responsibility to bear "the burdens of all who are heavily laden," though actually it was "the blessed Apostle Peter [who] bears them" in Siricius. Moreover, the bishop of Rome stated his belief that Peter "protects and watches his heir (*haeredes*) in all the cares of his office," an allusion to Paul's words of apostolic care in 2 Corinthians 11:28.[42] In this letter there is also the assertion that in the person of each bishop of Rome, who is now said to be the heir (*haeres*) of Peter, the apostle continues to lead the church.[43] Here then we have a fairly distinct claim to Roman primacy. It is also noteworthy that this letter is modelled after imperial decrees: in it Siricius gives instructions as to various practical issues and problems. In time, these *decretals*, as they would come to be known, would amount to a sizable body of "case law."[44]

Along with the claim of historical succession to Peter was the argument that the bishop of Rome had been granted the juridicial powers of the apostle to bind and to loose according to Matthew 16:18–19.[45] One sees this in a letter of Innocent I (401–417) to Decentius of Gubbio, written in 416:

> Who is unaware or does not observe that what was handed down to the Roman church by the Prince of the Apostles, Peter, and is

---

41 On Siricius, see Kelly, *Oxford Dictionary of Popes*, 35–36 and Chadwick, *Church in Ancient Society*, 325–328; for Himerius of Tarragona, see Mary Augusta Ward, "Himerius (3)" in Smith and Wace, ed., *Dictionary of Christian Biography*, III, 83–84.

42 Siricius, *Letter to Himerius of Tarragona* 1.1 (Patrologia Latina 13.1133A), trans. Robert B. Eno, *Teaching Authority in the Early Church*, Message of the Fathers of the Church, Vol.14 (Wilmington: Michael Glazier, 1984), 154.

43 Eno, *Teaching Authority in the Early Church*, 153. According to Walter Ullmann, this is the first occasion when a bishop of Rome described himself as an heir of Peter; Ullmann, "Leo I and the Theme of Papal Primacy," 30–31.

44 Robert Louis Wilken, *The First Thousand Years: A Global History of Christianity* (New Haven: Yale University Press, 2012), 167–168.

45 Chadwick, *History and Thought of the Early Church*, 239–240.

still kept up to now, must be observed by all; further, that nothing is to be brought in or introduced which does not have authority or seems to have other origins? This is even more obvious when you realize that no church was ever founded in all of Italy, Gaul, Spain, Africa, Sicily or any of the islands unless the venerable Apostle Peter or his successors appointed bishops for them. See if, in any of these provinces, there is any mention of another Apostle teaching there or even being there. If they do not discover any, as indeed they cannot, then they must follow the practice of the church of Rome.[46]

According to this theoretical reflection by Innocent, all of the churches in the western Roman empire ultimately trace their origins to Rome, and as such, must conform in both teaching and praxis to the pattern in the Roman church. In actual practice, however, Roman episcopal jurisdiction was limited to disciplinary matters in a number of the western provinces such as Gaul and Spain, and definitely did not include North Africa, as Innocent's successor Zosimus (417–418) would discover.[47]

During the latter years of Innocent's episcopate, the mid-410s, the teaching of a British monk, Pelagius, had become a major issue of controversy. He argued that the human will was sufficiently free to obey God and his commands without the aid of divine grace, and therefore, a person was potentially able to lead a sinless life.[48] In the words of J.N.L. Myres, Pelagianism encouraged an "attitude of self-reliance" and emphasized "the saving quality of a virtuous life."[49] Innocent had formally condemned this perspective on the Christian faith. Zosimus, however, came close to reversing his predecessor's condemnation of Pelagius as he was deeply impressed by the moral seriousness

---

46 Innocent I, *Letter to Decentius of Gubbio* (Patrologia Latina 20.552A–B), trans. Eno, *Teaching Authority in the Early Church*, 155.

47 B. Studer, "Papacy" in Angelo Di Berardino, ed., *Encyclopedia of the Early Church*, trans. Adrian Walford (New York: Oxford University Press, 1992), II, 461, cols.1–2.

48 Gerald Bonner, "Pelagianism" in Trevor A. Hart, et al., ed., *The Dictionary of Historical Theology* (Grand Rapids: Eerdmans, 2000), 422–424.

49 J.N.L. Myres, "Pelagius and the End of Roman Rule in Britain," *The Journal of Roman Studies* 50 (1960): 28–29.

of the Pelagians and their profound respect for his authority as the bishop of Rome. Having held a synod in Rome to discuss the matter of Pelagianism, in September 417, Zosimus informed the African bishops—including the man who would become Pelagius' main opponent, Augustine—that their view of Pelagius did not accord with reality. If Pelagius were judged on the basis of what had been at the heart of the main theological controversies in the previous century, namely, the doctrine of the Trinity, he must be regarded as orthodox.

The African bishops were outraged and informed Zosimus that Innocent I's ruling must be upheld. They sent Alypius of Thagaste (died c.430), a close friend of Augustine, to plead their position with imperial authorities at Ravenna. The upshot of Alypius' trip was an imperial edict issued at the end of April 418, by the western Roman emperor Honorius banishing the Pelagians from Rome as a threat to civic and ecclesial peace.[50]

Humiliated by these events, Zosimus eventually wrote the African bishops to reassure them that he had no intention of reversing Innocent's condemnation of the Pelagians.[51] But he was obviously deeply disturbed by the Africans' "lack of docility" and that they were not fully on board with the understanding of the Roman see that had been developing in Rome since Damasus.[52] He thus took the opportunity to reaffirm his authority as the bishop of Rome. Here is the relevant portion of that letter written in 418:

> The tradition of the Fathers attributed such great authority (*auctoritatem tantam*) to the Apostolic see that no one would dare dispute its judgment and has preserved this for all time by canonical rules. Up to the present, through these laws, ecclesiastical discipline gives due honor to the name of Peter from whom it also derives. The ancient canons assigned this great

---

50 Chadwick, *Church in Ancient Society*, 456–458.
51 For a discussion of these events, see Ullmann, "Leo I and the Theme of Papal Primacy," 32–33; Chadwick, *History and Thought of the Early Church*, 230; Green, *Soteriology of Leo the Great*, 17–18
52 The words of "lack of docility" are Chadwick's; see his *Church in Ancient Society*, 457.

power to the Apostle from the very promise of Christ our God so that he might loose what was bound and bind what had not been bound. A like condition of power has been given to those who have merited the inheritance of this see with his assent.

For he has, along with the care of all the churches, above all the care of this see where he sat. He permits no wavering of its privileges or its teachings because he has made its foundations firm by his name. It cannot be shaken; no one may assault it except at his own peril. Since therefore Peter is the source of such great authority (*tantae auctoritatis*), he has confirmed the zeal of all our predecessors who came after him so that the Roman church is strengthened by all laws and discipline both human and divine. ...So great is our authority that no one can reconsider our decision (*tamen cum tantum nobis esset auctoritatis, ut nullus de nostra possit retractare sententia*).[53]

As Ullmann has pointed out, this letter marks a key step forward on the road to the papacy.[54] The episcopal power of the bishop of Rome—the phrase "such great authority" occurring no less than three times in this short text—stems ultimately from the apostle Peter, which he derives from Christ's promise to him in Matthew 16:16–18 to "loose what was bound and bind what had not been bound." Such juristic power comes to the bishop of Rome since he is the heir of Peter—it being understood that Peter founded the church at Rome—and since in Roman law there is a "juristic continuity between the deceased and the heir," Peter is still living, acting and exercising solicitude in the person of the bishop. What this entails is this: due to the "Petrinity" of the apostolic see of Rome, no one can question decisions made by its holder.[55]

LEO I

Zosimus' letter was taken to North Africa by an acolyte named Leo, who is most probably the Leo I who became the bishop of Rome

---

53 Zosimus, *Letter 12 to Aurelius of Carthage* (Patrologia Latina 20.676A–B), trans. Eno, *Teaching Authority in the Early Church*, 156–157, altered.

54 Ullmann, "Leo I and the Theme of Papal Primacy," 32–33.

55 For the neologism "Petrinity," see Ullmann, *Short History of the Papacy*, 15.

twenty-two years later.⁵⁶ Remembered for his important Christological contribution to the Council of Chalcedon (451) and his saving Rome from the ravages of Attila and the Huns, Leo also drew together the assertions of his predecessors about the bishopric of Rome and, through the exegesis of a number of familiar Petrine texts, created the theoretical foundations of the mediæval papacy.⁵⁷ In a sermon that he preached on the third anniversary of his election as bishop, he exegeted Matthew 16:16–19 thus:

> When…the Lord had asked the disciples whom they believed him to be amid the various opinions that were held, and the blessed Peter had replied, saying, "You are the Christ, the Son of the living God," the Lord says, "Blessed are you, Simon Bar-Jona, because flesh and blood has not revealed this to you, but my Father, who is in heaven. And I say to thee, you are Peter, and upon this rock I will build my church, and the gates of Hades shall not prevail against it. And I will give you the keys of the kingdom of heaven. And whatever you will have bound on earth, shall be bound in heaven; and whatever you shall loose on earth, shall be loosed also in heaven."

The dispensation of truth therefore abides, and the blessed Peter persevering in the strength of the rock, which he has received, has not abandoned the helm of the Church, which he undertook to control. For he was ordained before the rest in such a way that from his being called the Rock, from his being pronounced the Foundation, from his being constituted the Doorkeeper of the kingdom of heaven (*regni coelorum janitor*), from his authority as the Umpire to bind and to loose, whose judgments shall retain their validity in heaven—from all these mysti-

---

56 Green, *Soteriology of Leo the Great*, 18–19, n.72. For Leo's thought and career, see especially T.G. Jalland, *The Life and Times of St. Leo the Great* (London: SPCK, 1941); Philip A. McShane, *La Romanitas et le pape Léon le Grand* (Tournai: Desclée, 1979); Susan Wessel, *Leo the Great and the Spiritual Rebuilding of a Universal Rome* (Leiden: E.J. Brill, 2008); Bronwen Neil, *Leo the Great* (London: Routledge, 2009).

57 Here I follow Walter Ullmann, "Leo I and the Theme of Papal Primacy"; William Dennis Lindsey, "Christology and Roman Primacy at Chalcedon," *Toronto Journal of Theology* 1 (1985): 37–38; Wessel, *Leo the Great*, 285–321.

cal titles we might know the nature of his association with Christ. And still to-day he more fully and effectually performs what is entrusted to him, and carries out every part of his duty and charge in him and with him, through whom he has been glorified. And so if anything is rightly done and rightly decreed by us, if anything is won from the mercy of God by our daily supplications, it is of his work and merits whose power lives and whose authority prevails in his see. For this, dearly-beloved, was gained by that confession, which, inspired in the Apostle's heart by God the Father, transcended all the uncertainty of human opinions, and was endued with the firmness of a rock, which no assaults could shake.[58]

According to Leo's reading of Matthew 16:16–19, Peter's faith in declaring Jesus to be the Messiah merited his being appointed the foundation of the church, the doorkeeper of the kingdom of heaven and the judge whose earthly decisions are guaranteed heavenly confirmation. Critical to Leo's application of Matthew 16 is the Roman law of inheritance, which made its appearance in Zosimus' letter to the African bishops cited earlier. According to this legal perspective, a true heir replaces the deceased person, stepping into their shoes, as it were, and inheriting not only their possessions and wealth, or debts, but also taking over their responsibilities and duties in society. As Ullmann puts it: "Legally...there is no difference between the heir and the deceased: the latter is literally continued in the former."[59] It is obvious that Leo had this Roman understanding of inheritance in mind when he emphasized that Peter's ministry was still ongoing. It was such because he lived and acted through his heir, the bishop of Rome.[60] As

---

58 Leo, *Sermon* 3.2–3 (Patrologia Latina 54.146A–C), trans. C.L. Feltoe in Philip Schaff and Henry Wace, ed., *A Select Library of Nicene and Post-Nicene Fathers*, 2nd series, 1895 ed. (reprint, Edinburgh: T&T Clark/Grand Rapids: Eerdmans, 1997), 12:117, cols.1–2, modernized and slightly altered.

59 "Leo I and the Theme of Papal Primacy," 34.

60 A little later in the sermon Leo describes himself as "an unworthy heir (*indigno haerede*," *Sermon* 3.4 (Patrologia Latina 54.147A). On this term, see Ullmann, "Leo I and the Theme of Papal Primacy," 34–36; Michael M. Winter, *Saint Peter and the Popes* (London: Darton, Longman and Todd/Baltimore: Helicon Press, 1960), 179.

Leo declared in a sermon preached two years later:

> not only the apostolic but also the episcopal dignity of blessed Peter... has not ceased to preside over his see...for the solidity which he, having been made Peter the rock, received from Christ the rock, he has passed on to his heirs.[61]

So as to defend his right of primacy over all other bishops, Leo also emphasized that Peter's primacy was exercised even during the lifetime of the other apostles. Taking his cue from Luke 22:31–32, he argued:

> As his passion drew near, an event that was going to shake the fidelity of his disciples, the Lord said, "Simon, Simon, Satan has asked for you, to sift you like wheat. But I have prayed for you, that your faith may never fail. You in turn must strengthen your brothers, lest you enter into temptation." The danger from the temptation to fear was common to all the Apostles and all had equal need of the aid of divine protection since the Devil wished to upset them all and cause them to fall.
>
> And yet the Lord shows a special care for Peter and prays in particular for the faith of Peter, as if the future situation would be more secure for the others if the spirit of the leader remained unconquered. Thus in Peter the courage of all is fortified and the aid of divine grace is so arranged that the strength which comes to Peter through Christ, through Peter is transmitted to the Apostles.[62]

As Leo reads the Lukan text, he asks, "What does this passage say about Peter's authority among the apostolic band?" The answer seems obvious: just as the grace of fortitude at the time of the passion of the Lord Jesus came from Christ to the apostles through Peter, so it was

---

61 Leo, *Sermon* 5.4 (Patrologia Latina 54.155A), trans. Eno, *Teaching Authority in the Early Church*, 162, altered.

62 Leo, *Sermon* 4.3 (Patrologia Latina 54.151B–152A), trans. Eno, *Teaching Authority in the Early Church*, 161–162, altered.

the apostles derived their authority not directly from the Lord, but from him by means of Peter. If Peter had such a primacy among the apostles, should not his heir, the bishop of Rome, hold such a primacy among his fellow bishops? For Leo, all ecclesial power ultimately stems from the heir of Peter.[63] As he put it quite plainly: "Through Peter, the holy prince of the apostles, the Roman Church possesses the sovereignty over all the churches in the whole world."[64] With such far-reaching claims for papal authority, it is no surprise that Leo's words to his fellow bishops are so frequently terms of governance and obedience to the statues issued by the apostolic see.[65] In essence, Leo has established that communion with Rome is a necessary condition for communion with Christ and God.

TWO OTHER HISTORICAL REASONS FOR THE DEVELOPMENT OF THE PAPACY

There were two other critical reasons—non-theological ones—for the emergence of the papacy. The total collapse of Roman rule in Western Europe removed the Church of Rome from its patristic context and its vital relationship with other ancient Christian centres like Alexandria, Antioch and Constantinople that rejected the claim of Rome's primacy. Then, the advent of Islam in the seventh century and the loss of North Africa to the Christian world further isolated the Church of Rome, on the one hand, and, on the other, enabled her to argue her claims with more vehemence as she was now the mother church for so much of Europe.[66] North Africa had been a principal source of spiritual and intellectual vitality in the Latin-speaking western church and was, in R.A. Markus' words, "the only area in the western church which could look Rome in the face."[67] If neither of these events had taken place, it is extremely doubtful if Rome's claims for universal obedience to her bishop could have succeeded to any extent at all. But these events did happen—and down to the present-day there have been and are multitudes for whom the pope was and is the "blessed gatekeeper of

---

63 Ullmann, "Leo I and the Theme of Papal Primacy," 44.
64 Leo, *Letter* 65.2 (Patrologia Latina 54.881B).
65 Ullmann, "Leo I and the Theme of Papal Primacy," 25.
66 Markus, "Papacy and Hierarchy," 21–25.
67 "Papacy and Hierarchy," 22–23.

heaven,"⁶⁸ to use words that Hilary of Poitiers once used to describe the apostle Peter.

POSTSCRIPT: AN EVANGELICAL REFLECTION

Roman Catholic historiography often regards the development of the papacy detailed above as being providentially ordered. Thus, John Rist, though very conscious of the failings of the papal theocracy of the Middle Ages, has argued that the development of the papacy was essential to "the maintenance of theological purity" as well as for "the possibility of an expanding culture which in all its ramifications was to remain catholic, that is, universal."⁶⁹

R.A. Markus, a Roman Catholic layman, however, regarded the development of the papacy in late antiquity as fraught with problems. Writing in the wake of Vatican II, he emphasized that the dominant idea of Christian ministry during its early centuries was "loving service rendered to the community of believers." Markus stressed that among the early fathers, Augustine definitely knew this. As the North African bishop reminded his congregation on the anniversary of his ordination: "For you, I am a bishop; with you I am a Christian. The former is the name of an office undertaken, the latter, a name of grace; the former means danger, the latter salvation."⁷⁰

Like Cassian, who was cited at the outset of this chapter, Augustine was well aware of the dangers of episcopal office; yet, he deemed such an office as necessary for the good of the church. Markus stressed, however, that this concept of ministry was overlaid by another concept in the patristic era, namely, that of hierarchy: the bishop was over the rest of the Christian community, and in the case of the bishop of Rome, he was over the entirety of the episcopate. In this idea of ministry, the bishop became a mediatorial figure and the conduit of God's grace to the community, an idea clearly seen in Leo I's exegesis of Luke 22:31–32.⁷¹

---

68 Hilary of Poitiers, *Commentary on Matthew* 16.7 (Patrologia Latina 9.1010A).

69 Rist, *What Is Truth?* 232, 254–257. Quote from page 232.

70 Augustine, *Sermon* 340.1 (PL39.1483), trans Michael A.G. Haykin. Cited Markus, "Papacy and Hierarchy," 4. As Ray van Neste has noted, this whole sermon is "a beautiful portrait of pastoral ministry" (Oversight of Souls; http://rayvanneste.com/?p=1434; accessed December 16, 2013).

71 See Markus, "Papacy and Hierarchy," 6–13, 26–28.

Markus wanted to differentiate between the papacy in late antiquity, where the biblical concept of ministry as service has not been completely lost, and the later mediæval institution, where one has a full-blown papal monarchy or theocracy and "obedience has become the fundamental ecclesiastical virtue."[72] But, the roots of the papal monarchy of the Middle Ages lie clearly in the soil of the papal primacy worked out by the bishops of Rome from Damasus to Leo I. One cannot have the former without the latter, and the latter was rooted in distinct historical circumstance and tendentious exegesis.

Leadership is indeed critical for the *esse* of the church, as is apparent from a quick overview of the earliest of Christian texts, the letters of the apostle Paul. In Paul's letter to the Galatians, for instance, the earliest book in the New Testament next to James' letter, Paul states that the "one who is taught the word must share all good things with the one who teaches" (Galatians 6:6, ESV). Again, in 1 Thessalonians, also a very early text, Paul encourages his readers: "We ask you, brothers, to respect those who labour among you and are over you in the Lord and admonish you" (1 Thessalonians 5:12, ESV). And in Philippians 1:1, Paul and Timothy greet not only "all the saints in Christ Jesus who are at Philippi," but also the "overseers and deacons" (ESV). The key question for the early Christians was not whether they should have leaders or not. Leadership was a given. Rather, the key questions were: What model of leadership was to be promoted? And how should the church relate to her leaders? Standing in the tradition of Puritanism and eighteenth-century evangelical Nonconformity, which respectfully listened to the fathers but refused to read the New Testament solely through their coloured spectacles, I heartily affirm what P.T. Forsyth once said about the confidence of that tradition: "Out of village Bethels God is always, by the word of his Gospel, raising up children to Abraham and successors to Peter and Paul, though bishops be ignorant of them and priests acknowledge them not."[73]

---

72 See Markus, "Papacy and Hierarchy," 26–37. Quote from page 37.

73 P.T. Forsyth, *The Church and the Sacraments*, 3rd ed. (London: Independent Press, 1949), 46. The phrase "coloured spectacles" comes from Forsyth on the same page. "Bethel" was a favourite name for many eighteenth- and nineteenth-century Nonconformist chapels.

13

A concluding word

The patristic era, though not a golden age as some would depict it, is nonetheless one of the most significant eras in church history. To be sure, there is a sense in which every era of church history has importance, but the reality is some are more important than others. For Christians of my evangelical persuasion, the era of the church fathers has to be deemed one of the most important. For both good and ill, it gives us such things as the canon of the New Testament, the doctrine of the Trinity, the Constantinian settlement that united church and state, the papacy and the legacy of Augustine—all Western Christians are Augustinians to some degree! The entire history of the church in the West has been built on these foundations. In some cases (the union of church and state and the papacy) later generations challenged what was established in this era. In other cases (the doctrine of the Trinity, the canon and the legacy of Augustine), the church has often unwittingly assumed these gifts as a given. It is salutary to know the historical context in which these gifts were first formed and enunciated.

What I have sought to do in this book is to help God's people appreciate the rich heritage of this period, both its strengths and weaknesses.

I am thoroughly convinced that the strengths of this era far outweigh the problems, hence my longing that this era be on the radar of contemporary Christianity. We need to listen to these older brothers and sisters and learn from their wisdom, imitate their strengths, and yes, avoid their weaknesses. May the various essays be an aid to such growth in what I can only regard as spiritual maturity.

Index

abortion, 89–96
Aelia Flavia Flaccilla (356–386), 181
Aelia Pulcheria (385–386), 181
Alaric (died 410), 73, 138
Alexamenos, 12–13
Alexander (died 328), bishop of Alexandria, 101–103, 105
Alexander of Phrygia, 24
Alexandria, 45–46, 51, 101, 103, 167–171, 186, 202
Alypius of Thagaste (died c.430), 197
Ambrose (Origen's patron), 45, 169
Ambrose, bishop of Milan, 137, 146, 147, 149
amillennialism, 38–39

Ammianus Marcellinus (325/330–c.391–400), 190
Amphilochius of Iconium (c.340–395), 58–59, 92, 96, 114, 126
Anastasia, 78
Anicetus (c.155–c.166), 21
Antioch, 13, 53, 57, 184, 186, 189, 194, 202
Apollinaris of Laodicea (c.315–392), 39, 53–59
Arian controversy, 55, 101–109, 116, 138, 181, 189–193
Aristotle (384–322 B.C.), 94
Arius (c.250/256–336), 101–104
Asterius of Amasea (c.350–c.410), 171, 176–179

Asterius the Sophist (died 341), 105–106
Athanasius of Alexandria (c.299–373), 55, 87, 104–109, 113, 121, 189–190
Athaulf, 138
Athenagoras (133–190), 90, 92
Attalus, 23
Augustine of Hippo (354–430), 1, 86, 94, 135–161, 166, 171–175, 176, 197, 203, 205
Augustus Caesar (63 B.C.–A.D. 14; r.27 B.C.– A.D. 14), 142

baptism, 56, 62, 64–66, 71, 114–115, 188
Bar Kochba revolt, 47
Basil of Caesarea (c.330–379), 39, 53–59, 86–87, 89–96, 97, 109–121, 126–127, 136, 171, 176, 179–182,
Battle of Adrianople (378), 137
Battle of the Milvian Bridge, 81–83
Bithynia, 10–11
Brown, Dan, 5–7, 10

Caecilianus, 63
Calvin, John (1509–1564), 144
Cappadocia, 53, 58, 91, 127, 171, 175–182
Caracalla (r.211–217), 77
Carthage, 62, 72, 166, 172–173, 189
Cassian, John (c.360–c.435), 184, 203
Chi-Rho, 82

Chrysostom, John (c.347–407), 53, 136
Comma Johanneum, 71
Constantine (c.285–337, r.306–337), 6–7, 10, 38, 73–87, 104–105, 141–143, 166, 186–187
Constantinople, 91, 105, 118, 120, 139, 202
Constantius I (died 306; r.293–306), 78–80, 84,
Constantius II (317–361), 106, 190
Council of Alexandria, 108–109
Council of Ancyra, 95
Council of Chalcedon, 199
Council of Constantinople, 54, 57, 98, 100, 118–120, 181, 193
Council of Elvira, 95
Council of Ephesus, 126
Council of Nicæa, 6–7, 10, 18, 38, 98, 100–105, 108–109, 189
Cyprian of Carthage (c.200–258), aka. Thascius Caecilius Cyprianus, 61–72, 188, 192

Damasus I, bishop of Rome (366–384), 189–194, 195, 197, 204
Decentius of Gubbio, 195–196
Decius (r.249–251), 45
deity of Christ, 5–18, 55, 87
Demetrius (died 232), bishop of Alexandria, 45
Demosthenes (384–322 B.C.), 176

Diocletian (r.284–305), 72, 77–80, 133
Diodore of Tarsus (died c.390), 53
Dionysius of Alexandria (died c.265), 38–39, 44–53, 58–59
dualism, 20

Edict of Milan, 81, 166
Edict of Thessalonica, 193
Edwards, Jonathan, 76
Eleusius of Cyzicus, 118
Ephesus, 23
Epiphanius of Salamis (c.315–403), 53
Eusebius of Caesarea (c.260–339), 24, 46, 49–51, 59, 79, 82, 85–86, 106, 142–144, 158–159, 186–187
Eusebius of Nicomedia (died c.342), 104–105
Eustathius of Sebaste (c.300–c.377), 111–115, 118

Felix II, bishop of Rome (355–365), 190
Firmilian of Caesarea (died c.269), 188
Flavius Valerius Constantius, see Constantius I

Galerius (died 311), 78–80
Galla Placidia (c.388/390–450), 138
Galliani, Abbé, 137
Gibbon, Edward, 136–137

Gnostic, Gnosticism, 14, 20–35, 186, 42–45, 48, 100, 169, 170
Great Persecution, 78–80
Gregory of Nazianzus (c.330–389), 54, 120, 176
Gregory of Nyssa (c.335–c.394), 91, 117, 118, 120–121, 127, 134, 170, 171, 176, 181–182
Gregory of Tours (died 594), 24
Gregory Thaumaturgus (c.210–c.270), 91, 170

Hilary of Poitiers (c.315–c.367), 136, 183, 203
Himerius of Tarragona, 195
Hippo Regius, 146
Holy Spirit,
  deity, 97–121, 127
  ministry and work, 32–33, 59–60, 61–72, 98, 123–134
  power, 66–68
Honorius (r.395–423), 138, 197
house churches, 165–166
Hyginus (c.138–c.142), 21

Ignatius of Antioch (died c.107–110), 10, 13–15, 184–185
Innocent I (401–417), 195–197
Irenaeus of Lyons (c.130/140–c.200), vi, 19–35, 38, 39–44, 50, 59, 100, 188, 194

Jerome (c.347–419/420), 53, 69, 73–74, 86, 138–141, 143, 191–192
Jewish War (66–73), 47

Lactantius (c.240–320), 38
Leo I, bishop of Rome (440–461), 189, 198–204
Leonides (martyred 202), 44–45
Liberius, bishop of Rome (352–366), 189–190
Licinius (r.308–324), 81, 83–84
Lucan, 140
Lucian of Samosata (c.125–c.180), 11–13
Luther, Martin, 144
Lyons, 23–24

Macarius (300–c.391), 120–121, 123–134
Macrina (c.327–380), 91
Magnesia-on-the-Meander, 14
Manichean, 145
Marcellus of Ancyra (c.285–374), 104–106,
Marcion (fl.150s–160s), 21, 23, 27, 100
marriage, 176–179
Martyr, Justin (c.100/110–c.165), 20, 23, 38
Maxentius (r.306–312), 81
Maximian (r.286–305), 78–79
Mede, Joseph, 38
Meletius of Antioch (died 381), 112–114
Melito of Sardis (died c.190), 167–168
Messalians, Messalianism, 126–127
Messianic movement, 40, 47

Methodius of Olympus (died c.311), 38
millenarianism, 38, 51
millennium, 37–60, 158
Monica (331–387), 145
modalism, 9, 55, 100, 101, 102, 104–106, 116

Nag Hammadi, 20
Nepos of Arsinoë, 49–53
Numidia, 141, 145

Olympias (c.360/365–408), 182
Origen (c.185–254), 8, 20, 37–39, 44–58, 141, 164, 168–171, 182

Palestine, 45, 46, 80, 170
papacy, 183–204
Patricius (died 371), 145
Pelagianism, 148, 196–197
Pelagius (fl.400–420), 180, 196–197
Peregrinus, 11–12
Peter of Sebaste (c.340–391), 91
Pliny the Younger (61/62–c.113), 10–11
Pneumatomachi, 54, 109–121, 127
Phrygia, 80
Platonism, neo-Platonism, 145, 155
Polycarp of Smyrna (69/70–155/6), 22–23, 185
Pontus, 10, 11, 91, 170, 176
Porphyry (c.233–c.303), 79
Pothinus (c.87–177), 24

premillennialism, 38–39, 44, 46–60
Prudentius (c.348–c.405), 143–144

Quartodeciman controversy, 24, 187

Ravenna, 139, 197
Rutilius Namatianus (fl. fifth century), 139

Sabellian, Sabellianism, 102, 114, 117
Sabellius (fl.215), 102
sack of Rome, 135–141, 152–154, 160
Scriptures,
   canon, 26, 45, 52, 59, 153, 158, 205
   exegesis, 97–121
   perfection, 25–28, 94
   preaching, 163–182
   unity, 27–31
Serapion of Thmuis (died after 362), 106–108
Shapur II (r.309–379) of Persia, 84
Silvanus, bishop of Tarsus (died 369), 110–111
Simplicianus (died c.400), 147
Siricius, bishop of Rome (384–399), 195
Smyrna, 14, 22
Socrates, 118, 169
Speratus (died c.180), 141
Spurgeon, C.H., 170

Stephen, bishop of Rome, (254–257), 65–66, 70, 188
Synod of Philippopolis, 105
Synod of Side, 126
Synod of Tyre, 105

Tertullian (fl.190–215), 32, 38, 69–70, 74, 100–101, 104, 141, 149, 193
Tetrarchy, 78–80
Thascius Caecilius Cyprianus, see Cyprian of Carthage
Theodosius I (347–395; r.379–395), 57, 118, 159, 181
Theodotus of Nicopolis (died 375), 112–114
Thmuis, 106, 107–109
Trajan (r.98–117), 10–11
Trinity, Trinitarianism, triunity, 32, 71, 91–92, 97–121, 127, 181, 189
Tyconius (died c.400), 149

Ursinus (died c.385), 190

Valens (328–378), 118, 137
Valentinus (fl.138–166), 21, 23
Valerian (r.253–260), 71, 77
Vatican II, 203
Vettius Agorius Praetextatus (c.315–384), 191
Victor I, bishop of Rome (189–198), 24, 187–188
Vienne, 23–24
Virgil, 143–144
Visigoths, 73, 138
von Harnack, Adolf, 98

Warfield, Benjamin B., 7, 99, 144–145
Wesley, John, 76, 87, 123–125

York, 74, 80, 84, 141

Zosimus (fl.491–518), 139
Zosimus, bishop of Rome (417–418), 195–197

BOOKS, CONFESSIONS, CREEDS

2 Clement, 167
Against Asterius, 105–106
Against Heresies, vi, 21–35, 39–44, 100, 194
Against Praxeas, 70, 100–101
Against the Christians, 79
Church History, 46, 49
Chronological Canons, 158
Confessions (397–401), 1, 145, 146, 148
De instituto christiano, 127
Ecclesiastical History, 79
Edict of Thessalonica, 193
Fifty Spiritual Homilies, 125–134
Great Letter, 127
Latin Vulgate, 53, 73
Letter to Diognetus, 5, 10, 15–17
Nicene Creed (325), 87, 98, 104–106, 109, 111, 112
Niceno-Constantinopolitan Creed (381), 87, 98–99, 105, 118, 120, 181, 193
On First Principles, 46–48
On the Holy Spirit (375), 54, 91, 114–117
On the Passover, 167–168
On the Promises, 49–53
On the unity of the Catholic Church, 71
Refutation of the Allegorists, 49
Testimonia, 69
The City of God (413–426), 86, 135–161
The Da Vinci Code (2006), 5–7, 10
The Passing of Peregrinus, 11–12
To Demetrian, 65, 70
To Donatus, 61–72
Tome to the Antiochenes, 113

Also available from Joshua Press

| THE CHRISTIAN MENTOR | Volume 2

THE CHURCH FATHERS AS SPIRITUAL MENTORS: "HOPE IS KINDLED"

Historian Michael Haykin examines the lives of such Reformers as William Tyndale, Thomas Cranmer and John Calvin to see how their display of the light of the gospel in their day provides us with a "usable past"—models of Christian conviction and living who can speak into our lives today. Born in a time of spiritual darkness, they model what reformation involves for church and culture: a deep commitment to God's Word as the vehicle of renewal, a willingness to die for the gospel and a rock-solid commitment to the triune God. As a reminder that at the heart of the Reformation was a confessional Christianity, an essay on two Reformation confessions is also included.

The Puritan figures who are studied are Richard Greenham, Oliver Cromwell, John Owen, Richard Baxter and his wife Margaret, and John Bunyan. In addition, a study of the translation of the King James Bible (KJB) reminds us that the Puritans, like the Reformers, were Word-saturated men and women—may we be as well.

ISBN 978-1-894400-39-8; 196 pages

Deo Optimo et Maximo Gloria
To God, best and greatest, be glory

www.joshuapress.com

www.ingramcontent.com/pod-product-compliance
Lightning Source LLC
Chambersburg PA
CBHW020230170426
43201CB00007B/382